Exploring Lewis and Clark

Exploring Lewis and Clark

Reflections on Men and Wilderness

THOMAS P. SLAUGHTER

Alfred A. Knopf

New York

2003

THIS IS A BORZOI BOOK
PUBLISHED BY ALFRED A. KNOPF

Library of Congress Cataloging-in-Publication Data
Slaughter, Thomas P. (Thomas Paul)
Exploring Lewis and Clark : reflections on men and wilderness /
Thomas P. Slaughter.—1st ed.
p.   cm.
Includes bibliographical references and index.
ISBN 0-375-40078-8
1. Lewis and Clark Expedition (1804–1806)
2. West (U.S.)—Discovery and exploration.
3. West (U.S.)—Description and travel.
4. Explorers—West (U.S.)—Biography.
5. Lewis, Meriwether, 1774–1809.   6. Clark, William, 1770–1838.
7. Sacagawea, 1786–1884.   8. York, ca. 1775–ca. 1815.
9. Indians of North America—West (U.S.)—History—19th century.
10. Wilderness areas—West (U.S.)—History—19th century.
I. Title
F592.7 .S67 2003
917.804'2—dc21   2002069376
Manufactured in the United States of America
First Edition

To Louis P. Masur

*It is not often that someone comes along
who is a true friend and a good writer.*

—E. B. White, *Charlotte's Web*

It is always necessary to look forward and backward at the same time. Only in that way can we preserve our identities and live truthfully. You know the end of things as well as I do. We cannot pretend not to know them or deny that they exist. When we relate events from the past we know the results and must acknowledge them, whether or not they bring us understanding, or consolation, or shame.

—Ward Just, *A Dangerous Friend*

Contents

William Clark by Charles Willson Peale, circa 1810.
Independence National Historical Park.

Meriwether Lewis by Charles Willson Peale, circa 1807.
Independence National Historical Park.

Introduction

Exploring Lewis and Clark is about the expedition that Meriwether Lewis and William Clark led across the North American continent and back to St. Louis between 1803 and 1806. It is about the journals that they and other members of the expedition kept, the people who accompanied them and those they met along the way, and the animals they killed and those that transformed them. It is about dreams, spirits, myths, writing, and history. It examines how the explorers' possessions possessed them. It is about people who write and those who do not; it is about time, place, and spirituality. It is about naming, discovery, being an explorer, finding yourself, and losing your way.

The documentary filmmaker Ken Burns has called the Lewis and Clark Expedition "one of the great, but also one of the most superficially considered, stories in American history." About this, and on both counts, he is undoubtedly right. Bernard DeVoto and Stephen Ambrose have written gripping narratives that capture the courage of the expedition's leaders and the challenges they faced. No one will ever tell the story as well as DeVoto, because of his stylistic brilliance and because attitudes toward heroism, race, and the imperial and ecological impact of exploration were less troubled by complexity when he wrote in the early 1950s than they are now or ever can be again. Ambrose is also a brilliant storyteller. His biography of Lewis, *Undaunted Courage,* is a more racially enlightened narrative that benefits from forty years of scholarly research since DeVoto's *The Course of Empire* appeared. It is charged by Ambrose's knowledge of place, his love of nature, and his admiration for Lewis as a soldier, a leader, and a man.[1]

Nonetheless, Burns is also correct in saying that the Lewis and Clark Expedition remains one of the "most superficially considered" stories in American history. This reflects a curious paradox, because it is also the most heavily documented exploration in all of recorded history up to the twentieth century and hundreds of authors have written books about the expedition over the past one hundred years. The new edition of the expedition's journals is thirteen large volumes, over 1.5 million words by the editors' count. It also includes the journals of five members of the party and is one of the best-annotated, most comprehensive historical editing projects that have ever appeared.

In addition, there is a two-volume edition of the expedition's correspondence and a two-volume edition of first-person accounts of the expedition's path called *Before Lewis and Clark*. From this documentary record we get a Lewis and Clark newsletter, web sites, and a minor academic industry of conference proceedings, edited books, journal articles, and monographs on aspects of the expedition. What we have not gotten are many deep readings of the texts, although there are a few, or expansion of the relevant universe of historical records. *Exploring Lewis and Clark* seizes this hugely fascinating story, this mountain of contemporary records and scholarship, to widen our vision and to look beneath the explorers' narratives for different meanings than those they intended us to find.

The sweep of the journals' narrative across the continent and over time propels histories of the Lewis and Clark Expedition. Historians generally adopt the same chronological, episodic approach as the journal writers took. This is true even of such important topically focused books as James P. Ronda's *Lewis and Clark Among the Indians* and John Logan Allen's *Passage Through the Garden,* as well as those on botanical, medical, military, and diplomatic aspects of the expedition. The chronological organization is not a problem, and my observation is not a criticism of those fine books, but there are other ways to organize and focus discussions of the explorers. By eschewing the chronological for the topical, *Exploring Lewis and Clark* is closer in its structure to Ronda's *Finding the West* and Albert Furtwangler's *Acts of Discovery.*[2]

The journals and the cultural imperatives behind them remain powerful, indeed overwhelming to those of us who write about the Lewis and Clark Expedition. Scholarship most often continues to focus on the principals—Lewis, Clark, and Thomas Jefferson—as historians define them, with Indians and the forty-eight other members of the Corps of Discovery playing cameo roles. There are nods, and more, to the Indians and to the one woman associated with the endeavor in popular imagination, but rarely do we glimpse beneath the journals' narrative, around the two men whose names have become one—"LewisandClark"—except for the fantasy creations of a Shoshone woman who never lived.

Exploring Lewis and Clark uses the documentary record of the Lewis and Clark Expedition to different ends than most other books about the men and the event. It considers the meetings between peoples of different races in places that gave those encounters meaning. It is about Indian perspectives as well as those of whites, although I am often left to imagine what those may have been from the information that survives. It is about Clark's slave York, whom at least some Indians found the most impressive member of the expedition. It is about a Shoshone Indian woman who was also a slave—bought, sold, and gambled for among men.

The book engages ways that we process information. Cultural anthropologists have long known that humans react to the "new" through a sequence of emotional responses that include how we anticipate meetings. We filter such experiences through myths, dreams, hope, fear, and our sense of self. Then we rationalize newness through our own devices of knowing and crediting our senses. Next we reach an emotional/intellectual place where communion with the persons and/or things is possible. Finally, we "own" the knowledge, taking possession in some fashion that gives "newness" order and meaning. Typically, on the American frontier men exhibited a need for control that resulted in violence, sometimes in silence, not often enough in awe. Sometimes our ancestors felt lost; occasionally they were "found" in some mystical sense.

With this process and historical record in mind, the Lewis and Clark Expedition is an occasion for contemplating first meetings on the American frontier. There were other "firsts" and previous meetings on this continent, but not for these explorers of the American West. The richness of the historical record is an obvious enticement for a historian interested in the emotional dimensions of exploration. The variety of intercultural, interspecies, and geographical engagements is another lure.

Nineteenth-century Americans eventually forgot the Lewis and Clark Expedition. Leading citizens offered toasts, hosted several dinners, and congratulated the leaders, but the expedition was irrelevant to the continent-wide expansion that had already begun before the explorers' return. The westward movement would have continued without a moment's hesitation had all the expedition members died on the trail. Lewis's and Clark's place names were lost, their "discoveries" rediscovered, and their moccasin tracks obliterated by boots, hooves, and wagon wheels. Five years' delay before publication of the journals in heavily abridged form contributed to the expedition's irrelevance.

During the second half of the nineteenth century, the explorers and what they accomplished faded from the nation's collective memory. The recovery of the expedition and its construction as a national triumph was a twentieth-century process, one that came after the passing of the American frontier. New editions of the journals and hundreds of books blending fact, fiction, and myth have buried the explorers under a mountain of celebratory words. Historians often lose, and thus readers seldom get, critical perspective on the journals, the journalists, and the journey.

This book favors no single perspective on the expedition. Some chapters examine the explorers' journals internally, looking more deeply within the texts for their meanings. Others reach outward for contexts and sources that help elucidate the journal entries. A third approach focuses more on external contexts that the journals enlighten. Collectively, these different vantage points illustrate, without exhausting, a range of ways that the expedition can still be explored.

The journals are fascinating sources—beguiling, perplexing, complex, and far richer than historians have generally appreciated. They are foggy windows which admit and distort light on the men who wrote them. It is necessary, therefore, to explore their nature as sources, as chapter three does, in order to use them as subsequent chapters do.

The ordering of the chapters neither duplicates the expedition's chronology nor is it random. Chapter one considers the spiritual and mythological foundations of the journey and the journals. Chapter two looks to the secular and historical ambitions of the explorers. Chapter three examines the journals themselves. Chapters four through eight and my final reflections then use the journals in ways consistent with the approaches illustrated in the first three chapters. Chapters four, five, and six gaze outside the journals for what they can tell us about one liminal creature and two liminal people who, although elusive quarry, are essential to the expedition's spiritual, mythical, and historical standing. Chapters seven and eight and "Reflections" look internally toward the same ends.

Chapters one, four, five, and six, then, take an external perspective on the journals, one that looks outward for their meaning. Alternatively, chapters two, three, seven, and eight gaze inward to the texts and the men who wrote them. The starkest, and thus most illustrative, contrast is between chapters four—"Why Snakes?"—and seven—"Hunting Themselves." While chapter four is more about the wider culture's influence on the journals, chapter seven explores the personal and thus psychological dimensions of journal writing.

Given the nature of what the journalists wrote about snakes, it would not be possible for me to flip the analytical perspectives of those two chapters. What the journals actually say about snakes does not permit a deeper historical analysis of the kind that I pursue. A much longer chapter or a monograph on the subject of chapter seven could combine the internal and external perspectives. Such a contextualized discussion of hunting would be worth having, but not in a book of this sort that addresses other subjects too. In other words, the journals resist interrogation on the subject of snakes and thus propel the reader outside to the wider culture for meanings while they simultaneously embrace the reader who delves inside them for engagement with hunting and the self.

If *Exploring Lewis and Clark* is more about writing than exploring, that is because the written record is what survives and because writing is the explorer's defining task. First and foremost explorers are writers, and so are historians. Written words are the bridge across time that connects us to Lewis and Clark. If it were not for the journals, the expedition would be a footnote to history, of little or no enduring significance.

Neither the journals nor the explorers are what they seem. That is a story worth telling in the twenty-first century. It is not my intention either to celebrate or to vilify. The goal is to understand the Lewis and Clark Expedition differently than we now do. I do not aim to debunk myths. I am interested in the differences between myths and history, and I believe that the distinction is an important one. There is recoverable history buried under our national origin myths which can teach us relationships between the present and the past—who we are, what we have done, and what we can become. Lewis and Clark matter now more than ever and more than they ever knew—as mythical figures, as heroic ideals, but as humans too.

Exploring Lewis and Clark

CHAPTER ONE

Dreams

"IN THE BEGINNING the surface of the earth was all water and there was darkness." In this darkness and on these waters First Creator and Lone Man walked. They came across a duck—a mud hen in some versions—diving under the water and were curious. They asked the duck what she ate and she returned from a dive with sand in her beak, which they used to create the earth.

> The First Creator made broad valleys, hills, coulees with timber, mountain streams, springs, and, as creatures, the buffalo elk, black-tailed and white-tailed antelope, mountain sheep and all other creatures useful to mankind for food and clothing. He made the valleys and coulees as shelter for the animals as well as for mankind. He set lakes far apart. Lone Man created for the most part level country with lakes and small streams and rivers far apart. The animals he made lived some of them in the water, like beaver, otter, and muskrat. Others were the cattle of many colors with long horns and long tails, moose, and other animals.

First Creator and Lone Man compared their creations and found fault with each other's. "First Creator said of the land north of the Missouri River, 'The things you have created do not meet with my approval. The land is too level and affords no protection to man.' " Lone Man thought that First Creator had made the land south of the Missouri too rough. They agreed, though, to leave all as it was and to allow humans to use the south side until its resources were exhausted and then move across the river to the north. "So it was agreed between them and both blessed their creation and the two parted."

Lone Man watched humans multiply and was pleased. He worried, though, about evil spirits among them and decided to be born as a man. He chose a Mandan virgin for his mother, turned himself into a kernel of corn, and entered her when she ate him. "In the course of time the child was born and he grew up like other children, but he showed unusual traits of purity and as he grew to manhood he despised all evil and never even married. Everything he did was to promote goodness."

There are other stories about the creations, about the origins of Lone Man and his good deeds on behalf of humans. Mandans said they had come from a cavern on the north bank of a river at the ocean's shore. They told Lewis and Clark that they came from a village under the earth, from which they climbed on a grapevine. They knew that Lone Man never married or engaged in a sexual act. They believed that light-complexioned people would come from the east, because that was prophesied from the time of creation. And they anticipated trouble from the white men when fur traders and explorers arrived. When First Creator saw the whites that Lone Man created, he disapproved. "You have made a queer kind of men—they will always be greedy!"[1]

"In the beginning God created the Heaven, and the Earth." Important stories repeat. The earth is created three times in Genesis, and the Mandan told their creation story in multiple versions too. "So God created man in his own Image, in the Image of God created he him; male and female created he them." Again: "And the LORD God formed man of the dust of the ground, & breathed into his nostrils the breath of life; and man became a living soul." Lone Man also breathed life into his creations, and not always in the same way.

Myths vary in the repetition. Both the variation and the repetition are essential. "And God spoke to Noah, saying, Go forth from the Ark, thou, and thy wife, and thy sons, and thy sons' wives with thee: Bring forth with thee every living thing that is with thee, of all flesh, both of fowl and cattle, and of every creeping thing that creeps upon the earth, that they may breed abundantly in the earth, and be fruitful, and multiply upon the earth." Myths, by their very essence, can be and must be replicated. We repeat them—both the telling and the acts—over and over again.

Myths create binaries—heaven and earth, man and woman, good and evil, beginning and end, first and last, God and man. The middle ground between these binaries is scary, violent, evil or holy, and unnatural—a place to avoid (taboo) or approach through ritual in an attempt to resolve the danger of the binary or opposite. These are places for shamans. Even Jesus and Lone Man faced great danger in these liminal (in-between) spots when they became humans. "Now the serpent was more subtle than any beast of the field, which the LORD God had made." That, it seems, was its undoing. "And the LORD God said to the Serpent, Because you have done this, you are cursed above all cattle, and above every beast of the field; upon your belly shall you go, and dust shall you eat, all the days of thy life." Cursed, again, the serpent remains between God and humans, man and woman, nature and the unnatural, although always identified more closely with the second in each of these binaries—humans, woman, and the unnatural—thereby branding each by association. We are, in the Genesis myth, forever snake and not snake over and over again.[2]

Where, Lewis and Clark asked the Mandan, did your people come from? We live under the water, where we have a village and gardens. Then, before we remember, we come out through a hole and settle on the Missouri River. Lone Man is born to a Mandan virgin, who conceives him by ingesting a kernel of corn. . . . "Several little anecdotes told me today," Clark wrote, not even bothering to enter the (to him) silly stories that he dismissed charmingly. Ignoring the belief of some Mandans that they came from the south—First Creator's land—and the west—a cavern on the banks of a river at the ocean's edge—Clark postulated that they were descended from "a more civilized state" to the east.[3]

The explorers believed that the Mandans were too "white" to be full-blooded Indians. The tribe's comparatively fair complexion was a sign of racial connections to Europe, Lewis and Clark reasoned. The Indians spoke of a garden and a great flood, demonstrating shared mythical origins. The explorers sought other evidence of the Mandans' biblical knowledge, since an American "lost tribe" remained a distinct possibility, as did a Welsh genealogy. There were stories about Prince Madoc's discovery of North America and possibly some Mandans had heard about fair-complexioned ancestors who came from the east with stories about a garden, a snake, and a flood.

Such apparently simple issues as directionality were devilishly difficult to establish with the Mandan, though. Some came from below; some came from over there; some responded positively to Clark's suggestion that they came from the east. More than one traveler remarked that Indian responses to such questions were useless. According to the fur trader David Thompson, "persons who pass through the country often think the answers the Indians give are their real sentiments. The answers are given to please the querist." Hospitality dictated that answers please the guest, so the Mandan told Clark what they thought he wanted to hear. He did not appreciate their stories set westward, to the south, or underground. If he wanted them to say that they came from the east, they would provide that response, too. The eastern origin and the descent from civilization were Clark's theories. The directions were part of his mythical baggage. The desire for racial linkages between Indians and Europeans was his culture's, too. The Mandans knew better and did not share the dream that their peoples were one. Their "charming anecdotes" were true. They knew who the white men were and where they had come from.[4]

Mandans saw their myths unfolding in the present, as did Hidatsa, Nez Perce, Shoshone, and Sahaptan-speaking peoples whom Lewis and Clark met, while the explorers believed their culture's origin stories in the past tense if they believed them at all. These explorers, like most educated Americans of their day and ours, alienated the teller from the tale, the present from the past and future, and humans from the natural world in which the stories were embedded. When Lewis or Clark asked a question in the past tense, Mandans gave answers that seemed unresponsive. The explorers wanted "facts" they could write down. What they got often seemed inappropriate for transcription. Readers of their journals are left, then, with vague references to the stories and ridicule of the storytellers.[5]

Where are you from? Lewis and Clark asked the Nez Perce. We are the Nee-mee-poo, the "People," who live in this place. But where did you live before you came here? Ah, there are stories about a time before the memory of humans when the earth was covered in water.

The water wandered among the pine trees with no paths to follow. There were only animals then, which made the earth ready for the arrival of the People. Skunk, who was a great mystery man, and Bear wanted to dig a path for the water so that the People could find berries and roots on dry land. Coyote, who liked to do big things, volunteered to dig a ditch from the ocean, through the mountains and onto the level plains. He dug high, which is the falls, and low, which is the valley. "So were the rivers formed and things made ready for The People."[6]

Lewis did not bother to write such answers down and neither did Clark on the outward leg of their journey. They could, however, try to rephrase the question. How is it that your people came to live in this valley? Ah, you want to know about Bear and the boy.

A boy wandered in the mountains at the time when the People were coming to take the place of animals on earth. He could not find his parents, but did meet up with the grizzly bear. "Bear growled until the mountains shook and echoed his anger." The boy, unlike the animals, did not show fear and answered bear's growls in calm words. "I can only die. Death is only part of life. I am not afraid." Bear was full of wonder at the boy's bravery and declared him a member of a superior race. In admiration, Bear flipped the boy up on his back and showed him the homes of beaver, moose, elk, deer, and buffalo. He showed the boy the path through the mountains to a beautiful valley full of edible game, berries, and roots. Bear then took the boy back to the People and the boy showed them the way to the valley and all the secrets that Bear had shared with him.[7]

How frustrating for Lewis and Clark. Even if you want to, even if you take it seriously as an origins myth, the story cannot be captured in writing. Its essence is embedded in the telling—the voice that growls the grizzly's words, the teeth that chomp, and the snarling mouth. The audience should include children. The listeners must display the boy's fear, speak his lines courageously, and portray the excitement in his eyes as he tells of the wonders he has beheld. They should know the landmarks to which the story refers—the particular rock, the specific river, the mountain pass through which Bear carried the boy. The meaning is not in the words alone; it is in the telling.[8]

The Indians whom Lewis and Clark met lived in much closer proximity to the nonhuman world than the explorers ever would. Those who used bows and arrows literally had to get closer to their prey than the long-rifled hunters of the expedition. They were in better communication with nature, listening more effectively and feeling more listened-to. They were emotionally and empathetically closer to nature, apprentices to the animals around them and ever alert to the wisdom, the power, and the mysteries that nature has to share.[9]

Clark fared no better with Hidatsa informers than he had with the Mandan, than he would with the Shoshone or Nez Perce. Hidatsa men told him "many extraordinary stories." When he redrafted the entry for that day, Clark noted again that he walked with the Hidatsa chief and interpreters, but left out even the vague reference to their stories. Clearly their answers were "extraordinary" in a pejorative sense only, and thus not worth writing down. They were unbelievable, incredible, fantastic, and unresponsive. Clark wanted facts, not superstitions, and he wanted honest answers to his straightforward inquiries. Where did your people come from? There is a lake on the bottomlands of the Missouri River. People live under the water, which is very deep. You can hear their voices talking or singing. Sometimes you can hear their dogs barking and their drums when they are dancing. The past and the present, nature and humans, are one in the story.[10]

Where did you come from? "The [Mandan] chief pointed out several places," Clark wrote on the expedition's return journey, "where he said his nation formerly lived and related some extraordinary stories of their tradition." Let me show you; we come from here—this rock, that lake, the mud or outcropping over there. Places were not passive settings to Clark's Mandan respondent. Experiences were not separable from the places where they occurred. Locales were not interchangeable. Places were active participants and often the source of an event. Space was undifferentiated from time. Space and time apparently existed in a continuum, a cycle that was neither linear nor past; the future came in its own time as it did before.[11]

It made sense to the Mandan, Hidatsa, and Nez Perce respondents that the explorers were looking for places, but they may have failed to comprehend why the white men wanted to know where the ocean, the mountains, or the source of the Missouri was. It made less sense to them than it did to Lewis and Clark that the explorers were in a hurry to get to a mountain, felt late reaching the source of a river, or had no time to be here rather than there. The expedition's journals embodied Lewis's and Clark's sense of linear, sequential time as an objective entity divorced from experience in the present.

another myth

How could you be late for a mountain? The notion made no sense at all. To those Mandan, Nez Perce, and Hidatsa who experienced place as animate and experience as inherently spontaneous and temporally dynamic, the explorers' race to be "first" would have appeared irrational.[12]

In one story that Clark did write down during his second visit with the Mandan, the people he spoke to recalled coming out of the ground where they lived. A grapevine grew up from their village through a hole in the earth. When they looked up the vine, they could see light. Some of the braver ones among them climbed the plant. When they got to the top, they saw buffalo, grapes, plums, and other animals and plants good to eat. They tasted the fruit and found it good. Others, including women and children, joined them, climbing to the surface of the earth. In time, a pregnant woman climbed the vine and it broke under her weight, leaving her and the rest of her people below, where they continued to reside. When the Mandan died, they returned to this subterranean village.[13]

When the Mandan found the game good, they crossed another one of those in-between places that harbor the greatest dangers of all. Just as the mythical binaries fall on either side of a dangerous divide, so do hunters and their prey. The hunt takes place at a boundary between the human and nonhuman. The hunter, with one foot on each side of the chasm, risks both his identity and his life. In Genesis, the wild places where animals dwell are signs of our fallen condition. In the Hidatsa, Nez Perce, and Mandan origin myths recounted here, arrival at the animals' dwelling place is a blessing and often a great gift of the animals themselves.

These tribes were not banished to the wilderness as were Adam and Eve. Instead they discovered it. These Indians received what the Europeans called "wilderness" as a gift. Toward the end of his journey, Clark began to comprehend this alternative perspective on people in nature. "To its present inhabitants nature seems to have dealt with a liberal hand," he realized. This was a profound insight for a man from his culture; it represents an enlightenment that few of his contemporaries ever experienced. Nature gave, nature "dealt" with an active, perhaps—in modern Western terms—even conscious intent.[14]

The animals gave themselves too, which the explorers never appreciated any more than the hunters who followed them west. They witnessed, but did not fully appreciate, the ceremonial preparation that accompanied the hunt. The ritual attached to the buffalo was simply "superstition" to them. Feeding a buffalo skull, entreating its spirit to favor the hunters, made no sense. To Lewis and Clark, and the hunters who accompanied them, it appeared that the Indians they met entered the hunt with greater trepidation than European-Americans did, but the expedition's journals suggest that the opposite was true.

The Sun Dance, which the explorers heard about, and the buffalo-calling ceremony were beyond their appreciation, if not their comprehension, in spiritual terms. For all their culture's celebration of hunting, and for all the explorers' documentation of their hunting skills, they never experienced killing as a spiritual act. They saw themselves as possessing their prey and never as the vulnerable, weaker parties in the hunting relationship.

Where are you going? the Mandan and Hidatsa asked the explorers. What are you looking for? We are traveling up the Missouri River to its headwaters, where we expect to find great mountains and a short portage to a great river that runs down the western side of the mountain range to a great ocean. Do you know where that is? Is it far? No, not far. You will have an easy trip. That is what the explorers wanted to hear and their hosts wanted to please them. The Indians' response was a kindness, a blessing, a wish for the travelers' trip. Great mountains, a mythic river, and a body of water too large to see or to paddle across—this was a mythic journey to sacred places of great mystery.

Lewis and Clark described a magnificent valley watered by a grand river, one even greater than the Mississippi or Missouri. They sought transit to exploitable agricultural resources—new land for American farmers—and another trade route to the Far East. They saw rivers as conduits, mountains as obstacles, and natural beauty as exploitable fertility. Some of their Indian respondents misunderstood, believing that the explorers sought mystical places—mountains, a river, and a garden on the edge of a mythical body of water. The explorers contemplated a passage; some of their hosts comprehended the expedition as a quest for spiritual power derived from specific locales. *[handwritten: two stories equally mythical]*

If Lewis's and Clark's words evoked images of a passage to a sacred garden, they were close to engaging the northern Plains Indians on shared mythical ground. The Mandan spoke of Edenic origins themselves, where animals and people shared language. The difference was not immediately obvious to either group, but the Mandan still lived in their garden while the explorers had been expelled from theirs, left to wander the planet in a futile quest to find the way back. *[handwritten: We are losers]*

Eve speaks lucidly with a snake; now that made sense to a Mandan or Nez Perce. The snake gives her access to wisdom—"mystery," the Mandan would say, which made sense to them, too. Lone Man communicates with a mud hen. First Creator becomes Coyote when he wishes. Bear shares his secrets with a Nez Perce boy. People live under the lake. Coyote digs a trench from the ocean to hold the water. Indians sought power and knowledge of "mysteries" from animals. American farmers consulted the moon about when to plant their crops and graft fruit trees, fur-bearing animals about the winter to come, and domestic livestock about an impending storm. Euro-Americans and Amerindians all communicated with nature, but one was "science" and the other "superstition" in Lewis's and Clark's eyes.

Toward the end of their journey, though, when Clark and Lewis had taken separate paths, Clark fused the perspectives. A short passage in the journals chronicles communication that never occurred across these cultural lines, at least not during this expedition. He drafted a speech in anticipation of finding the Crow Indians along the Yellowstone River, a meeting that never took place.

The passage can be read as a cynical attempt by Clark to manipulate Indian "superstitions" for his own ends or as a wise attempt to speak to the Crow on their own terms. Either way, the goal would be to impress them with a spiritual power that their culture valued and his denied. What should not be dismissed in any interpretation of the speech, though, is the possibility that Clark believed and meant what he said. And what he intended to say to the Crows was this: "Children I heard from some of your people [blank] nights past by my horses who complained to me of your people having taken four of their comrades."[15]

The passage's significance transcends Clark's claim of having received a message from horses he knew well. It was not in the least unusual for people in his culture to talk and listen to their domestic animals. Direct verbal communication from animals to humans was not as common among Euro-Americans in Clark's day as it had been in the century before his birth, when the devil's "familiars" took on animal forms among the New England Puritans. Speaking dogs and whispering birds were never entirely welcome in Anglo-America and their existence was roundly denied by the most educated Americans, especially after such ephemeral creatures contributed to the deaths of so many innocent people in the Salem witchcraft trials. In folk culture, though, there were stories and "documented" events. Clark was more closely connected to this folk culture than Lewis and thus spiritually closer to the belief systems of the expedition's enlisted men than the more book-educated Lewis. As is clear from the journals, too, and not just from this passage, Clark was becoming more spiritually attuned to the cultures of the Indians the longer the expedition proceeded.

There are three other aspects of this passage that are also significant. If Clark was simply fabricating an event for the indulgence of Crow "superstition," he might just as well have filled in the number of days since the fictional event took place. In other words, the best reason for leaving the number of days blank has little to do with his inability to anticipate the exact date when he would deliver the speech. To be sure, he could not pick a number higher than the number of days intervening between the horses going missing and his anticipated meeting with the Indians whom he believed had stolen them, but he could choose any lower number if he was simply making the whole thing up. The better reason for not filling in the blank was that he had a particular date in mind and intended the speech to reflect the actual evening when the horses communicated with him.

In this same regard, Clark might have named the actual number of missing horses—twenty-four—rather than the significantly lower number of four. Again, if he was fabricating, why not create a story that better served his purposes of recovering as many of the twenty-four horses as possible right up to the full count? The better answer is that he named the number four because that is the number his horses actually told him were taken by the Crow. Unless, of course, he simply made a transcription error by writing "four" when he meant to write "twenty-four."

Finally, and most ephemerally of all, it is significant that the horses complained to Clark at night rather than in the morning. One possible explanation is that Clark was implying that the communication came to him in a dream. That would bring Clark's story into line with both his own culture's mainstream beliefs about animal communication and with those of the Crow. Horses do not generally speak—in either culture—during what we would call conscious states of the recipient's mind. It is more likely that Clark would hear from his horses in a dreaming state that would be associated with sleep in his own culture, but that the Crow would entertain as possible in a waking trance too.

Early in the expedition, both Lewis and Clark scoffed at such Indian "superstitions" and claimed to believe that the spirit world is impermeable by humans. "They are a very silly and superstitious people," Patrick Gass wrote in his journal about one Indian tribe, mistaking spirituality for superstition, a distinction that is always in the eye of the beholder. When Indians appeared "silly" for not sharing the explorers' comparative valuation of trade goods, for example, the whites discounted the spiritual values associated with items valued more highly by their hosts. "These Indians had the appearance of being very poor, and set a great value on the most trifling article," noted Joseph Whitehouse in his journal. As the explorers saw it, esteeming mirrors, red cloth, or blue beads more highly than iron tools was a sign of the Indians' ignorance, but that is because they failed to observe the ceremonial function of trade goods in the Indian societies.

> The hunting party found several pieces of red cloth at an Indian camp, which we expect the Indians had left there the last winter as a sacrifice to their maker, [which] the Indian woman mentioned is the custom when they break up their encampment and which shows that they have some knowledge of the supreme being.[16]

In societies where the accumulation of goods was neither a goal nor a measure of wealth, the power to give them away was greater than the power to keep them. So, too, the function of trade goods to further spiritual growth was more deeply appreciated than the explorers realized. Mirrors, for example, were among the most popular items left behind by Lewis and Clark. Merchants found cheap looking glasses mounted on pasteboard a trade item valued more highly by Indians than their cost to the traders. Those whites who speculated on the Indians' high valuation of mirrors assumed that they were vanity items. Prince Maximilian, a German traveler who visited the Mandan about twenty-five years after Lewis and Clark, observed that many of the Indians actually wore mirrors around their wrists.

These Indians are vain, and in this respect childish, like all savage nations. They are very fond of ornament, and the young men have always a little looking-glass suspended from their wrists. The traders sell these looking-glasses in a pasteboard case, which, however is immediately changed for a solid wooden frame, and attached to the wrist by a red ribbon or a leather strap. The looking-glasses are framed in various ways; the rude frame is often painted red, or with stripes of different colours, with footsteps of bears or buffaloes carved on it. Nay, sometimes these frames are of a considerable size, divided at one end like a bootjack, and ornamented with brass nails, ribbons, pieces of skin and feathers. Some had very ingeniously fastened this important appendage to their fan made of an eagle's wing.[17]

What Maximilian understood no better than Lewis and Clark was that the mirrors were easily integrated into Plains Indian culture as a variation on items that already had spiritual functions. Reflective objects—water, crystal, and polished metals and stones—were used for divination before the arrival of the explorers. Reflections, generally distorted by ripples in water or surface variations in solid objects, helped the dream seeker focus—we might say meditate, self-hypnotize, or hallucinate. The inexpensive mirrors circulated by Lewis and Clark, as well as by fur traders, may have clarified the dreamers' image, thereby altering and possibly even enhancing the visionary's soulful gaze. Liberating the soul from the body connected a dreamer to the spiritual power of the natural world, which was much more highly valued among these tribes than the ritually impoverished goods that Europeans esteemed.[18]

Everything Maximilian saw is consistent with the ceremonial significance of mirrors. The wooden mount he describes was designed for planting the mirror in the ground, thereby freeing the dreamer's body from earthly attachments and enabling the soul to fly. The ornamentation reflected the mirror's association with powerful animal spirits—bears, eagles, buffalo, and snakes—and a closer observation would likely have revealed that each mirror was personalized to incorporate the dreamer's association with particular animal spirits.

Wearing the mirrors reflected their value and the dreamer's attachment to this most valued trade item.

How odd, the Plains Indians may have pondered, that the bearers
of these remarkable gifts had so little appreciation of their worth.
How peculiar that the white men were so dismissive of the spirit
world to which their mirrors facilitated access. In a double-edged
way, the gift of mirrors may have contributed to Indian suspicions
that Lewis and Clark were on a vision quest and to the Indians' belief
that the explorers' lack of interest in mirrors reflected the white
men's dispirited souls.

This meant that the power of Lewis's and Clark's trade goods could
be both positive and negative, as the explorers should have known.
They expected the Indians to admire the medals struck for distribu-
tion among "chiefs." The medals bore President Jefferson's image on
one side and hands embraced in friendship on the other (see illustrations on page 187). Handshaking was a novel concept to some of the
Indians they met, as was the notion of a two-sided image-laden
adornment. As the Nez Perce long remembered, "each man in a turn
took the right hand of Big Eagle and moved it up and down, up and
down, in a way never seen before." How strange; what could it mean?
It was a physical presumption—taking a man's right hand—and
could seem aggressive. At least one "chief" reacted negatively in the
presence of the explorers to a gift of the handshaking coin. Clark
reported the event.

> I gave a medal of the small size to the Cheyenne chief &c., which
> appeared to alarm him. He had a robe and a fleece of fat buffalo
> meat brought and gave me with the medal back and informed me
> that he knew that the white people were all *medicine* and that he
> was afraid of the medal or anything that white people gave to
> them.[19]

Perhaps the chief was merely being polite and meant to say that
the whites were all "bad" medicine and he wanted nothing to do with
their tainted gifts. Certainly that is what other Indians along the way
meant, as those who followed Lewis and Clark learned. According to

the fur trader Alexander Henry, for example, the Hidatsa determined that Lewis and Clark were evil and that the medals, flags, and other items the white men left behind were full of their bad mystery, and therefore "supposed they could not better dispose of those articles than by giving them to the natives with whom they frequently warred, in hope the ill-luck would be conveyed to them." The Hidatsa told Henry that Lewis's and Clark's manners "disgusted" them. The explorers were haughty. They believed themselves above nature and other men. They impolitely dismissed stories that the Hidatsa told them in response to their questions. They were, the Hidatsa concluded, spiritually bankrupt.[20]

Other Indians also found Lewis (especially) and (sometimes) Clark closed-minded and considered one or both of them spiritually impoverished, perhaps soulless, and possibly evil. The white men sought to demonstrate, but not to share, their power—firing guns to impress their Indian hosts. The Indians were more impressed by other "mysteries," though—mirrors, magnifying glasses, medications, compasses, and the color of a "black-white man's" skin.

Lewis and Clark tried to awe Indians with a loud air rifle. It was a minor and ineffective "mystery" to the Hidatsa and Nez Perce, who nonetheless tried to be polite. When Indians attempted to return favors or gifts with some of their own mysteries, Lewis and Clark were impatient, which at least some Indians perceived as rude. Others, probably most, had no desire to share their mysteries with the explorers in any event. The white men were not interested in spirits. They did not want to converse with a grizzly bear, understand the coyote's howl, or gain favor with the buffalo. Lewis disbelieved knowledge derived from animals in visions. He, at least, did not know how to dream in the Indians' sense.

On the outward journey, Lewis and Clark did not show respect for Indian origin myths. Some Hidatsa and Nez Perce, at least, saw the white men as spiritually deficient and were prescient in their assessment of the expedition's purpose. Could it be a war party? Not likely with a woman along. They certainly were not merchants; they did not bring enough trade goods and did not seem all that interested in furs. They might be the remnant of a lost tribe, the black man being their fiercest warrior honored by painting his body black, the woman and child being the only ones not captured by their enemies.

They looked more like the survivors of several tribes, though—with red, black, and brown hair, curly and straight; blue, brown, and black eyes; various complexions, including a black man and a Shoshone woman. They surely did ask many questions. They seemed curious, but unable to comprehend the mysteries that Mandan and Hidatsa informants shared. They were looking for mountains, the sources of rivers, and an ocean. Perhaps they were on a vision quest, seeking spiritual power from mysterious places. They certainly needed deeper spirituality. Group quests were not unprecedented in Plains Indian experience, and neither was soliciting visions at the variety of ages represented in the group. Ah, that must be it; the white men needed to learn how to dream.

A dream can be a conscious hope or ambition. In that sense of the word it is about the future. Dreams are also the unconscious state of REM sleep. In that meaning they are products of the moment, although often understood as processing the past or predicting the future. Nocturnal dreams are not at all the same as waking dreams or visions, which can be spontaneous or induced but are often more "real" to the dreamer. In each of these senses—waking fantasy, sleeping horror or ecstasy, and visionary full-sense engagement of realities seen only by the dreamer—dreams are culturally bound. That is true for the experience, memory, reporting, and interpretation of dreams.

To be human is to dream, but other creatures also dream. To live is to dream. The earth lives—rivers and mountains, rocks and trees too. To dream is to live. Does death bring an end to dreaming or is it simply another dream? The sun sleeps, oral traditions teach us, and so does the moon. Perhaps we are the dreams of the heavens and the earth, of spirits that animate life.

To Amerindians of the Great Plains, the white men's distinction between waking and dreaming makes no sense. Visions are actual encounters with mythic sources of power. The successful dreamer merges states that Europeans experience only autonomously. Conscious/unconscious is not a binary that makes sense in Plains Indian cultures. It is replaced by a distinction between what is known and what remains mysterious. Dreaming is a way of breaching that divide, of achieving knowledge about the mysterious and thereby moving it to the category of the known.[21]

Dreaming, then, is a reflection of a mythic worldview that provides the symbols for interpreting meanings. Whether dreams are significant and powerful communications with a natural world external to the dreamer is a question of culture and skill. The proof of the dreamer's empowerment can be practically demonstrated by a display of previously unknown ability, of mystery solved, or of knowledge revealed. The dream of a cure can be validated by healing, of good fortune in war by a successful raid, or of the coming of strangers by their arrival.[22]

Within such a mythic tradition, it makes sense to induce dreams. Vision quests were often associated with youth, but in Plains Indian cultures they could be pursued at any age, by either gender, and alone or in a group. It was possible to seek collective empowerment or a personal vision within a structured group ritual, in addition to the personal vision quest associated with coming of age. Since visions were a gift bestowed at the whim of the giver, rituals of preparation were significant.

Lewis and Clark professed disbelief in an active spirit world, having shed their culture's fear of witches and their familiars long ago. They also dismissed Indian rituals of preparation and active solicitation of spiritual empowerment. Their conscious protestations of disbelief, their dismissal of "superstition," and their attempt to reduce experience to a science of tangible "fact" bely the depth of their self-doubt. The expedition became, then, an unacknowledged vision quest for some of its members, who opened themselves to spiritual enlightenment even as they denied the power of "unconscious" revelation. Lewis fought hardest and most visibly against dreaming, endorsing his culture's secular worldview in rigid, strident tones that attempted to wall off experience he was unprepared to accept.

Clark, too, believed in hard facts retrievable and verifiable only in a conscious state. Clark was more open to his doubts, though, more accepting of the unreliability of his senses, and experienced greater spiritual growth. A number of Indians from several tribes noticed this

Lewis - book educated
Clark - less "formal" ed.

difference between the two white men and recognized that neither was the same man on the return trip that he had been on the way out. Lewis was spiritually drained, emotionally exhausted, a nervous wreck. Clark was calmer, more open, wiser, and more powerful by journey's end. Vision quests, the Plains Indians knew, do not work for everyone. Lewis was already dead; only his body was still alive.

Some of the clues are subtle, to be sure, but there are reasons to believe that Lewis's and Clark's rational science was, in part, a pose rather than a full and accurate reflection of their inner selves. Certainly they were writing for Thomas Jefferson and his circle of Enlightenment philosophers. They knew the anticipated audience for their journals and Jefferson had schooled Lewis in the language and values of the American Philosophical Society, the Library Company of Philadelphia, and their members. The farther they got from Philadelphia, though, the harder it was to maintain the rational perspective of the "philosophical" mind.

Early in the expedition Clark prayed, but caught himself before revealing the depth of his spirituality in writing. "My father I am sorry that the first man I brought." The phrase certainly has a prayerful form and entreats forgiveness, but forgiveness for what is not clear. The written prayer was a partial lapse, caught almost in time. It is a touching admission of frailty and an expression of regret. The rest of the entry for August 18, 1804, suggests that Clark felt badly about the physical disciplining of Moses Reed, a deserter caught and returned to camp. "The first man I brought" is also unclear, but implies that Clark felt a personal responsibility for this outcome. Perhaps Clark recruited Reed himself. Maybe Reed was "the first man" Clark had "brought" himself to whip as part of the five hundred lashes inflicted on the man's back. In any event, the entry is one brief glimpse into Clark's soul, into his comparative emotional accessibility, his humanity, and his belief in a higher spiritual being to which he felt responsible. It is also unlike any revelation made by the more guarded, professional, deistic, and unyielding Lewis. Lewis shows himself as less likely to pray, less likely to be caught in the written act, and also less forgiving of others and of himself. It seems less likely that he would have regretted whipping a deserter however much pain he inflicted.[23]

Clark was also open to dreams right from the beginning of the journey. Here, too, he regretted this lapse from the scientific rationality of his day and attempted to expunge the fact that he acted in response to a dream. "This creek I call Roloje a *name given me last night in my sleep.*" When he transcribed the entry into his fair copy, Clark left out the words that I have italicized.

Again, this is a shard rather than a complete artifact of Clark's belief, which seems insufficient to embark on an interpretation of the dream. Since Clark knew, though, that this was not the sort of revelation an audience of Jefferson's peers would value and since Clark tried to expunge the reason he chose this name, it is a particularly revealing insight that we might easily have lost. It is also significant that even though he was embarrassed for people—perhaps including or possibly even especially Lewis—to know why he chose the name, Clark did not change it, remaining instead loyal to the nocturnal message he received.[24]

Not surprisingly, the Christian God and his own dream were more credible than Indian spirituality to Clark and equally incredible to Lewis if we take the tone and content of their discussions of Indians' spiritual sites at face value. Knowing as we do, though, that Clark had a spiritual bent that he tried to suppress in the journals, we can discern clues that the explorers were not as confidently rational, by their lights, as they attempted to portray themselves. There is a dogged debunking quality to such entries. There is also evidence of active hostility to spiritual artifacts, which suggests an engagement born of insecurity. Finally, there is also a certain whistling-in-the dark quality to the entries, suggesting that the journal writers boyishly tried to hide how spooked they could sometimes be in a place feared *only* by "savages."

On August 25, 1804, a party of ten armed members of the expedition set out to explore a "mountain of evil spirits" that people from several Indian tribes had told them about. Clark wrote the journal entry for this day, which again provides a different sort of opportunity for analysis than it would if Lewis were the author. It was a solitary hill on a vast open expanse of the Plains. This itself seemed mystical to the Indians, suggesting either a significant creative event or, to the explorers, the hand of man. But, as Clark explained, the force of the prairie wind was enough to make the hill; there was no cause to jump to superstitious conclusions based on this thoroughly explicable outcropping. We might suspect Lewis's voice in the explanation. We should also suspect that the confidence came only in retrospect, after they left this eerie place.

Indians experienced the hill as one of those in-between places, a spiritually potent locale. "It is supposed to be a place of devils or—" wrote Clark, who then tore off the rest of the page. What did Clark write that so upset him, which he had to keep us from reading? The entry continues on a separate sheet.

> They are in human form with remarkable large heads and about eighteen inches high; that they are very watchful and are armed with sharp arrows with which they can kill at a great distance; they are said to kill all persons who are so hardy as to attempt to approach the hill; they state that tradition informs them that many Indians have suffered by these little people and among others that three Omaha men fell a sacrifice to their merciless fury not many years since. So much do the Omahas, Sioux, Otoes and other neighboring nations believe this fable that no consideration is sufficient to induce them to approach this hill.[25]

As they climbed, Lewis's dog "gave out" and returned to camp. A small detail, but worth reporting for some reason. Perhaps it was an omen; animals often sense trouble before humans can see it. In the context of Clark's feelings during the ascent this detail took on meaning that it otherwise would have lacked. From far below the summit, they could see "great numbers of birds hovering about the top." Undoubtedly they wondered why.

All this is reported in sequential time, because the feelings—fear, mystery, and perhaps enchantment—came from not knowing what lay ahead. We have to imagine the men's frame of mind, their posture, their thoughts, as Clark only tells us in retrospect what they found. It was simply the presence of vast numbers of flying ants that attracted the birds, Clark reported—nothing mystical about that, only irritating bites. The Indians' belief that "unusual spirits" drew the birds was only evidence, according to Clark, that the "savage mind" was easily frightened. This fear was irrational, Clark would have us believe, and a sign of the Indians' inferiority to European-Americans. And yet Clark reported that York was exhausted by the party's pace, "he being fat and unaccustomed to walk as fast as I went." Why the quickened pace if the place did not spook the explorers too? Clark, for one, was enchanted by the view from the summit; it was a special place in more ways than one and the subject of one of Clark's longer physical descriptions, which he expanded greatly in his second journalistic retelling.[26]

Clark was not even sure whether the "hill" or "mountain" was a natural phenomenon. It was neither clearly human nor not-human in design. The hill was scarily unnatural to the explorers and they wanted to believe that it was a "natural" place. Clark expressed disbelief in "devils." Patrick Gass thought they were looking for "small people," which are not necessarily the same at all. Gass's "people" sound more human. Clark's "devils" were otherworldly. These were liminal creatures, mysteriously between people and animals, the tangible and the spiritual. To Clark they were evil creatures for their deviation from the human, who quite possibly could not be killed with guns. Gass, who stayed back in camp while other volunteers climbed the hill, was frightened.

> Captain Lewis and Captain Clark went to see a hill on the south side of the river where the natives will not or pretend that they will not venture to go, and say that a small people live there, whom they are afraid of.

This entry is full of Gass's disdain for Indians, which he couches in disbelief. Interestingly, he suspects pretense rather than delusion. Nonetheless, even after the party's breathless return, he is unprepared to dismiss the possibility that the little people exist. "About 10 o'clock," Gass reported, "Captain Lewis and Captain Clark with the party accompanying them came to camp, but had not been able to discover any of those small people."[27]

If the explorers mentioned their uneventful climb to any of the Plains people who had told them about the hill, the Indians would not have been surprised by their failure to locate the spirits of that place. The explorers lacked ritual preparation for their encounter; they climbed the hill in the wrong frame of mind. Something bad might have happened to them, but whites often seemed unaffected by witchcraft. Alternatively, something may have happened and they were not yet aware of their misfortune or were simply not yet affected, but nothing good could come from such an unprepared state. Preparation was essential for spiritual growth.

The explorers had noticed the severed fingers of Mandan warriors and asked for an explanation of the multiple digits sawed from their hands. Was it an enemy's torture? There could not be so many who had suffered accidental losses, sometimes on both of their hands. Mandans told them about the Sun Dance, about the rites that gave them access to the spirit world. Lewis and Clark found the explanations disgusting rather than enlightening. Such "superstitions" made no sense to them.

Had they visited the Mandan, the Sioux, or other Plains tribes practicing the Sun Dance ceremony at a different time of the year, they might have witnessed the mutilation in its ritual context. They could have seen naked men painted yellow and brown shaking rattles threateningly and others with brown torsos, blue shoulders, and red noses. They would likely have recognized the dancers as costumed snakes and vultures. They would have understood the symbolic intent of those in wolfskins who pursued others wearing antelope antlers about their heads. They could have identified the grizzlies by their skins and growls and the beavers by their tails. It is unlikely, though, that witnessing the Mandans' Sun Dance would have given the explorers an appreciation of Indians' dreams.

After four days of dancing, fasting, and sleeplessness, all of which enhanced the dream state, some of the Sun Dancers submitted to the next stage of preparation. Mystery men, themselves bearing conspicuous scars from their personal experience of the pain they inflicted, used knives to rip through the chest, arm, leg, and back muscles of the dreamers, and passed splints of pointed bone attached to leather cords through the incisions. Buffalo heads and other ritually weighty objects hung from the cords to tug on the wounds, and the dreamers were suspended some three or four feet from the ground. At this point, assistants used a pole to poke and turn the hanging dreamers, as the artist George Catlin described the next phase of the ordeal.

> The turning was low at first, and gradually increased until fainting ensued when it ceased. In each case these young men submitted to the knife, to the insertion of the splints, and even to being hung and lifted up, without a perceptible murmur or a groan; but when the turning commenced, they began crying in the most heartrending tones to the Great Spirit; imploring him to enable them to bear and survive the painful ordeal they were entering on. This piteous prayer, the sounds of which no imagination can ever reach, and of which I could get no translation, seemed to be an established form, ejaculated alike by all, and continued until fainting commenced, when it gradually ceased.[28]

It was generally after about twenty minutes that bystanders cut the dreamers down. Upon reviving sufficiently to crawl, they offered a finger for ritual excision. With the splints still through their muscles, the thongs still bearing the weight of the skulls and other weights suspended from them, and their bloody hands untreated by any meliorating care, those who could stand began to dance until the weight and tugging brought on by the movement tore the splints through their flesh. Sometimes, when the dancing was ineffective in this regard, other dancers assisted by stomping on the thongs or ripping them off.

Lewis and Clark were capable of witnessing the pain, appreciating the courage, and cringing at the bloodshed, but not of getting the point. The explorers lived in a different world, in which the dancers could be recognized as symbolically costumed, but not as representative of animal spirits. They, even more than we, were unable to suspend a state of disbelief to appreciate the dreamers' alternative reality. These were lines across which communication failed. The openings to spiritual conversation, which some Indians thought they perceived with members of the expedition, were misunderstandings of the possibilities for shared dreams. The distance between the cultures of the explorers and the people they "found" was greater than the Indians believed, if less than the explorers asserted, for all their posturing about science and civilization. The gap between dreaming and science was narrower than the explorers claimed. Plains Indians had science and were interested in the explorers' botany and astronomy, if not in their zoology, but nonetheless the gap was unbreachable from either culture's perspective.

If he would not learn to dream, Lewis could neither achieve understanding of the Indians' natural world nor grow spiritually. If Clark would not acknowledge his belief in dreaming, his vision quest would remain a private one. As a vision quest, the expedition failed collectively, but York, Clark, and the Shoshone woman found themselves on the journey. It is possible that others did too, but the historical record on the souls of the rest of the expedition is slimmer still. By the time of the second visit to the Mandan, the future looked dim for Lewis, grizzlies, buffalo, and snakes. As for the animals' spirits, their power endured in the souls of believers like the Mandan, Hidatsa, Nez Perce, and, perhaps, Clark.

CHAPTER TWO

Being First

a European concept?

EXPLORATION IS COMPETITION. It is a game, a sport, deadly serious and dangerous. Explorers are hunters and believe themselves prey. Death stalks the explorer; he tracks plants, animals, people, and terrain. What he does not eat is a discovery, most of it just as valuable dead and easier to carry. The explorer is a killer, a man to be feared. He is also afraid.

Exploring is a race with no second place. The discovery must be cast as a first. Winning defines the explorer, who always finds something new. Pilgrims seek the old and familiar. Travelers report on the strange or forgotten. An explorer discovers the unknown.

The explorer prepares for his journey by studying "facts." Myths are the window through which he views maps. Imagination is the lens that focuses his reading of journals published by other explorers. He carries these maps and journals—some in his mind, some in his hand—with him on his travels. Of course, the myths and imagination also go with him, but of this he is largely unaware. He believes himself above such "superstition," a man of facts, objective in his vision and evaluation of data, a "philosopher" in the eighteenth century, a "scientist" by the middle of the nineteenth century.

He carries the great explorers from the past with him too. They are his guides, models, and competitors. These are the men he measures himself against. They are his idols, who in life embodied his ambitions, dreams, fears, and expectations and who in death are the only court fit to judge him. Such an ego, one that perceives itself in extraterrestrial terms, as a god and on God's journey, is typical of an explorer. It often makes him an impossible person anywhere except on an expedition, and he is sometimes unbearable there as well.

So the explorer packs a heavy load of cultural and personal baggage, some of which he bears lightly, even unconsciously. The burden of "fact" he carries gladly; it is his chief weapon against his greatest fear—the truly novel, entirely unanticipated, totally unknown, and hence unassimilable experience. He knows quite a lot, much of it wrong, but nonetheless essential for his travels. His path is from one "known" to another, never into an unimaginable wilderness.

Explorers, unlike travelers, do not get lost. They find "new" places or new ways to places that are themselves "lost" or "remote." They map, giving order to their journey no matter how disorderly it may be. They name, possessing all that they see, plotting the relationship of places, objects, and living creatures to themselves. They collect; they write; ultimately they must publish or lose their claim to all that they have "found."

The explorer's journey is as much across time as through space. In the middle of an ocean, a jungle, or a desert, the explorer aims for precise temporal location in reporting events. To mistake the day of the week is to be truly lost. He often reports the hour of the day, even when that recollection is far less precise than he pretends. This exaggerated, or fabricated, precision comforts him and lends credibility to his observations. It is evidence of his "objectivity," his scientific method, and establishes a clear chronology.

Chronology *is* the explorer's story—what happened first, next, and as a consequence of what came before. He fears being lost in time as much as being lost in space. To explorers, "savage" time is circular; "civilized" time is linear. The explorer's sense of causation is also linear. He is wrong to assume that Indians are unable to comprehend linear time and he ignores the circularity of his own culture's temporizing cycles, but the simplicity of the distinction is essential to him precisely because he fears "going native." Such assumptions are part of his "science," his authority embedded in the texts that his journals become.

Time is the explorer's talisman against savagery. The explorer brings time to the wilderness. No "savage" was ever early before his arrival, at least as far as he knows. Only after him, he believes, is anyone either late or lost. His questions about "when" elicit incomprehensible replies from *discovered* peoples. Answers to queries about "where" are only marginally more intelligible and, he eventually discovers, "unreliable" in terms that he comprehends.

Partly the obsession with time is a function of the explorer's desperation to be "first," an accomplishment defined in temporal terms, but it is more than that. It is fear that clocks him. He fears losing his way, his civilization, and himself. Exploration challenges his identity. In ways that the explorer never fully comprehends, his greatest discovery may be of himself, and that can be the scariest prospect he will ever face on any continent, at any altitude, and in any weather. In the end, in this sense, the explorer is truly alone.

Pilgrims and travelers collect people. An explorer expunges them. He describes discovery as a solitary event, although that is almost never literally true. He recalls being first and alone. Companions create narrative problems for the explorer. Christopher Columbus's infamous theft of the credit and bounty due Juan Rodríguez Bermejo for first sighting land was not simply a quirk of personality. Other explorers might resolve the dilemma differently, although Columbus's lie is far from unique in the history of exploration. They all would see Bermejo's keen eyesight as a problem requiring at least a narrative solution, at worst a violent one.

"Discovered" people present challenges too. They, like those on the explorer's team, must be eliminated as potential claimants to *his* glory. They must be devalued as Others, lost and savage. Then the explorer can trumpet *his* finds.

Found people are specimens, like seeds, stones, plants, and animal skins. They are also witnesses to his triumph, so he tries to bring back a few survivors to testify in his behalf. Good "savages" admire, preferably worship, the explorer and seek to emulate him. They are thrilled to be no longer lost and crave the civilization that the explorer represents. They are in awe of his courage, declare him the epitome of manliness, and defer to his leadership. Obviously, any "volunteer" returning with him qualifies on all counts. Bad "savages" are enemies who need to be tamed, banished, or eliminated. There is no fourth alternative for "discovered" people occupying the explorer's "discovered" land. Declining the imposed status of discovered savage, refusing to be found, claiming not to be lost, and offering neutrality are all unacceptable. Rejecting the hierarchical relationship between savagery and civilization is incomprehensible from the explorer's perspective.

The explorer is often a Christian and characterizes himself as such. This was true from the late fifteenth through the early nineteenth century, even though explorers are often the most secular and least God-fearing men in their cultures and even when, late in the period, the cultures have themselves secularized. He is a proselytizer, whether or not he believes in a deity; he is a missionary for "civilization." He is a salesman, an advocate, a promoter of his culture, which he characterizes in commercial, religious, technological, ethnic, and national terms.

The explorer, as a European, is both assertive and insecure about his superiority to whatever and whomever he discovers. If he were not the product of a culture at once curious, restless, and greedy, he would have stayed home. It was, after all, such marginal European powers as Portugal and England, unable to compete on the Continent, that led the search for discoveries to redress the balance of power in Europe. If he had been successful back home, the explorer would not have left. It is difficult to separate the explorer's uncompromising assertion of his civilization's superiority over others from his personal doubt that this is so. The combination of the two, though, is what makes every encounter with a recognized Other, whether human or not, a tense and potentially violent event. Constantly triangulating his insecure sense of self against all comers, the explorer frequently asserts his superiority by killing what he finds.

The reader probably discerns by this point that the explorer is often wrong about himself and others. The "savages" do not really worship him. The men accompanying him on *his* expedition may very well hate him. The longer he is away from home, the less sure he is about his self-worth, the more violent he becomes, and the more mistakes he makes. The "facts" he brings with him and the "facts" he reports are often untrue. He is far from objective, frequently miscomprehends interpersonal exchanges—language being only one of many barriers to communication—and is a poor judge of people, especially himself. His all-consuming desire to be first, to find people, places, and things that are new, overwhelms his judgment and often leads him to exaggerate and lie.

[handwritten margin note: Some pretty strong generalizations — Marie overcomes this]

At the center of the paradoxes, confusions, contradictions, and lies that contribute to the explorer's construction of his journey is the inflexibility of the definition of "explorer." If he is second, he is nothing—a traveler at best, more likely a laughingstock who has wasted other people's money or, worse yet, a mere mortal who is ignored. He must, he will, find a way to define his journey as a "first" and what he sees as a discovery, however far-fetched that should seem to us in retrospect. This need not be conscious fabrication; indeed the explorer often convinces himself that he was the first to find exactly what he and countless others over the ages were looking for. His alternatives are failure, depression, despair, ending his days in a delusional state— as Columbus did—or dying by his own hand—as in the case of Meriwether Lewis.

To die while exploring is heroic. To be killed by "savages" the explorer discovered martyrs him, as happened to Captain James Cook. Ideally, the martyred explorer is not on his first journey, in his first meeting, but has returned triumphant after achieving acclaim for the discoveries of a previous voyage. The worst fate for an explorer is to die of old age, forgotten and surpassed by the discoveries of others.

Although the explorer seeks discovery in rhetorical isolation, he achieves glory only after—often long after—returning home and publishing his findings. The explorer must assert his claim as "first"— his names, maps, and vision of what he has seen—to a sometimes disbelieving, always insufficiently appreciative audience. No matter how celebrated he is, it cannot be enough. In his mind, others cannot comprehend his sacrifice, his ordeal, or his achievement.

As a man of action, the explorer often faces the greatest challenge after his welcome home. When the celebration ends, he must become a writer. This is essential for self-promoting his discoveries. He must compose himself, make order out of disorderly notes that he took in the wild before he knew what his story would be. This can be scarier than the journey. He must publish or his discoveries may perish along with him. He must survive this sedentary task without the stimulation of the wilderness, the adrenaline rush of physical danger, and the joy of the hunt. Now he must really work alone.

Explorers, circa 1492–1806, are men. Exploration defines their gender, racial, and species identity. They triangulate who they are in relationship to what they are not. In other words, they discover themselves through contacts with such Others as mountains, deserts, rivers, weather, animals, women, and other men. This exploration of self is unacknowledged, often unrecognized, and not what explorers think they are writing about. Indeed, to the extent that they are aware that their journals could be self-revelatory, explorers often "edit"—suppress or excise—what they can. They want to report facts—the anthropology, botany, diplomacy, geography, geology, and zoology—of the journey. To achieve these ends they create fictive selves based on idealizations of other explorers. So their journals tell us more about the standards against which they measure themselves than about who they are; or, at least, that is the journal writer's intent.

For all these reasons, treating the journals of explorers as if they are chronological narratives of fact is a colossal mistake. It uncritically buys into the myth that explorers seek to create. It retells their story, perhaps better than they tell it themselves, but does not deepen our understanding of them, what they did, and the significance of their trip. Granting the journals of any expedition autonomous standing as "truth" is myth, not history.

Explorers are not prophets, although that may be exactly how they see themselves. Their journals are not gospel, regardless of the authoritative tone explorers take in their writings. Explorers are more interesting, what they see and do is more complicated, and their journals are more revealing than that. Explorers' journals provide, at best, the perspectives of individuals rather than the whole or the only story that can be told. They are partial, skewed, self-serving, and incomplete. Others preceded them; others were there; others came later. There is more to know, more to imagine, and more to say. There are more stories to tell.

Race, culture, and religion are essential definitional components of "explorer," which makes the whole notion of exploration a lie. Inevitably, explorers' "discoveries" were already known to non-Europeans. Asians, Africans, and Indians—women, children, and men—preceded the explorers, traveling great distances, enduring weather, terrain, animals and insects, and reaching the far corners of the earth. The first great human travelers were African and Asian. The discoveries of millennia previous to ours were not made by "explorers." Even those of the past five hundred years were usually to places already peopled by racial Others, but the non-European discoveries lacked one or more of the essential components of exploration.

It goes without saying, then, that the explorer of the fifteenth through early nineteenth century was often the first *white man to claim a discovery and to report it in print in a European language.* The first woman to make the ice age passage from Asia is not America's "discoverer," because she is disqualified by gender, race, religion, and culture, and because she is anonymous and did not report that journey in print in a European language. So, too, any Asian who sailed the Pacific to the Americas or any African who traversed the South Atlantic would be similarly disqualified. Why is Leif Eriksson not the "discoverer" of America? As a European man whose accomplishment was reported in an epic poem and whose presence in North America long before Columbus is confirmed, he certainly seems to qualify, but he was not a Christian and Columbus, although later to arrive, beat Eriksson into print with the "discovery." Habit, politics, and subsequent endorsement by the explorers who "followed" Columbus all play a role, but it is also critical that followers were successful in promoting his myth.

There are two "discoveries" that have mythical standing in the United States. One is that of Columbus, which has sustained serious, perhaps ultimately mortal, blows in the past two decades. No informed reader any longer takes Columbus's journals as gospel. No one should still see Columbus's "discovery" the same way that he did, which is not necessarily to question the significance of his four voyages across the Atlantic, his courage, or his accomplishment. We know that Columbus's journals do not represent a full telling of the events they report and that no single reading, in his time or ours, can be definitive. Clearly there are more and other stories to tell, stories that reflect a fuller comprehension of meanings than Columbus or his historians have ever had. This, too, is not necessarily a criticism of Columbus or his historians, because no singular perspective can ever encompass the variety of meanings that first meetings provide and no single reading could exhaust the stories that the journals can tell.

America's other mythical expedition is that led across the continent and back by Meriwether Lewis and William Clark between 1803 and 1806. Lewis and Clark aspired to the first rank of exploratory fame as well as to be the "first" explorers to discover Welsh Indians, a Lost Tribe of Israel, and a water route across the continent. They saw themselves as the last great North American explorers and the first Americans—white citizens of the United States—to achieve that standing. They aimed to be the first to connect Christopher Columbus's "discovery" of the East Coast with James Cook's West Coast landfalls.

Lewis's and Clark's emulation of Cook and Columbus was sometimes subtle and at other points explicit. Lewis, for example, imagined himself a ship's captain, which helped him cast his enterprise in the company of the great seaborne explorers. "I steered my course through the wide and level plains," he wrote, "which have somewhat the appearance of an ocean." No explorer had yet achieved fame without crossing an ocean, so Lewis created waves to fulfill his need. No captain achieved renown without triumphs over water and land, savages and beasts, and Lewis and Clark battled them all heroically in the pages of their journals.

As near contemporaries of Cook, who died at the hands of Hawaiian Islanders in 1779, Lewis and Clark sought to extend his tradition across time. They fancied themselves descendants of Columbus and embodiments of Cook's legacy, much as Americans saw themselves as the torchbearers of English liberty in their revolution against British rule. The coincidence of Cook's end and the beginning of the United States would have seemed providential to men more divinely inspired than Lewis and Clark. Clark (b. 1770) and Lewis (b. 1774) were just old enough to be literal descendants, which is mythically useful but unnecessary. Such auguries are for myth-tellers, not for myth-makers, and were of no significance to Lewis and Clark.[1]

All such legacies are, of course, fictions. Nonetheless, self-delusion is essential to the exploratory enterprise, whether in North America, South America, Africa, or the Pacific Rim. The exploring process is irrational, contrary to explorers' claims and beliefs, subjective, out of control, and expeditions are frequently lost in space and time. It is really quite marvelous that Lewis and Clark were able to sustain the fantasy of controlled, objective "discovery" so long and in the face of so much evidence to the contrary. In that way they were typical of explorers before and after them, who explored every ocean and continent of the globe.[2]

Lewis clocked the moment when he became "first." It was on the morning of April 7, 1805, when the expedition left Fort Mandan in present-day North Dakota, launching boats up the Missouri River into previously unexplored terrain. Or, at least, that is the way Lewis saw it and how historical tradition has preserved the triumph down to this day. Lewis, embracing and creating the historic moment, postured for the ages in his journal entry of that date.

> Our vessels consisted of six small canoes, and two large pirogues. This little fleet although not quite so respectable as those of Columbus or Capt. Cook were still viewed by us with as much pleasure as those deservedly famed adventurers ever beheld theirs; and I dare say with as much anxiety for their safety and preservation. We were now about to penetrate a country at least two thousand miles in width, on which the foot of civilized man had never trodden: the good or evil it had in store for us was for experiment yet to determine, and these little vessels contained

every article by which we were to expect to subsist or defend our-selves. However as this the [*sic*] state of mind in which we are, gen-erally gives the coloring to events, when the imagination is suffered to wander into futurity, the picture which now presented itself to me was a most pleasing one. Entering as I do, the most confident hope of succeeding in a voyage which had formed a dar-ling project of mine for the last ten years of my life, I could but esteem this moment of my departure as among the most happy of my life. The party are in excellent health and spirits, zealously attached to the enterprise, and anxious to proceed; not a whisper or murmur of discontent to be heard among them, but all act in unison, and with the most perfect harmony.[3]

Columbus and Cook see Lewis off on his "voyage." Lewis acknowl-edges the "party" manning his "fleet," but then reduces the moment to the explorer's singular and possessive accomplishment. "My departure," he writes. He reduces the rest, including his cocaptain Clark, to the status of crew. He defines the meaning of "first" as broadly as he ever will, ever can even in bad conscience. His, theirs, will be the first feet of "civilized" men to tread this ground once they disembark. Again, the image evokes Cook's and Columbus's island landings, flag-plantings, and ceremonial claims in behalf of their monarchs.

Lewis's claims were less regal, more republican, as befit the new nation whose empire he stretched. The logic remains the same, though, the tradition long-standing. The "civilized" man who steps in a predecessor's footprint obliterates the "savage's" right to walk there again. Thereafter, natives are subject to civilization's whims.

The expedition or "project," as Lewis now called it, was no longer Jefferson's. It was "a voyage which had formed a darling project of mine," Lewis wrote, seizing the initiative, the credit, and the glory from his patron-president. The feat had a singular hero as all great expeditions did. Not even a cocaptaincy, however muddled by an already overweening bureaucracy that demoted Clark to lieutenant, could eclipse an explorer's singularity. Only one civilized man could be first. It would be Lewis's footprint that obscured others already there.

Lewis believed himself under control. His decade of planning made him optimistic. Success was in his hands whatever "good or evil" lay ahead. He had purchased and packed—not literally himself, but figuratively in the explorer's singular "I"—everything they needed to face any contingency. Lewis was so confident that he "suffered" his imagination "to wander into futurity" just as he had allowed it to travel back in time to Columbus and Cook. How awkwardly, calculatedly, put. Lewis felt so in control of everything around him and, most important here, of himself that he let his imagination loose, without fear that it would wander away. Lewis allowed that he had an imagination and denied at the same time that it would be a significant influence on his actions or the journals. The here, the now, and the real were essential. In the future, he would act on and record just the facts. That, at least, is what he intended, and what he expected readers of his journals to believe.

Seven days later, in his entry of April 14, Lewis acknowledged that his earlier claim to be "first" was an error. He did so in passing, even as he staked out the ground for a second claim to preeminence.

> Passed an island above which two small creeks fall in on Lar[boar]d side; the upper creek largest, which we call Charboneau's Creek after our interpreter who encamped several weeks on it with a hunting party of Indians. This was the highest point to which any whiteman had ever ascended; except two Frenchmen who having lost their way had straggled a few miles further, though to what place precisely I could not learn.

Imprecision frustrated Lewis; he could not tell exactly which step made him "first." Since the anonymous Frenchmen were lost when they wandered farther west than Charbonneau, their claim to precedence was dubious, and undocumented, but a challenge that Lewis aimed to overcome quickly and with as much certainty as he could create.[4]

Lewis racialized the meaning of "first," which was previously implied in "civilized." He also gendered the accomplishment by creating the compound "whiteman" to supplement the masculine nationalization of "Frenchmen." His ambition for a gendered and racial achievement superseded any mere national, linguistic, or cultural "first." He knew that his would not be the first step, and he knew that his moccasined footprint would be indistinguishable from an Indian's to any "civilized" eye, but Lewis's imprint would be documented in a text and certified by the journals of other expedition members. Such a textual "first" eluded both the Frenchmen and Indians who walked ahead of him.

On April 26 Lewis felt he could safely reassert his claim to be "first" even though he did not know where the Frenchmen had wandered. Upon reaching the confluence of the Missouri and Yellowstone Rivers, Lewis sighed, smiled, and celebrated his accomplishment.

> After I had completed my observations in the evening I walked down and joined the party at their encampment on the point of land formed by the junction of the rivers; found them all in good health and much pleased at having arrived at this long wished for spot, and in order to add in some measure to the general pleasure which seemed to pervade our little community, we ordered a dram to be issued to each person; this soon produced the fiddle and they spent the evening with much hilarity, singing and dancing, and seemed as perfectly to forget their past toils as they appeared regardless of those to come.

This was the first time that Lewis allowed himself to celebrate the achievement. It was not the end, but only the beginning of his exploratory accomplishment. He knew that much more lay ahead than they had left behind, but he had achieved the first of his goals.[5]

Lewis was wrong. He knew he was wrong. He persisted, nonetheless, in the lie that was essential to defining his success. He was not the first "civilized" man to cross the continent; he was not even the first English-speaking man to make the overland journey to the Pacific. Indeed, the Canadian Alexander Mackenzie had already made the trip a decade before Lewis and Clark, and got his account into print two years before their journey began. Lewis and Jefferson read Mackenzie's book and it was the specific spur to Jefferson's long-held ambition to sponsor an American mission that did the same thing.[6]

Historians and the editors of the journals need Lewis and Clark to be "first" too, and the expedition's myth is so powerful that they redefine Lewis's aim. "From the Great Plains," the editors explain, "semi-arid and largely treeless yet teeming with game, they had entered the Rocky Mountains, the first English-speaking whites to do so with the exception of Alexander Mackenzie's Canadian party to the north a few years earlier." No matter how you trim it or how positive a slant you put on the facts, Mackenzie's expedition did it first, and ten—not "a few"—years before Lewis and Clark took off. The Americans were, at best, second even with the racial and linguistic qualifiers that hardly enhance their accomplishment.[7]

All that is left are the patriotic roots of the claim that Lewis made and historians attempt to sustain. Lewis and Clark can be the first white Americans to make the trip for those who take pride in a national "second," which counts for little in the history of exploration, or the bigotry implied by their racial triumph. The racial qualifier diminishes the simultaneous arrival of York and the Shoshone woman with the rest of the expedition just as it dismisses the continent's exploration from west to east by Native Americans.

Lewis was less immune than historians have been to the increasing evidence that he was not first no matter how he defined it. On August 26, 1805, his journal entry distanced him from the circumscribed claim to be first. Clark was the actor, but Lewis was the writer, who acknowledged logical tension between claiming the status of "first" and knowing that others watched their every step.

> He walked on shore a small distance this morning and killed a deer. In the course of his walk he saw a track which he supposed to be that of an Indian from the circumstance of the large toes turning inward. He pursued the track and found that the person had ascended a point of a hill from which his camp of the last evening was visible; this circumstance also confirmed the belief of its being an Indian who had thus discovered them and ran off.

It was critical that the footprints belonged to an Indian, not a "civilized" man. So Clark's discernment of difference—whether or not it was mistaken—was necessary and therefore assured.[8]

Shaken by the evidence that they were discovered rather than being the discoverers of the people and places around them, the explorers resorted to naming as a way to reassure themselves of their precedence. Clark asserted the honor for Lewis: "I shall in justice to Capt. Lewis who was the first white man ever on this fork of the Columbia call this Louis's River." If Lewis was "first," rather than one among the other white men of the expedition, then it is unclear what gave Clark the standing to name what is today called the Snake River. Modesty ill becomes an explorer; it is an improbable aspect of his character, and impossible for him to sustain. Was the idea really Clark's? Why did he render "Lewis" as "Louis," a name that he knew perfectly well how to spell the first time? We might suspect deception here—whether of himself or just of us is unclear—and perhaps even a spelling lapse barely concealing the writer's knowledge that his claim is disputable.[9]

The problem associated with claiming themselves "first" increased exponentially in November 1805. Not only had they "savage" contenders and textual evidence of Mackenzie's accomplishment; they faced material evidence that other whites had been there before them. On November 3 Lewis and Clark passed the easternmost point achieved by a member of George Vancouver's 1792 expedition. "Our commanding officers are of the opinion that it is Mount Hood," Patrick Gass wrote on the same day, "discovered by a lieutenant of Vancouver, who was up this river 75 miles." So Lewis and Clark knew about Vancouver's precedence but kept the knowledge from readers of their journals.[10]

The next day they began meeting Indians who had all the trappings of contact with "civilized" men. "The Indians at the last villages have more cloth and European trinkets than above," Clark observed. "I saw some guns, a sword, many powder flasks, sailor jackets, overalls, hats and shirts, copper and brass trinkets with few beads only."[11]

The Indians who joined the explorers on November 5 wore red and blue sailor jackets, overalls, shirts, and hats. They carried muskets, pistols, and tin flasks to hold their powder. They were "assuming and disagreeable," according to Clark, which meant the Indians were unimpressed by the explorers. The Indians were shrewd traders, which angered the explorers, esteemed the explorers' trade goods little, having already acquired more and better items than what these white men brought, and were less hospitable than Lewis and Clark required.[12]

Worse yet, the Indians "spoke a few words of English." When queried about contacts, the Indians described "Mr. Haley" as a frequent visitor. The Indians had learned curse words and the names of trade goods from the crew of the brig *Lydia* out of Boston, which was captained by Samuel Hill. Americans—not just Canadians and Englishmen—had already visited these shores. Lewis and Clark would have to suppress, deny, or ignore evidence that they were not first by even the narrowest measure of their accomplishment. They were not the first white men, the first "civilized" men, the first English-speaking men, or even the first white, English-speaking Americans to reach the West Coast.[13]

[handwritten margin note: when was this?]

To reassure themselves in the face of such devastating news, the explorers asserted their "discovery" repeatedly. "At a run and island near the shore here the traders anchor and trade," Clark acknowledged: "We passed at each point a soft cliff of yellow, brown and dark soft tones. Here Capt. Lewis, myself, and several of the men marked our names, day of the month, and by land &c &c." This passage implies a new claim, that they were the first to reach this point by land. Such a "first," of course, would have to exclude Indians and would still leave them second to Mackenzie, but at least it would give them standing as the first white Americans to reach the West Coast of North America by land.[14]

[handwritten margin note: sounds like current explorer first blind woman to climb to all of CO's 14,000 ft peaks in winter, etc.]

They followed this with a volley of naming—Clark's Point of View, Lewis's Point—and carving their names in pine trees and rocks. One of the sailors had bested them, though, by tattooing his name on the arm of an Indian woman. "I saw the name of J. Bowman," Clark noted, "marked or picked on a young squaw's left arm." It would be hard to beat or delete that.[15]

The explorers persisted, inconsistently, in recognizing the priority of others and in claiming their standing as first. Clark explained in his entry of December 7, 1805, that he explored a bay and therefore claimed the right to name it. "I have taken the liberty of calling [it] Meriwether's Bay," Clark explained, "the Christian name of Capt. Lewis, who no doubt was the first white man who ever surveyed this bay." In fact, as far as we know, the first white man to explore the bay was William Broughton, a member of Vancouver's 1792 expedition. He named it Young's Bay after Sir George Young of the British navy and that is how it is still known today. Whether or not Clark knew the previous name or the namer, he knew that Vancouver's expedition had preceded his own. He knew better than to claim that Lewis was "first," especially since Clark had explored the bay himself.[16]

What is more, Patrick Gass wrote that they found evidence of recent habitation by whites. "About the same time Capt. Lewis and his party returned," according to Gass, "they had been around the bay and seen where white people had been in the course of the summer, but they had all sailed away." In the face of their previous knowledge, despite the physical evidence they found, Lewis and Clark persisted in their claim to be first. Such is the irony—the deception, delusion, and construction—of naming. Such is the subjectivity of naming, which bestows names irrationally.[17]

There was also visible evidence that Vancouver's men and the traders the Indians described were not "first" themselves. Clark reported another person, who embodied evidence of "first" contacts earlier than those of the woman with the tattooed arm.

> With the party of the Clatsops who visited us last was a man of much lighter color than the natives are generally. He was freckled with long dusky red hair, about twenty-five years of age, and must certainly be half white at least. This man appeared to understand more of the English language than others of his party, but did not speak a word of English. He possessed all the habits of the Indians.

An "Indian" with red hair inherited the trait from both parents, so a liaison between a white sailor and an Indian woman could not have accounted for this offspring. Patrick Gass described the man as having

recessive genetic trait" [handwritten margin note]

"the reddest hair that I ever saw, and a fair skin much freckled." Such physical features suggest contact going back forty to fifty years earlier, which would be several decades before the arrival of Vancouver's men.[18]

Since Clark, himself redheaded, and Lewis did not comprehend the genetics of red hair, they could not have estimated the antiquity of claims to discovery of the West Coast. They did regard the red-haired Indian's existence as an incontrovertible challenge to their priority, though, and saw his knowledge of English as an additional problem. There were also legends among the Indians, which Lewis and Clark do not report, of a Spanish shipwreck dating back to the early eighteenth century that deposited both redheaded and African survivors among the Northwest Coast Indians. The Astorians, who arrived during the decade after Lewis and Clark, told of a red-haired Indian whom they called Jack Ramsey, because that was the name tattooed on his arm. Ramsey's father, who was perhaps named Jack Ramsey himself, was believed to be either a deserter or survivor from an English shipwreck, but whether the Indian Ramsey and Lewis and Clark's red-haired Indian were the same man is unclear.[19]

We can only imagine how Lewis and Clark reacted to the mounting evidence that they were not first—no matter how you cut it— because they did not share their despair. The whole trip west was a race against being late. They sprinted to the Pacific Coast only to find a red-headed Indian, another with an English name tattooed on her arm, and more Indians outfitted with European clothing and weaponry. What a succession of blows to their ambitions. What a challenge to their imaginations. Reconstructing their journey as "first" would prove as great a challenge as making the trip.

The news kept getting worse. Eventually, Clark made a list of thirteen English and American traders who had beaten them to the Northwest Coast. These thirteen were in addition to the explorers— Cook, Vancouver, and Mackenzie. This was besides the settlement on Nootka Sound that Lewis figured out, erroneously, must be trading with the Indians from there. They would hear different names, in addition to the thirteen, over the course of the winter. The more

Indians they talked to, the more English-speaking white men they learned about.[20]

What was left for Lewis and Clark to be on their return trip? They could supersede those who came before them—correct mistakes, add information, embellish the known, and discover what others had missed. They hoped that even Cook, their hero, had made mistakes. According to Clark, ornaments on native canoes were seashells, not teeth, as Cook believed. Nowhere in Cook's journals did he identify the decorations as teeth, though, so it is unclear why Clark fabricated a false identification by Cook, unless it was just to correct him, thereby establishing a standing above those who got there "first."[21]

explorers are wrong

Naming was another variant of "first," which staked a claim to what no one else had ever found or, at least, what no one else had ever documented finding, which is far from the same thing. Sure, there were people living on and among these "new" finds, and some of the "discoveries" were themselves humans, but Lewis and Clark personalized their "firsts" by naming places and objects after themselves, their men, or someone dear to them. "Fanny's Bottom," named for Clark's youngest sister, Frances, was perhaps a bit too personal, so they changed that one to "Fanny's Valley," but they named something for everyone on the expedition and numerous sites after themselves.[22]

Logically, it would be even more difficult, even more interpretively challenging, for the explorers to be "first" on their return trip. At best, it would seem, they could be second to themselves. Nonetheless, they were up to the challenge of finding "new" people and places. They had missed one whole native village on their way out because seasonal hunting patterns left the Indians in a different spot. "They had now, therefore," explained Lewis, "the gratification of beholding white men for the first time." So the explorers were a "first" for the Indians, who beheld the white men with awe. Or, at least, that is how Lewis constructed the encounter as a discovery.[23]

The return trip also provided opportunities for renaming and therefore recasting the explorers' discoveries as "firsts" even on their second pass. "The river here called Clark's River," wrote Lewis, "is that which we have heretofore called the Flathead River. I have thus named it in honor of my worthy friend and fellow traveler Capt. Clark. For this stream we know no Indian name and no white man but ourselves was ever on its principal branches." They had never let an Indian name stand in the way of renaming before, so that detail is more significant as an acknowledgment that their right to naming, and renaming, was compromised by the fact that Indians were there first. Likewise, the qualified claim to being the first white men on the "principal branches" of the river is a subtle admission that they knew they were embellishing existing maps based on information provided by other white men who had been through today's western states of Montana, Idaho, and Washington before them.[24]

The final, crushing blow to Lewis's and Clark's ambitions came with their meeting of white men whose journey west was unencumbered by any of Lewis's and Clark's discoveries. During the second week of August 1806, where Lewis expected only to find Clark or Indians, he stumbled upon "civilized" Americans.

> Being anxious to overtake Capt. Clark who from the appearance of his camps could be at no great distance before me, we set out early and proceeded with all possible expedition. At 8 a.m. the bowsman informed me that there was a canoe and a camp he believed of whitemen on the N.E. shore. I directed the perogue and canoes to come too at this place and found it to be the camp of two hunters from the Illinois by name of Joseph Dickson and Forest Hancock.

This is the last entry that Lewis wrote, even though the expedition would be another month in the field. Lewis's excuse was his injury, suffered when one of the hunters mistook his captain's buttocks for the haunches of an elk. "As writing in my present situation is extremely painful to me," Lewis concluded, "I shall desist until I recover and leave to my friend Capt. C. the continuation of our journal."[25]

No, the coincidence of meeting up with the white men and Lewis's cessation of writing was cause and effect. The pain intensified and was not entirely physical. Even when Lewis recovered the use of his rear, he did not resume writing. Why write? There could be nothing more of significance to document. They were neither first nor essential to those who would come next. The journals would languish until after Lewis's death because they revealed the explorers' failure. Editing the journals required a great deal of forgetting before the explorers could write their way first.

CHAPTER THREE

Writing First

IN AUGUST 1806 Lewis and Clark were almost home, almost safe from the human and nonhuman threats to their lives and their fame. While still on a stretch of the Missouri River where they had imagined themselves the "first" white men on the journey out, they began to meet others headed west. At first there was one canoe, two men, news, and understandable excitement. Then more men, more news, and a return to the commonplace drudgery of travel and the taken-for-granted experience of greeting others who spoke the same language, shared the same culture, and who divided "us" from "us" rather than just from "them."

Ultimately, the explorers met over 150 white men on the Missouri. Two things about these successive meetings must have perplexed Lewis and Clark. One, they learned that their countrymen had believed them dead. Two, their presumed deaths made no difference in the westward course of empire. Without their discoveries, their maps, their journals, their specimens, or their completion of the race to be "first," others were extending commerce westward just the same. Whether they were alive or dead, first or not, found a water route to the Pacific, Welsh Indians, a lost tribe of Israel, or man-eating monsters around the next bend, the hawkers of "goods" made their journeys unencumbered by what Lewis and Clark "knew."

How depressing. Oh, they put on their best front to others and tried to fool themselves. They acted the roles of heroes as long and as well as they could. They shared their stories, but these were mainly of adventure, of travel rather than discovery of what they had hoped to find. In the immediate aftermath of their return, the expedition was, as even champions of Lewis and Clark have recognized, "at best a disappointment and at worst an embarrassing failure." Could fame be based on the negatives of lost tribes not found, of nonexistent water routes, and of Indians who had already traded and bred with other white men? Was the world truly waiting for what they wrote?[1]

Such questions had to be disconcerting, if only because of how much they risked, endured, and invested in writing. The physical burden of the writing materials was great under the conditions they traveled. The act of writing was burdensome too. But the real issue was fame, and the discomforts were a small price to pay for immortality. The journals staked their claims to discovery, their rights to name what they found, and thus their legacy as explorers. Unpublished, they were irrelevant, as the fur traders who passed them already demonstrated could be the case. Dead or alive, they were failures if their findings never made it into print. Alive or dead, it was the written word alone that would carry them across the finish line.

The odd thing about all this uncertainty is that the journals are generally read as fonts of fact rather than as honed reflections designed for effect. As a recent editor of the journals asserts, "what sets this romantic and stirring event apart from other western epics is the true and undisputed evidence upon which it is based." Well, yes and no; the "evidence" of the journals is largely undisputed, but it is certainly not indisputable.[2]

"True" is not that simple either. The journals contain lies, deceptions, errors, inconsistencies, internal contradictions, differences among the six journal writers, and contestable perspectives. They embody suppressions, exclusions, ignorance, bias, and partial knowledge. In other words, the journals are reflections of human fallibility and are the product of explorers' ambitions. They are, then, just as false as they are true.

Readers should not assume, for example, that the journalists told time accurately. When the explorers reported what happened "today," that is often untrue. They took notes, but not always on the same day as events, which they then copied to field notebooks, and then recopied to neat fair copies in the red leather notebooks they carried. This process usually took days, as nearly as we can tell, often weeks, and sometimes years to complete. "Copying" included rewriting—adding, deleting, and moving passages. The texts that modern editors consult are generally third generation and much of the first and second drafts are now lost.

Twentieth-century editors of the journals even disagreed about whether the bulk of the explorers' written work lay before or behind them when they returned to St. Louis. Clark did send about one year's worth of journals—May 13, 1804, to April 3, 1805—to Thomas Jefferson in mid-1805, so those are clearly "field" journals. Internal evidence also suggests that the bulk of the journal entries, if not all of them, were redrafted before Lewis's and Clark's return to St. Louis. In one entry, for example, Clark explained that the Missouri River was so rough and the boat he rode in "so unsteady that I can scarcely write." Since that journal entry is in the same steady hand as those before and after it, we can tell that he transcribed, and perhaps also revised, his shaky notes once on shore.[3]

The journals are retrospective. They are not contemporaneous transcriptions of "fact." When Clark's notes blew overboard in a squall on July 14, 1804, it was "a most unfortunate accident" which made it difficult for him to construct journal entries. John Ordway noted that two days' notes were lost, so Clark was drafting entries at least three days late and disguising the lapse of time by using the present tense and such language as "today," "this afternoon," and "this evening" to discuss events. Another entry, for October 13, 1804, refers to "last night," suggesting that Clark wrote either the entry or the note from which it was "copied" the next day, but possibly that was not true either. There is, in other words, no consistent pattern to when they wrote, and the explorers obliterated much of their editing trail from notes through fair copies. We do know, though, that they tried to hide from us how much time had elapsed between events and the creation of their "original" written versions of them.[4]

The journal writers took notes and wrote and revised daily entries on the trail—at least once and sometimes more often—and the journals were edited again for publication. "I am much engaged in rewriting," Clark explained while the expedition was still traveling west. He was "rewriting" to a fair copy that he nonetheless called his journal "in its original state."[5]

The published journals contain entries that are fourth and even fifth drafts. We know there were "field notes" and "field journals." All of these lost texts predated the entries neatly transcribed into the small red leather notebooks that historians and editors call "originals." Perhaps there were more field journals, and there were certainly "notes" that the explorers destroyed after "copying" entries into the red books. In the surviving journals, there are often double entries that were significantly altered in the revised accounts. After all of that revising we get the editors' organization and interpretation of the texts, which counts as another generation removed from the ideal "original."

One scholar has speculated that Lewis and Clark were surprised, and undoubtedly disappointed, that the "neat journals they brought back from the expedition were not acceptable to publishers exactly as written." Perhaps, but the explorers had revisions that they wanted to make when they returned. In Clark's entry for September 18, 1805, for example, he suppressed information that he did not want to share with the rest of the men. Only when he returned to St. Louis did Clark explain—in red ink that he did not carry with him on the journey—the rationale for action that he and Lewis took on that day.

> The want of provisions together with the difficulty of passing those immense mountains dampened the spirits of the party, which induced us to resort to some plan of reviving their spirits. I determined to take a party of the hunters and proceeded on in advance to some level country, where there was game [to] kill some meat and send it back.

Clark intended this and other insertions to be published without editorial comment as part of the "original" text. The additions included his memory of motivations for his actions. Although it made perfectly good sense not to share with the men at the time either his diagnosis of their spirits or the reason he took them hunting, Clark

how events in change in the act of writing

did want the published journals to explain his reasoning as he recalled it.[6]

It is significant that Clark made this change, among others, as much as five years after the event that the entry reports. Such an understanding helps us to appreciate the journals in their fuller complexity as something more, and something less, than the quick and unconsidered recording of facts. It helps us see the entries as crafted perspectives consciously framed with a view to their effect on audiences—in this case, first the other men of the expedition and then the larger public imagined for the published version.[7]

There were things that Lewis and Clark did not want readers to know. They wanted to control our knowledge about them and our views of their accomplishments. We see this repeatedly in the movement from the earliest surviving entries to subsequent ones. They believed, for example, that explorers' journals should be dispassionate. Clark was never entirely successful at hiding his emotions, and the longer he wrote the less successfully he suppressed what he felt. The general pattern for him is revealed in the two drafts of comparatively short and uneventful entries for December 16, 1805. In the first, Clark revealed that he was "cold and wet" and that it was "certainly one of the worst days that ever was!" He deleted his feelings for the fair copy and thereby stuck closer to the spare "facts" that he thought would enrich his journal.[8]

In other ways, too, the explorers attempted to control our perceptions of them. The surviving drafts of Clark's entry for January 8, 1806, show him editing out information about an Indian plot against the life of one of the expedition's men. The story had sex, jealousy, intrigue, lingering fear, and an Indian heroine who saved the man's life. Although it is unclear why Clark decided to leave the story out of his fair copy, we can reason that the full account was too revealing for his taste. Possibly he did not want us to know that the men were having sexual relations with Indian women or that Indians had less than affectionate feelings for the explorers.

controlling the reader's perceptions

Whatever Clark's motives for suppressing the story, the two surviving drafts give us clues to his model of an explorer's journal and reveal how difficult it was for him to sustain the posture of his ideal.

The earlier drafts also reveal more facts and sometimes different or even contradictory perspectives to the ones honed for publication. There are stories that never made it from the notes to any draft of the journals, drafts that were destroyed, and stories that the explorers never wrote down at all. What we have are selections of experience edited multiple times.

Patrick Gass said as much in his journal, making explicit what Lewis and Clark implied.

> If this brief journal should happen to be preserved, and be ever thought worthy of appearing in print, some readers will perhaps expect that, after our long friendly intercourse with these Indians among whom we have spent the winter, our acquaintance with those Indians lower down the river and the information we received relative to several other nations, we ought to be prepared now, when we are about to renew our voyage, to give some account of the fair sex of the Missouri and entertain them with narratives of feats of love as well as of arms. Though we could furnish a sufficient number of entertaining stories and pleasant anecdotes, we do not think it prudent to swell our journal with them as our views are directed to more useful information.

Sexual adventure, personal conquests, and stories of romantic liaisons, while entertaining, were not "useful." Editing toward fair and publishable copies of the journals systematically sought to delete references to the men's sexuality—even while blaming Indian women for the venereal diseases the explorers apparently contracted in places where they claimed to be the "first" white men.[9]

The ideal authorial posture minimized the personal experiences—including thoughts, feelings, and impressions—of everyone except Lewis and Clark. The journals thereby supported claims that the expedition and its accomplishments were theirs. Historians have always rightly portrayed the expedition's dual leadership as remarkable in the history of discovery. It is truly extraordinary that given the competitiveness of exploration each was willing to share being "first" with the other. More typically, though, the explorers' generosity with fame ended there.

Lewis, for example, described one of the expedition's historic departures in his entry for May 15, 1804. He implied his own participation in the group's disembarkation from the mouth of the River Dubois and claimed that the entry explained what occurred "today." Since he did not join the party until May 20, he would not have had the information contained in the entry before May 20 and therefore could not have written his entry until at least then. It was important to Lewis that he appear to be there at this beginning, however artificially constructed it was as a start, but since other expedition business kept him away, he wrote himself into the scene at least five days later and tried to disguise the inaccuracy of this claim to fame.[10]

Clark's exaggerations are typically less grand, reflecting a different sense of self and ambition than that of his fellow explorer. When Clark wrote "killed a wolf on the bank," a reader might assume that Clark killed it himself. Indeed, though, we know from other journals that Lewis wounded the animal and John Colter finished it off. Hunting mattered to Clark, whose journal reads like a scorecard reporting who shot the largest and the most animals. He prided himself on his hunting prowess and was loath to accept a long streak without an impressive kill. One of the many ways that we know how much hunting mattered to Clark is internal evidence that he sometimes drafted his journal entries and left a space for the results of his "walk" later in the day. When he returned, he either entered his score or left the space blank.[11]

This comparative elevation of Lewis's and Clark's significance is not confined to the journals written by them. The four other journalists buried themselves in the written record. "The man who was frostbitten informed us that he felt much easier than he had done since he was frost bitten," Joseph Whitehouse wrote in his entry for January 16, 1805. When we find from his own slippages in voice and confirm by reference to other journal writers that Whitehouse was "the man" to whom he referred, it seems a curious distancing of self from the subject of his entry. Five months later, Whitehouse explained that "one of our party was very sick all this day." Again, it was him.[12]

There are two surviving drafts of the entry Whitehouse wrote for June 26, 1805. The earlier of the two reads as follows: "I took sick this evening, I expect by drinking too much water when I was hot." The revised fair copy addressed the same personal debility: "One of the party was taken very ill and it was supposed his sickness proceeded from drinking too much water when he was warm." Whitehouse used the same process of distancing to describe his recovery the next day.[13]

All four of the sergeants whose journals survive—Joseph White-house, John Ordway, Patrick Gass, and Charles Floyd—generally referred to members of the expedition without naming them. They are all but anonymous in their own journals. The third-person references to themselves and the nameless description of anyone except the captains are two devices by which the sergeants effectively edited themselves out of their stories, achieved an objectified impersonal self, and elevated Lewis's and Clark's experiences even when those were secondary in the events they described.

because Jefferson expected it?

The sergeants minimized their own presence and that of the other enlisted men in their journals to the point of vagueness. It is hard to see the men and one woman in the dim light that the sergeants' journals shed on them. Lewis's and Clark's presence is hard to assess for the opposite reason. They stand in a glare. Not only do the sergeants shine the light of fame on the captains; Lewis and Clark reflect more on themselves. They exaggerate their own participation. They elevate their experiences, feelings, and assessments over those of anyone else. Sometimes they push the truth even further, making claims for their accomplishments that are patently untrue.

After their return, Lewis referred to the expedition's collective accomplishments as if he had traveled alone. "My late tour to the Pacific Ocean," he called it. News that Patrick Gass intended to publish his own journal threw Lewis into a rage. In a public letter "warning" the public against "spurious" texts, Lewis described the "deceptions" that would challenge his claim to sole control over all the journals. He even issued a prospectus intended to warn off competitors. "This work will be prepared by Meriwether Lewis," he claimed, without mentioning Clark. Lewis went on to describe "his literary labours" as singular. He brooked no competition and entertained no alternative perspective or voice. The expedition and the writing were "his" and the fame would be his as well. In the end, Lewis never published

tour?!

sad guy...

anything and the journals became the collective endeavors of Clark, George Shannon, and the editors who have worked since with the texts.[14]

As the history of the journals' publication reveals, they became as much a product of editors' hands as of the authors'. Francis Biddle, in cooperation with Clark and Shannon, elided the various voices of the journals into one smooth narrative; Elliott Coues selected heavily and imposed his own order on the disorderly journals; and the twentieth-century editors Reuben Gold Thwaites and Gary Moulton organized the journals into "chapters" of their own creation. So we have hugely complicated texts to work with, ones that in published and manuscript form are often quite distant from any literal "truth" and are often deceptively remote from even the authors' first impressions of the experiences that they recount.[15]

It is undoubtedly easier, then, to inquire of the journals what Lewis and Clark (and their editors) wanted us to know about the expedition rather than what actually happened on any given day. The illusion of precision has misled readers for two centuries about what the journals reveal. It is fascinating, to be sure, that journals kept in the wild would give us not only the day and date of events but often the precise hour and minute at which they occurred. Obviously, the claim is often untrue, but who is fooled—us or them—and to what end?

Lewis's very first journal entry—that of August 30, 1803—is misdated. He apparently forgot that August has thirty-one days, but he knew that he had left Pittsburgh the day before September 1. There is no entry for August 31, and in a letter he contradicts the journal's dating of his departure. This small error is hardly worth noting—and is certainly no cause for berating Lewis—except it reveals that right from the start the journals are something different from what the journal writers and their celebrators have claimed.[16]

After writing an entry for every day between August 31 and September 18, 1803, Lewis stopped. Blank pages follow the entry for September 18, some of which Nicholas Biddle—the journals' first extraexpeditionary editor—used for his notes. Lewis intended to go back and silently fill in entries for the intervening days, but never did. The "blank" period was one that Lewis did not consider forward motion—a week in Cincinnati, a visit to fossil beds at Big Bone Lick, Kentucky, and a side journey to Clarksville, Indiana Territory, to pick up William Clark and several recruits. After two more weeks in Clarksville, the expedition began again for Lewis and the entries resumed when the party reached Massac, in southern Illinois.[17]

When Lewis started again, he got the dates wrong for a week. The expedition moved "forward," which was westward, and he wrote—a short entry for November 11 and another for November 12. Then the entry for November 13:

> Left Massac this evening about five o'clock—descended about three miles and encamped on the S.E. shore. Rained very hard in the evening and I was seized with a violent ague which continued about four hours and as is usual was succeeded by a fever which however fortunately abated in some measure by sunrise the next morning. I then took a

Poor man; he was ill, quite possibly from a malarial attack. That would explain why the entry is inconsistently timed—"this evening" and "the next morning." Lewis did not really write that same evening, but sometime later than he claimed. He was trying to write as if the entry was drafted on the same day as events, but slipped into the admission that he wrote the entry sometime after "the next morning," which had already passed.[18]

The most interesting thing about this entry, though, is the way it ends. "I then took a" is an interrupted thought, an unfinished sentence to which Lewis never returned. In his next entry, that for November 14, Lewis recorded that his fever continued through that day. Perhaps he began the previous entry before his health permitted. Again, the November 14 entry has internal contradictions about time. The initial claim is that the entry was written "this evening," but Lewis also referred to his recovery in the past tense, which makes it unlikely this entry was written on the day that he claims.[19]

It was a story about heroic engagement—in this instance of Lewis with his own body. Possibly he left the sentence unfinished intentionally, so that we can admire the struggle, sympathize with the hero, and thereby appreciate the eventual triumph all the more. That would only be human, fitting, and "true" to the way Lewis felt on those days.

Again, the point of my analysis of the journals is not to criticize Lewis and Clark or their writing. They were humans (that is, fallible), incapable of fully grasping their own limitations (who is?), attempting to conform to journalistic standards of their day (as men of science), and working under the stresses of environment and ambition (as explorers and men). My observations are intended as correctives to our readings, usages, and understandings of the journals, not as a knock on the journalists or what they wrote. All texts are vulnerable to close readings, but explorers' journals are interestingly, revealingly, and essentially so.

critique directed at us [handwritten marginal note]

The clues multiply that the journals are not what the explorers, editors, and historians claim. They are not daily recordings of "fact" but crafted recollections designed to control public knowledge of the expedition and disguised as daily logs. Those who support the heroic model of Lewis and Clark historiography want the journals to be "true" in a literal way that they are not. The expedition's historians and editors want the journals to be fountains of fact and chronologically accurate. The story they want the journals to tell is a shallow, simple, straightforward narrative of movement across space and through time. They want to believe that the journals are a guide, in one fluid interchangeable voice, to what happened and when. They read the journals as narratives of greatness—great men accomplishing great deeds against great odds for great ends.

There are disagreements among journal writers about the dating of events, which means they cannot all be accurate. John Ordway wrote in his entry for September 12, 1806, that

> Mr. McLanen informed us that the people in general in the United States were concerned about us as they had heard that we were all killed then again they heard that the Spaniards had us in the mines &c.

Clark's entry for the same day made no mention of such a conversation, but five days later he reported a similar exchange. Since both Clark and Ordway noted that the expedition met up with "McLanen," possibly the merchant Robert McClellan, in passing on September 17, how could Ordway possibly have had this conversation on September 12?[20]

Again, such minor discrepancies matter as a warning against reading the journals as gospel. They also matter, though, as a clue that time passed between events and entries, leading to some mistakes that we can discern and others that we cannot. Chronology matters as linkage in a chain of causal sequence. In other words, if Ordway was mistaken in his memory of the date on which he spoke with "McLanen," we should then assume that nothing in the intervening five days could have been the result of the meeting, because it had not yet taken place.

The conjunctions of time and place also matter as causal contexts. Joseph Whitehouse says that the expedition passed the Buffalo River on May 25, 1804; Clark says May 26. They cannot both be correct. Sorting out the "truth" in this case and others like it can be difficult. On balance, it seems more likely that Whitehouse got this one right, because there is a pattern of internal evidence that he generally wrote his entries closer to the date of their occurrence than Clark often did.[21]

If the discrepancy is a function of the errant memory of either Whitehouse or Clark, then we might reason that Whitehouse probably wrote his entry in closer temporal proximity to the event and that therefore his recollection is more reliable. The problems, though, include the fact that we do not know who wrote his entry first in this case, which of the men had a better memory, or which of the two men kept better notes from which he composed his entries. So we are probably better off admitting that we do not know which one is correct and disclaiming any certain knowledge of the conjunction of time and place in reference to the Buffalo River and the expedition in May 1804.

The assertions of precision, and undoubtedly the attempts to be precise, were calculated even more finely than simply dates. The explorers aimed to report days of the week as well. After two years in the wilderness, for example, it mattered to Lewis and Clark that September 18, 1805, was a Monday and September 28 a Thursday. They were off by a mere two days—the eighteenth was actually a Wednesday and the twenty-eighth a Saturday—which is not bad reckoning unless you care enough to claim a precision of knowledge that was beyond them.[22]

[handwritten margin note: Claims of precision that was impossible]

It is more interesting that Clark described September 27 as a Wednesday in the earliest draft that we have and September 28 as a Friday in a revision. However lost Clark might have been in relation to the days of the week, and however desperately he wanted to appear more precise than his knowledge would support, it remains odd that he contradicted himself in such a way. We might expect more precision in his mistakes. A consistent two days off would be more understandable than a failure to note the passing of a day of the week along with a date.[23]

There are two possibilities that might explain the compounded errors. One is that Lewis and Clark knew they were unsure of the days of the week and simply listed days randomly—or based on their best guesses—as placeholders for later revision. Such a theory is consistent with the red-ink revisions that corrected the days after, perhaps long after, their return to St. Louis, when the editor(s) had access to a calendar. Another possibility, consistent with this theory, is that even the earliest surviving entries were made after the passage of time and memory rather than on the date of the events they report. That helps account for the sorts of mistakes that seem peculiar if Lewis and Clark really were making daily entries as they wanted readers to believe.

The chronological challenges of the journals are not limited to errors of day and date. Nor are discrepancies confined to the explorers' attempts to disguise the distance between events and entries and to hide the imprecision of their knowledge about time. The chronology of entries is further muddied by Lewis's and Clark's silent copying of information in total disregard of when they made observations and who made them.

Clark's entry of November 7, 1805, for example, contains a lengthy and intimate description of the pubic areas of Chinookan Indian women, which he found shockingly visible around their clothing when they bent down and he peered through their skirts. The passage is identical to Lewis's of March 19, 1806. The style, spelling, syntax, and perspective are Lewis's. Examination of the originals also supports the theory that Clark copied from Lewis.[24]

Joseph Ordway engaged in the same process of silent revision accompanied by an impossible chronological claim. His entry for March 22, 1806, includes the following passage.

> A sketch of the beginning of Sergt. John Ordway's journal which he commenced at River Dubois (14 May) in the year 1804 . . . also it being a minute relation of the various transactions and occurrences which took place during a voyage of two years, four months & 9 days from the U. States to the Pacific Ocean through the interior of the continent of North America.

That estimation of time for the journey accurately conveys the expedition's precise arrival date back in St. Louis—six months after the entry's date.[25]

If we accept the explorers' dating of their journal entries as "true," then Ordway recorded the exact date of the expedition's arrival back in St. Louis six months before it happened and Clark copied part of his entry for November 7, 1805, from Lewis's for March 19, 1806. If the journals were the sequential daily entries that their authors disguised them to be, neither Ordway's bull's-eye prediction nor Clark's cribbing from the future would have been possible. If the "originals" were first-generation texts, these two entries would defy our understanding of time. The recent editors are undoubtedly correct in their guess that Ordway wrote his expedition summary at least six months after he dated it and are probably right that Clark inserted Lewis's passage on Indian women into his earlier entry when he prepared the journals for publication in 1810. Whatever the explanations, though, this fluid sense of what the journal entries were and whose they were makes them less than authoritative guides to when observations were made and even who made them.[26]

We should recognize that dating practices such as Patrick Gass's estimates are more honest, self-conscious, and quite possibly more accurate than those that appear precise down to the day of the week and the time of the day. "About the 16th," Gass guessed in one November 1804 entry. We should accept that we have no better knowledge than that about the dates of events or about when the explorers wrote their entries no matter what explicit claims they made or how they used the present and past tense.[27]

The explorers' need to be "first" accounts for their claims to precision down to the date on which they reached each point on their outward journey. Indeed, the two are linked in Clark's carvings on rocks and trees. "I marked my name and the day of the month and year on a large pine tree on this peninsula," he explained in a typical entry of this sort. The assertion implicitly scratched into the pine's sticky bark was that Clark was there before anyone who could read or chop or burn the tree down. It is in those senses an ephemeral claim supplementing those scratched in rock. It was also a claim to precedence that Clark knew perfectly well to be untrue.[28]

There was no obvious reason, though, for Lewis and Clark to stretch for the days of the week. The days were a redundancy at best and at worst a contradiction of uncontestable claims as to the date. In other words, the possibility of error made inclusion of the days a risky venture that could only undermine the journals' authority. "The days of the month for January are right," Lewis noted on January 31, 1806, "but the days of the week as affixed are all wrong, nor did I discover it until this morning." Someone, at some point, corrected some of the days of the week for that month, but who, when, and why only some we cannot know. Lewis may have been hedging his bets here, recognizing that he had not a clue to the accurate days, but unable to correct the "mistakes" until after returning to St. Louis, at which point he either failed to complete the corrections or left them untouched for the later revisions of others.[29]

It must have been other needs that led the explorers to assert knowledge they knew, or at least suspected, they lacked. These reasons were quite possibly personal and not fully comprehended by them. The pattern of such stretches beyond their knowledge suggests

trying to hold onto precision out of need for control

that Lewis's and Clark's most ardent (and errant) attempts to be precise came at moments when they were least secure about the particular knowledge they claimed.

Right from the beginning of the expedition the explorers were
impatient. They felt rushed, late, ill at ease with the pace of "progress"
across the continent. They lacked time by some measure that is not
obvious. "For this enquiry I had not leisure," Lewis remarked in explanation for why he did not stop to examine an Indian mound. It is
unclear what rushed him past the site. Three years later, still hurry-
ing "ahead," Lewis was dismayed to admit that "this is the first time
since we have been on this long tour that we have ever been compelled to retreat or make a retrograde march." The elements had
pushed them back, set them back in time and space. They set out
"late," got "detained," and were repeatedly frustrated by their sense
of how fast they should go.[30]

After four months of struggling with time, Clark estimated the
length of the trip that lay ahead. By his calculations, they would
return to St. Louis in a little less than two years, not later than the
end of 1805. He underestimated the trip's length by about nine
months. The attempt to predict a return date reveals their temporal
stress at the end of 1803. The projection helps explain why they felt
late for the next two years and nine months.[31]

The explorers' unwarranted assertions about time came when
they were most worried about the pace of their progress, about
whether they were really "first," about meeting their schedule, and
about whether they would ever reach home. Statements about their
exact location in space came when they were feeling most lost. In
other words, precision masks confusion throughout the journals and
is a better guide to when Lewis and Clark felt lost than to exactly
where and when events occurred.

Confusion about time and dates in their entries for November
1803 may even have caused Lewis's and Clark's concerns about where
they were in space. They were temporally disoriented, took their first
measurements of longitude and latitude, and Clark drew a map. The
grasping for precision masks, perhaps from themselves, the utter
confusion revealed in a contorted sentence about where they were.

"Passed the Mississippi this day," Lewis wrote, "and went down on the other side after landing at the upper habitation on the opposite side."[32]

The confused sentence is a better map of the explorers' interior chaos than it is a guide to where they were. Lewis's insecurities led him to bury us in an avalanche of "authoritative" detail, thereby suffocating his own doubts. The next sentence is about an otherwise insignificant fish. "On our return," Lewis continued, "which was at five minutes after one o'clock, we were a little surprised at the apparent size of a catfish which the men had caught in our absence." Lewis then reported the length of the fish, the distance between its eyes, its head circumference, the dimensions of the mouth opened and closed, its width and weight, and the length of its entrails.[33]

This entry is a fascinating case study in the emotional challenges of exploration and the psychological compensation Lewis unwittingly made. He felt lost, so he reported the time he saw a dead fish down to the precise minute. He could not accurately calculate the longitude and latitude, so he measured the entrails of a fish. He juxtaposed detail and omission, precision and confusion, in what were for him wild extremes. This entry is not science in its mapping, dating, or measuring. It is neither systematic nor clearly useful to anyone. It is simply confused.

Lewis's mind at work

One week later, Lewis was still feeling lost. We can tell, in part, because he recorded the precise time the expedition departed. He then juxtaposed their reunion with Nathaniel Pryor, one of the enlisted men who had been lost, and his own inability to figure where the rest of the men were. "I am not confident with respect to the accuracy of the observation of this day," Lewis explained, "in consequence of some flying clouds which frequently intervened and obscured his disk at noon."[34]

Then, apparently reflecting his utter frustration, Lewis stopped writing journal entries and did not resume for four hundred days. ! "This morning left Capt. Clark in charge of the boat," he wrote. That is it. No explanation. Lewis's abdication of journal writing to his less literate partner should be viewed within its journalistic context. He recognized that journal writing was one of the principal responsibilities of an explorer and the locus of his fame. He knew that journal writing was one of the most significant instructions Thomas Jefferson had given him. He was frustrated by his powers of observation. No explorer ever achieved fame by measuring the entrails of a catfish, so it is possible that here Lewis was, indeed, "first."[35]

We need to ask, then, what the journals are if they are not "indisputable" records of "fact." If they are less reliable guides to external events than we have long believed, they are better guides to the interior wilderness—the minds and hearts of the explorers—than we have appreciated. Such a perspective opens the journals up for wider use in many more ways than they have yet been approached.

Accepting the journals' complexities renders them no less valuable. Indeed, they are more revealing, richer, and much more useful than generally recognized. They simply merit closer readings, alert to their possibilities. They warrant recognition of the roles played by personality and perspective in drafting the entries. We should accept that reading the journals is a creative act, just as writing them was. As contestable terrain, the journals can be opened to wider, but never definitive, interpretive possibilities, some of which are explored in the rest of this book and many of which have surely not yet occurred to explorers of Lewis and Clark.

CHAPTER FOUR

Why Snakes?

L EWIS AND CLARK had little commercial, diplomatic, or scientific interest in snakes. Thomas Jefferson had not included snakes on his list of curiosities for the explorers to pursue. They never ate a snake, no matter how starved they became and however meaty the supply. By their professional standards, then, there was no reason to mention snakes in the journals, except in the event that snakes crossed their path and became part of their story for better or, more likely, for worse.

Nonetheless, the journals are full of snakes even when there were no snakes to behold. "Snakes are not plenty in this part of the Missouri," wrote Clark early on. The explorers were wary of snakes. They expected encounters and feared even more the unseen snakes they assumed were lurking about. They knew snakes from personal experience and their culture's lore. As Anglo-American men, members of the Lewis and Clark Expedition had a mandate to seek and kill "serpents" as a defining act of their manhood.[1]

For Lewis's and Clark's seventeenth-century cultural ancestors there was no significant distinction to be made between snakes as reality and allegory. The identity was insoluble. Snakes were evil; evil was palpable; snakes were evil and real. Especially for seventeenth-century New Englanders, evil embodied in nature gave the world coherence. To the Puritans, in their ever beguiling way, snakes were necessary and reassuring as well as threatening and requiring extermination. Puritans needed nature to surrender meanings and—

so funny...

need for nature to provide symbols

through snakes, wolves, eclipses, droughts, and earthquakes—it did. The Bible and their own visceral reactions explicated snakes as natural texts.

The snake of the Puritans was the biblical "serpent" from Genesis. For Lewis and Clark, the snake could still be a "serpent," revealing the baggage they carried from our culture's origin myths. "Killed a serpent on the bank of the river," Lewis reported, and then went on to describe it at length in seemingly dispassionate scientific detail. The explorers found meanings in nature, although fewer spiritual ones than the Puritans and less apocalyptically freighted lessons than those of their cultural ancestors. The snake still represented evil, but it now had other roles as well.[2]

The snake was still powerful in Lewis's and Clark's more secular universe; it was still a formidable foe against which a man could define himself. Men of their day still killed rattlesnakes, if not in a conscious blow against sin, in an unconscious act of self-preservation even when the particular snake posed no personal threat. Such unprovoked attacks were part of their mission to clear, to civilize, and to Christianize North America, which were all the same thing whether they knew it or not, and to rid the continent of malevolence as part of God's plan. This was part of their legacy from the Puritans and to us.

As the nineteenth century began, Anglo-Americans still put bounties on rattlers, preached about the devil's appearance in the form of a snake, and labeled those who stood in their way as snakelike, which put a moral burden on the community to eradicate human serpents too. Such characterizations easily applied to Indians, those "snakelike" creatures—one tribe of which they even called "Snakes"—whom Lewis and Clark described in much the same ways—as evil, unnatural, and even as presumptive cannibals who feasted on raw entrails.

So the lines of cultural descent were direct, even though Lewis and Clark no longer believed—as the Puritans did—that nature was bound by the rules of grace. The Puritans looked backward, across the Atlantic, as they squinted with fear into the wilderness—to medieval forests full of spirits who meant humans no good, to a future that resembled the rural English past of cleared land, fenced fields, and safety from monsters that inhabited such an ungodly place. Lewis and Clark gazed west, into a wilderness that harbored a future with many of those same characteristics, and which still potentially harbored demons and ghosts.

fear of wilderness [handwritten marginalia]

Eighteenth-century stories about snakes, which influenced Lewis, Clark, and their men, were a product of both Renaissance "superstitions"—including those shared by the Puritans—and Enlightenment thought. Right along with Newtonian physics, Linnaean natural history, and Lockean psychology, the eighteenth century embraced belief in the four elements, the four humors, astrology, witchcraft, alchemy, and the Great Chain of Being. Almost everyone still believed that a balance of the four elements—fire (hot and dry), air (hot and moist), water (cool and moist), and earth (cold and dry)—and the corresponding four humors—choler or yellow bile (hot and dry), blood (hot and moist), melancholy or black bile (cold and dry), and phlegm (cold and moist)—was necessary for the health of all living things. Medical treatment, agricultural advice, and political theory reflected attempts to restore balance to systems that were out of whack.

Just about everybody still agreed that the stars and planets affected earthly events, and astrology could be studied in colleges, encyclopedias, and, of course, almanacs. "Judicial" astrology, which ascribes planetary causes to individual actions, was no longer part of the cultural mainstream, but "natural" astrology, which studies the influence of the heavens on material objects—the elements, weather, and the human body—was almost universally believed. And the Great Chain of Being, which posited a universal hierarchy descending from God and the angels down through classes, genders, races, animals, and plants to the lowliest of organisms, still gave a structure to nature, an order whose inflexibility was now being questioned, but one that continued to frame discussions about classification and meaning past the century's end.[3]

Serpents were no longer literal embodiments of the devil by Lewis's and Clark's day, but snakes did continue to have powers incomprehensible in mere biological terms. The linkage between snakes and evil had come into question during an Enlightenment age of reconsideration that still had significant ties to the Middle Ages. Charming, possession, division without death, and other supernatural qualities were still deemed possible, but were subject to scientific inquiry through direct observation and scrutiny of secondhand accounts.

John Ordway recorded such an event in the journals of the Lewis and Clark Expedition. "Delayed a short time," he wrote,

> for Capt. Lewis to take m. [meridian] observation. Proceeded on along the bank of a large prairie one of the men killed a large spotted bull snake under the bank. A number of birds which live in the bank [were] flying about this snake. It is supposed the snake charm[ed] them.[4]

Belief in the hypnotic power of snakes was the most durable of all the snake stories of Lewis's and Clark's day. "Charming" or "fascination" was a hybrid of the Renaissance occult and Enlightenment science, a naturalization of the spirit world that arose in the second half of the seventeenth century and endured through the middle of the nineteenth century.

The issue was how, exactly, snakes kill their prey. Since no one had ever actually seen a rattlesnake strike until the development of modern high-speed camera shutters and slow-motion film, fascination was a theory that filled the observational gap. There was logic to the theory, as there always is, which supported belief in the snake's power to charm its victims against competing theories and even visible facts. "The vulgar notion of their biting their prey," reasoned Christopher Witt, an eighteenth-century authority on the natural world, "and suffering it to die before they devour it, deserves no credit; they never bite their prey at all; if they did, they would surely destroy themselves by their own poison."[5] The logic was clear and the fact was confirmed time and again by observations such as the ones made by the men of the Lewis and Clark Expedition.

When snakes fix their eyes on an animal, reported J. Hector St. Jean de Crevècoeur, the prey becomes paralyzed,

[o]nly turning their head sometimes to the right and sometimes to the left, but still with their sight invariably directed to the object. The distracted victim, instead of flying its enemy, seems to be arrested by some invincible power; it screams; now approaches and then recedes; and after skipping about with unaccountable agitation, finally rushes into the jaws of the snake and is swallowed, as soon as it is covered with a slime or glue to make it slide easily down the throat of the devourer.[6]

cw!

Usually the victims were squirrels, birds, or mice, sometimes a rabbit, occasionally a horse, and rarely a man rescued from the snake's stare by an act of will or the intercession of another person who was not charmed. This was the raw data presented for analysis by curious men, who would try to explain how charming works, why the squirrel or the mouse did not run, why the bird could not fly but stumbled slowly, inexorably, in fear, right into the snake's mouth. This was science studying what we call the occult, looking for a biological or, again in our terms, psychological cause.

A purely occult explanation would satisfy some who still believed in the evil eye and legends attached to such malevolent practices. Some men of science still spoke about spells being cast, but that sort of thinking was more from the past and did not inform curious men like Lewis and Clark. Joseph Breintnall believed that snakes "have the power, and use it, of darting from their eyes some harmful effluviums, subtle as the rays of light, which through our optics find quick admission to the brain." The botanist John Bartram also spoke favorably of this theory, as had Christopher Witt earlier in the eighteenth century.[7]

Effluvia, exhalations of some vile sort, continued to explain much about nature and disease throughout the nineteenth century, but they were not an entirely satisfactory solution to the problem of snake charms. Reigning optical theory described the eye as a passive receiver of external stimuli, so attributing the active power of emission to a rattlesnake's eyes was unsettling because it meant that one theory or the other was wrong. For an explanation to satisfy the eighteenth century's curious men it had to have universal application in nature's law.

As a consequence of the problems with fascination theory—it had too much in common with the older world of spirits and spells and too little with the science of Bacon, Newton, and Locke—it was disputed right from the start. One of the first published reports of snake charming from English North America was John Lederer's, in 1672, and he did not believe it himself. He wrote off the story to superstitious Indians who told it to gullible white men.[8]

One Dr. Kearsley, writing from Philadelphia in 1735, also found accounts of snake charming incredible. From personal observation, Kearsley was convinced that fear, courage, or snakebite itself explained the behaviors that others described. One of the flaws in the snake-charming theory, he reasoned, is that under the right circumstances small animals act the same way with other predators, virtually running into their mouths. "Excess of fear," Kearsley explained, "counteracts its own purpose, and precipitates them into the danger which it should excite them to shun."[9]

Kearsley's explanation had the quality of universal cross-species application, as cowardly humans were known to act this way too—fear driving them to injury or death that a braver one would avoid. Counterevidence from the same species could simply reflect the time of the year: "[S]mall birds, especially in breeding time, are so disturbed at the near approach of birds of prey, snakes, cats, foxes, or any other creatures fatal to their young, that they will expose themselves to the greatest danger." So, under the right circumstances, cowardice or courage could explain the inexplicable behavior.[10]

Finally, some of the victims were undoubtedly bitten before the observer witnessed the scene. How long, a skeptic like Kearsley might ask, did the reporters of prey freed from a rattler's mouth follow the scurrying victim to see if it lived? "I conclude, therefore," this man of science advised, "that there is no more mystery in the manner of a snake's catching his food, than in a pike's or a heron's, who, by a common and ordinary stratagem catch such silly fish as come within their reach." So much for folk wisdom, so much for observed fact, so much for the world of charms, spells, potions, and such; there it all was, the sort of commonsense explanation that would throw the rest out, knocking the snake down yet another link in the Great Chain of Being.[11]

Yet the stories persisted, prospered, and endured. "In many of our country situations," Benjamin Smith Barton wrote in his *Memoir* on rattlesnakes, "there is hardly a man or a woman, who will not, when the subject comes to be mentioned, seriously relate some wonderful story as a convincing proof of the doctrine." Barton was not surprised that such beliefs remained common among ignorant folk: "[T]he human mind, unenlightened by science, or by considerable reflection, is a soil rich in the weeds of superstition and credulity." He was astonished to find that still, in 1796, such stories survived among "men of learning, of observation, and of genius, by those who have the book of nature in their hands; that book which will, in some future and some happier age, eradicate many of the prejudices which disfigure, and which mock the dignity of, human nature."[12]

Barton gave more credit to stories ascribing a hypnotic power to the rattlesnake's rattles or a mesmerizing gas than he did to those about effusions from the snake's eyes. Why some theories made more sense to him than others is unclear from the nature of the evidence. Those he found worthier of study than others tell us more about Barton and the fashions of science than they do about the stories, the tellers, or the "truth" of their tales.

There is the same fascinating mix of science and folklore in Lewis's and Clark's stories about snakes. They used the "science" of snake rattles as a medical treatment to ease the labor of the Shoshone Indian woman who accompanied the expedition. One of the traders assured Lewis that the treatment never failed to induce delivery.

> Having the rattle of a snake by me I gave it to him and he administered two rings of it to the woman broken in small pieces with the fingers and added to a small quantity of water. Whether this medicine was truly the cause or not I shall not undertake to determine, but I was informed that she had not taken it more than ten minutes before she brought forth. Perhaps this remedy may be worthy of future experiments, but I must confess that I want faith as to its efficacy.[13]

This skeptical approach to medical practice is appropriate to the "philosophical" perspective taught in Lewis's and our time. Replication was key. Lewis tried it once, but had only one subject, and an Indian woman at that, so he did not want to be gulled into complacent acceptance of what could have been a coincidence. His lack of "faith" is precisely the point, because in theory science gazes dispassionately into the face of "facts" and never blinks.

The affinity between snakes and Indians made the rattle "cure" of the Shoshone woman suspect. The eighteenth-century stories suggest that Indians knew snakes better than whites did—whether as sources of valuable information or as liars who duped credulous men. In part this reflected Euro-Americans' naturalization of Indians. In part it reflected the particularly snakelike qualities—evil, stealth, and deception—they associated with those two "unnatural" Others. Lewis and Clark found a literal connection, which they later took for granted when they encountered snakelike Indians. It was Clark and Charles Floyd who recorded the event.

> A short distance above the mouth of this creek [are] several curious paintings and carving[s] in the projecting rock of limestone inlaid with white, red, & blue flint of a very good quality. The Indians have taken of this flint great quantities. We landed at this inscription and found it a den of rattle snakes. We had not landed 3 minutes before three very large snakes were observed on the crevices of the rocks & killed.

Lewis, Clark, and their men found such places unsettling. For all their science, for all their secularity, for all their wilderness experience, they were spooked more than once by Indians' magical places. They could dismiss out of hand fantastic Indian stories about snakes taking human form and people who became snakes; they could kill rattlesnakes by the dozens, but they could not escape their fear or be sure that snakes were just another biological organism. They never did accept that snakes are, in that sense, just like us.[14]

Perhaps the most telling details of this particular story are the ones that Clark omits. He is vague about the "curious paintings and carvings," leaving our curiosity unsatisfied. What did the explorers risk landing to view and then hurriedly abandon when frightened by a "den" of rattlesnakes? We might conclude based on Clark's entry that they never got close enough to interpret the images, because if they did why would Clark withhold information about what the pictures portrayed? Charles Floyd tells us, though, that the explorers

> past [*sic,* passed] some springs [that] come out of a cliff 2 miles past a creek on the N[orth] side called the River of the Big Devil one mile past a rock on N. side where [there are] . . . pictures of the Devil and other things. We killed 3 rattle snakes at that rock.[15]

Snakes, Indians, and the devil—it sounds like a Puritan nightmare. Since the devil as such does not exist in Plains Indian cosmology, we can be certain that the "Devil" was Floyd's. Whether you consider Floyd's triad of details constructed or literal, its significance harbors in the reality of the experience for the explorers. Clark's exclusion of the devil betrays either the content's insignificance to him or his attempt to conceal—especially from himself, but also from readers—the chill that ran up his spine. Joseph Whitehouse left both the Indians and the devil out of his account. Patrick Gass did not even mention the snakes in his journal. This was science gone wrong, fact blurring with magic, fear aborting an experiment. It may have taken only three minutes from their landing until the discovery of the rattlesnakes, as Clark reports, but how long did it take after that for the expedition to disembark?[16]

As we know from other snake stories, the line between faith and facts was never clear. How was Clark to know, for example, that stories describing milk snakes sucking from cows' udders were folktales with no factual basis? When he encountered a persistent snake which appeared unaccountably interested in a doe he had shot, Clark reasoned that it was after her milk.

> (I will only remark that during the time I lay on the bank waiting for the boat, a large snake swam to the bank immediately under the deer which was hanging over the water, and no great distance

from it. I threw chunks and drove this snake off several times. I
found that he was so determined on getting to the meat I was
compelled to kill him, the part of the deer which attracted this
snake I think was the milk from the bag of the doe.)

As always with snakes and bears, Clark describes the creature as male.
The assumption is self-referential—a fitting opponent must share the
hunter's gender to heighten the threat. In order for the hunter to
achieve manhood in competition against nature, it must be a good
match. The parenthetical nature of the story is fascinating. Clark will
"only remark," thereby debasing his story even more than he did by
opening with a parenthesis. The story is thus doubly set off from the
journals. Clark is unsure whether it even belongs, whether he is reli-
ably reporting "facts."[17]

As Benjamin Franklin reminded readers of *Poor Richard's Almanac,* an
ounce of prevention is worth a pound of cure. Every snake killed was
one less to worry about, so Lewis and Clark documented that they
were doing their share. "We killed a large rattle snake," noted Clark.
"Several rattle snakes killed by the party" on a more successful day. "I
killed a snake near our camp, it is 3 feet 11 inches in length," Lewis
bragged. "During our halt we killed a very large rattlesnake," Lewis
recorded—the "we" revealing that it was not his kill. Gass, Ordway,
Whitehouse, and Floyd counted snake kills in their journals as well.[18]

Even with all the caution and killing, there were a number of scarily close calls. One man, unnamed, encountered a rattler in a bush as
he pulled a towrope along the riverbank. Another, also nameless in
the journals, "caught one by the head in catching hold of a bush on
which his head lay reclined." "Captain Clark was near being bit by a
Rattle snake this day," Whitehouse reported; "it got between his legs
whilst he was standing fishing, he killed it, & a number of the same
kind this day." Lewis records the same near miss as one of three:
"Capt. Clark was very near being bitten twice today by rattlesnakes,
the Indian woman also narrowly escaped."[19]

Clark found that day memorable for the close calls and commemorated it with a traditional explorer's gesture. "This mountain," he
wrote in his journal, "I call rattle snake mountain." That was a mere

five days after Lewis recorded the naming of "rattle snake cliffs." They also named a rattlesnake rock, creek, and island during the expedition. Clearly the snakes preyed on their minds and the names were meant to be warnings recorded on maps, signs for those who followed them into the wilderness.[20]

The closest near miss was Whitehouse's, when he "trod on a very large rattle snake. It bit my legging on my leg. I shot it. It was 4 feet 2 inches long, & 5 inches & a half round." When Whitehouse edited this entry, he shortened it considerably, leaving out how he killed the snake and where it bit him. The effect was to render the incident less dramatic. He also made it less personal—indeed impersonal—by switching to the third person and leaving himself unnamed. In the final draft, "one of the party was near bit by a rattle Snake, which he killed. It measured 4 feet 2 inches in length and 5½ inches round." What Whitehouse did was extract the fear along with the drama. He reduced the encounter from an upsetting experience to science. What remains is a set of dimensions with emotional depth suppressed.[21]

Superstition against science — both seem inadequate here

In keeping with this desire to construct dispassionate journals, an actual snakebite was reported as the most unremarkable of all the serpent encounters. "Joseph Fields got bit by a snake," Clark reported, "which was quickly doctored with bark by Capt. Lewis." No one even mentioned the type of snake or whether it was poisonous. Ordway added the detail that the bite was on the side of Field's foot. Gass remarked five days later that Field had recovered. So the details were inverse to the seriousness of the encounter, revealing that <u>control was best achieved through silence</u>.[22] *contradictory to achieving control through precise writing*

If fear was best concealed under the cloak of the commonplace, then apocryphal and other third-person stories could be the most emotionally revealing of all. The teller denied his own fear while trying to scare his audience. The power of snakes—the nature of danger and the danger of nature—is open for scrutiny in eighteenth-century stories that reported the threat and how it could be either avoided or met.[23]

The fear survives in a story, widely told during Lewis's and Clark's youth and long after their deaths, about a farmer, a snake, and a boot. There are two eighteenth-century versions, separated in the recording by about sixty-five years, but which had a life that extended far beyond where and when somebody wrote them down. These two tellings illustrate the story's apocryphal nature and the truth it held across time. The first came out of New England in 1714 and was read before the Royal Society, this time as part of a longer "Account of the Rattle-snake" by Thomas Walduck, a West Indian sea captain.

"Their venom is deadly let it be lodged anywhere so long as the snake lives but not longer," the passage begins. In some of the eighteenth-century stories, the victim needed the snake to die a real *and* a symbolic death, but in Walduck's telling the folk just want the snake dead. The story continues, to illustrate the point that the venom is potent at the moment of biting and across time as well.

> A man in Virginia being in the woods having a pair of boots on was bit by a R[attle] Snake through his boot, came home to his wife and died. His boots were hung up in the house and his widow married a second husband, who put on those boots and by riding a small journey complained with a pain in his leg and likewise died. The boots were hung up again and the woman married the third husband, who made use of the same boots, and the first time wearing them complained as the former of a small tumor in his leg and likewise died. Upon this the surgeon cut the boot in pieces and found the tooth of the Rattle Snake that bit the first husband, and did all the execution since [the tooth was] as small as a hair. They took it out with a pair of forceps and pricked a dog with it that within a few hours died. The surgeon took the tooth some time after, tried it upon another dog and it did him no hurt, and it was supposed then the snake was dead.[24]

Three husbands gone, and now the boots destroyed too. Perhaps I am being unfair to the apocryphal wife, but what the story does not say is also fascinating. I am struck by the wife's lack of curiosity, her frugality, her good fortune in finding three men in succession with the same-size foot, more or less, and the last two needing boots. I am intrigued by her serial marriages and wonder whether the second or third husband had any fear of her bad luck. But all this is beside the snake story's point.

Slaughter reveals
a lot about
himself here
/
learning
from folk
tales

It is important to note how the tale ends, with the experiments on dogs and the logic that *proves* the snake's death. Since it was *known* that the venom is effective throughout a snake's life, the loss of potency demonstrates that the toothless rattler is finally dead. This is precisely the kind of knowledge that survives from the past, but that now, in the eighteenth century, is subject to scrutiny as never before. The experimental mind-set that the story reveals is stuck in the past, but will not be for long, as the process of experimentation helps people think their way out of old boxes and into new ones that seem more modern, more scientific, to us.

The second version of the story is J. Hector St. John de Crève-coeur's, published in 1782, which also claims to be true. In this telling, the event occurs in New York, rather than in Virginia. This time a Dutch farmer is mowing his fields in his boots, a precaution designed to protect against snakes. Knee deep in his crops, the victim inadvertently steps on a viper, "which immediately flew at his legs," bit his boot, and then was killed with a scythe. Again, as we know from the other stories, the death of the snake is a critical point, although it is almost lost here, a withering member of the tale's old body as time passes and the snake's end no longer has a clear function for the teller and perhaps for the audience.

A scare to the farmer—a close call to be sure—but no harm apparently done, the boot having taken the force of the snake's venom. That night, his day's work done, "the farmer pulled off his boots and went to bed, and was soon after attacked with a strange sickness at his stomach; he swelled, and before a physician could be sent for, died." The poison invades the man's stomach this time, instead of his leg—a new limb branching off from the old story's trunk, which gives us a clue to how far the teller and the audience are from their traditional roots. This version of the story was written down by a man who never suffered or saw a snakebite for an audience of readers who had no greater knowledge of nature than he. As in the earlier version, no cause could be found for the victim's painful demise, but sudden, inexplicable death was still common enough, so people wondered, had their suspicions, and buried the dead.

A few days after, the son put on his father's boots and went to the meadow; at night he pulled them off, went to bed, and was attacked with the same symptoms about the same time, and died in the morning. A little before he expired, the doctor came, but was not able to assign what could be the cause of so singular a disorder; however, rather than appear wholly at a loss before the country people, he pronounced both father and son to have been bewitched.

The tug between science and magic continues, with the physician pulling both ends. Not that he believed in magic, but the doctor still *needed* magical causes to explain the failure of *philosophical* cures. He still required the ignorance of patients to hide his own.

In this telling of the story, the widow is not so quick to remarry and, blessedly, she apparently had only one son, so she sells her husband's clothes. Then, as you can probably guess, "one of the neighbours, who bought the boots, presently put them on, and was attacked in the same manner as the other two had been." There are not so many bodies in Crèvecoeur's story as there are in Walduck's, but the point is the same. A wise person again figures it out, not a surgeon, but an

eminent physician, who fortunately having heard something of the dreadful affair, guessed at the cause, applied oil, etc., and recovered the man. The boots which had been so fatal were then carefully examined, and he found that the two fangs of the snake had been left in the leather after being wrenched out of their sockets by the strength with which the snake had drawn back its head. . . . The unfortunate father and son had been poisoned by pulling off these boots, in which action they imperceptibly scratched their legs with the points of the fangs, through the hollow of which some of this astonishing poison was conveyed.[25]

This time, sixty-seven years after the previous telling, there is no need for the death of the snake. The narrator does not require it and he presumes, if it even occurs to him, that his readers have no need for that ending. The nature of the physician's cure is no longer interesting enough to report. In Walduck's version there was no cure at all. Now, it is taken for granted as a commonplace of modern medicine, with no folk treatment involved.

The two stories illustrate change over time, from the beginning of the century until near its close. Folk-thinking is not dying or dead, but it is buried deeper in the culture, falling into disrepute among philosophers and other curious men. An educated person such as Crèvecoeur no longer heard or even saw the same things as men of science did three decades before. The world was changing and so were the snakes. In both tellings, the story is about the triumph of science over ignorance, about the greater curiosity of the philosopher than of the folk.

Crèvecoeur's tale lacks the same storytelling bravado as Walduck's, the sort of details I can play for their humor as I pick it apart. Since both stories were presented as fact, changes in peripheral matter reveal something about the credulity of reading audiences across time. It would not be long, if the time had not already passed by 1781, before philosophers of nature would laugh at the principal claim of the story, that death can be caused by a scratch from a boot once bitten by a snake. Once bitten, and so recently, by such stories as this, curious men cast a more skeptical eye on all fantastic accounts of the natural world.

Lewis and Clark still had to contend with wonders just beyond their ken. The explorers report, for example, coming within five miles of a marvelous spot they apparently had no scientific curiosity to visit.

> George Drewyer gives the following ac[coun]t of a pond . . . ab[ou]t . . . five miles below [on] the s[outh] s[ide] past a small lake in which there was many deer feeding. He heard in this pond a snake making gobbling noises like a turkey. He fired his gun and the noise was increased. He has heard the Indians mention this species of snake. One Frenchman gave a similar account.

[handwritten marginal note: what in the world . . . ?]

The snake was "of immense size" and could be heard for several miles when it gobbled. Perhaps there was no need to confirm the story firsthand—George Drouillard, an unnamed Frenchman, and unspecified Indians having denied them any claim to discovery. Possibly the pressures of time left the expedition without leisure to pursue folk-snakes for five miles. Having just passed "the place of snakes," which Clark describes as "the worst place I have seen," they may have already beheld more than enough serpents to satisfy their scientific curiosity. They might have lacked confidence that they could find Drouillard's snake or the stomach to add ten miles to their trip for the sake of a snake.

Maybe they were scared. As hunters, Lewis's and Clark's men would be prey to a snake that imitated wild turkeys. According to the story, this snake increased the volume of its gobble when a gun was discharged. The snake was "immense" and may have consumed men. Possibly the pond was a seat of marvelous events and Drouillard delivered his tale as a story of narrow personal escape from a mystical force. For them, the danger was no less than that posed to Odysseus by the Sirens who lured sailors to their rocky deaths with a song. Told, as this story was, at the beginning of a journey Lewis and Clark equated with a quest, it alerted the men to the mysterious dangers of the unknown that awaited them. Clark reported this secondhand story because, however remarkable it was and although unconfirmed by firsthand sightings, it was a significant event in their trip. It was a story that affected men who still knew that snakes were mystical creatures possessing powers that transcended brute strength.[26]

That is what made snakes important enough to kill and led the explorers to report encounters as triumphs of courage and skill. It was not just that snakes could kill them—like a bear, a river, or an Indian. A man scratched by a bear would bleed. One engulfed by a river could drown. One tortured by an Indian would suffer excruciating pain. But a man bitten by a snake risked even worse—possession of his soul. "I have heard only of one person who was stung by a copperhead in this country," Crèvecoeur tells us.

> The poor wretch instantly swelled in a most dreadful manner; a multitude of spots of different hues alternately appeared and vanished on different parts of his body; his eyes were filled with

madness and rage; he cast them on all present with the most vindictive looks; he thrust out his tongue as the snakes do; he hissed through his teeth with inconceivable strength and became an object of terror to all bystanders. To the lividness of a corpse he united the desperate force of a maniac; they hardly were able to fasten him so as to guard themselves from his attacks, when in the space of two hours death relieved the poor wretch from his struggles and the spectators from their apprehension.[27]

This is a story about control by an evil force which comes right from traditions of spirit possession somewhat transformed for the late eighteenth century. The cause is now biological—the bite, in this telling the "sting," of a snake. The perpetrator is a natural entity that is only itself—not a devil, an elf, a cunning man, or a witch in disguise. It is a snake, just a snake, but an animal that has powers once reserved for supernatural beings.

The story is about humans in nature, about how different we are from snakes and how fragile the boundary is between us. Like tales *us again* about wolf-men and vampires which continue to prosper in the centuries ahead, eighteenth-century stories about people bitten by snakes reveal some of the primal fears that spirit possession once bore alone. The locus of the fear has not changed, for the forest was always the preferred home of evil spirits, but in this still largely forested continent Americans were secularizing and naturalizing evil at the same time. Along with other western Europeans, they were reconceiving nature as a parallel series of connections that included humans rather than the traditional hierarchical chain with us near the top.

Make no mistake about it: the explorers were scared of snakes. They killed what they feared, and killing snakes—rattlesnakes above all—was a defining act of manhood at the time that they lived. So Lewis and Clark documented each snake they saw, snakes they imagined, and snakes they failed to perceive. They found "a den of rattle snakes" curiously close to an Indian carving on an outcropping of rocks and killed three. A milk snake found them. They were bitten and nearly bitten by snakes a number of times. They killed snakes by the dozens, recording each triumph and near miss. Even when they found rattlesnakes cohabiting with prairie dogs, Lewis's and Clark's snakes occupied an autonomous spot in nature.[28]

As Lewis and Clark returned from the wilderness, the future of Indians was headed in one direction and snake stories were headed in two. Scientists remained interested in snakes, but no longer fascinated. "The power of fascination attributed to this genus is too absurd to require our serious consideration," Dr. D. Humphreys Storer concluded in 1839. To men of science, snakes were becoming just snakes—merely biological organisms no more mysterious than lizards or snails. Ministers still had the traditional biblical serpent, to be sure, which revived for every revival as an image of evil to be resisted and feared. "The devil, that old serpent," in Jonathan Edwards's words, could still be "dragged up out of hell" to inspire a congregation with fear. Snake oil dealers worked the mystical terrain, too, selling the power that no one could see, but all with a dollar could taste. The political snake of the newspaper devices became an even more common symbol of courage, power, and force. "Don't Tread on Me" or I will bite was the sort of image that endured. Racehorses and ships of war would continue to be named "Viper" and "Black Snake" as warnings to competitors and morale boosters for passengers and crew. And none of this positive imagery diminished the effect or frequency with which politicians described each other as slithering serpents who betrayed the public trust.[29]

The charming snake that possessed a man's soul was alive but unwell when Lewis and Clark finished exploring and the divided snake was perhaps already dead. *Harper's New Monthly Magazine* ran a story on snake charming in 1854 which took a middle path, endorsing belief in the power of snakes to charm their victims, denouncing "the vague and often sublime fancies of the ancients regarding the serpent," and standing on the authority of "interesting facts." The magazine recognized that naturalists no longer believed in fascination, but wrote off the academic scientists as ignorant men. "People living in crowded cities," *Harper's* explained,

> who receive from abroad "specimens" preserved in alcohol and
> bottled, or write dissertations from examinations of the "stuffed

skin," must feel assured, from what they *see before them,* that the power of fascination is a fable; and as doubting is a safe form of unbelief, it is freely expressed.[30]

At least as far as *Harper's* was concerned, the scientists' snake had not yet vanquished all others, but the Puritans' snake was extinct. To be sure, the snake of fable and legend was becoming harder to find in the nineteenth century, buried as it was more deeply below the culture of curious men. Gothic fiction is the place to look then, not natural history, explorers' journals, or travelers' tales, for this snake as he hissed his last hiss and bit his last boot.

Nathaniel Hawthorne, that savior of traditional tales, tells this one, too, for more modern ends. In "Egotism: or, The Bosom-Serpent," a snake possesses one Roderick Elliston and imbues him with qualities recognizable from the seventeenth- and eighteenth-century past.

After an instant or two, he beheld the figure of a lean man, of unwholesome look, with glittering eyes and long black hair, who seemed to imitate the motion of a snake; for, instead of walking straight forward with open front, he undulated along the pavement in a curved line.

The more modern twist on the eighteenth-century stories is the narrator's wondering whether the snake was real or imagined, whether the "bitten" man was "the victim . . . of a diseased fancy, or a horrible physical misfortune."

Eighteenth-century essays on snake fascination anticipated the reality question with their discussions of imagined snakebites. Hawthorne again: " 'It gnaws me! It gnaws me!' he exclaimed. And then there was an audible hiss, but whether it came from the apparent lunatic's own lips, or was the real hiss of a serpent, might admit of discussion." Hawthorne is sucking inspiration from the stale air of stories oft told, of jackets and boots, of skin taking on colors and spots, of arms writhing like snakes, of men hissing through their teeth and rattling in their throats. The story reeks of musty, brittle old paper that crumbles in Hawthorne's hands, which helps the reader imagine the strain on the historian's eyes as he reads the accounts of curious men, long since gone, who chronicled the lives and deaths of these snakes.

In Hawthorne's telling, the victim survives and so does the snake, another turn from the past, when one or both of them die, the snake sometimes twice.

> At that moment, if report be trustworthy, the sculptor beheld a waving motion through the grass, and heard a tinkling sound, as if something had plunged into the fountain. Be the truth as it might, it is certain that Roderick Elliston sat up, like a man renewed, restored to his right mind, and rescued from the fiend, which had so miserably overcome him in the battle-field of his own breast.

The narrator, like nature's philosophers of old, has to rely on the trustworthy reporter, who was always suspect. The poison comes now from within the victim rather than injected through the snake's teeth, for "there is a poisonous stuff in any man's heart, sufficient to generate a brood of serpents." The heart, not the soul, is the organ attacked. The snake is bound closer to earth than in the Puritan past, when adulterous women wore A's on their clothes, or in the eighteenth century of Bartram and Witt.[31]

The diagnosis comes from the victim himself, rather than from a man of science as in the older versions of folktales. The cure is the love of a woman, not oil and herbs. The wife saves her husband rather than just his clothes. Wisdom is found in the same place where terror lurks and tenderness dwells—in the mind, the heart, the ego, the self. The language of psychology supplants mystical tropes.

Clearing the wilderness had not proved enough. In some ways things had gotten worse. By chopping down trees, pulling up stumps, planting seeds, and burying fence posts, we wiped out our enemies who dwelled in the rocks and the forests that got in our way. By building the cities one house, one street at a time, we drove them away from the coast and ever deeper into the continent that Lewis and Clark explored. In the city and farm now cleared, fenced, and paved, in a land where wilderness is as rare as poisonous snakes, we find the real vipers dwelling deep in ourselves, the monstrous egos that harbor serpents in our hearts. To our horror we see that they became us.

Now, all that remains of the medieval snake is the stench of dead myth and the snakes in our souls. As for the biological ones, there are some carcasses frozen by taxidermy in space and preserved across time and a few hearty rattlers dwelling in New England's rocks, descendants of vipers the Puritans missed. One way or another the stories live too, hidden in books that few hunters can find, wonderful tales that curious men, like those who traveled with Lewis and Clark, took the time to write down.

Very little in here about L. & C.

CHAPTER FIVE

Porivo's Story

THERE IS MORE about snakes, bears, and buffalo in the journals of the Lewis and Clark Expedition than there is about her. There is no physical description of her. We do not know from the journals whether she was tall or short, fat or thin, attractive or unattractive to the white men around her. The explorers did not give her a voice.

And yet she is an irreplaceable character in stories about the expedition. She is a symbol of peace who distinguished the explorers from a war party. She is a mediator, an interpreter, and a guide to cultural as well as "natural" landscapes. Without her, so the stories go, all would have been lost.

Despite the vast silences of the expedition's journals, much was written about her during the twentieth century. Even more words have explored what the various twentieth-century creations of her reveal about our modern culture. Her story and ours are so intertwined that any claim to have separated them would be a lie. The stories about her are not just about us, though, and some of them are even arguably hers.

She is elusive, fictive, mythic, and real. She is the Indian princess required by myths of discovery and conquest. She becomes a princess of equal standing with Pocahontas when Lewis and Clark declare her brother a "great chief." The two princesses thereafter serve as complementary symbols of racial fusion by "saving" white men and bearing biracial sons. From their mid-racial place, the princesses guide the white men—John Smith onto the continent and Lewis and Clark across it—bringing interracial comity to Anglo-American conquest.[1]

She was probably born on the west side of the Rocky Mountains during the late 1780s, perhaps in 1788 or 1789. A monument to the event creates a location several miles southeast of Salmon, Idaho. While she was still a young child, her father promised her to a future husband, likely in trade for horses. Shortly before she reached puberty, when she would have been turned over to her husband, she was among a number of women and children captured by Hidatsas in a raid on her Shoshone band. She was about twelve or thirteen at the time. Subsequently her Hidatsa master sold her to Toussaint Charbonneau, a Sioux-French Canadian fur trader whom Lewis and Clark *Charbonneau* hired as a translator. Shortly before the expedition left the Mandan Indians, she gave birth to a son whom she carried with her on the *2 wives* journey. Charbonneau left his other Shoshone "wife" with the Mandan until his return.[2]

Anglo-American mythology has no place for her once she finishes "guiding" Lewis and Clark. As a "leader" of white men across the continent, she also becomes an awkward figure in Indian lore. She is like a character in a play who utters her essential lines in the first act. Killing her off is one means of getting her offstage. Keeping her alive alters the plot.

So we get two stories about her death. There is a story that she died in 1812, which saves her from becoming the dark side of an American Indian princess and prevents her from challenging Lewis's and Clark's status as cultural leaders. This is the story favored by historians, who "document" her death in several texts written by "reliable" white men.

For others, though, another story has attractive subversive implications. The story that she lived until 1884 restores her—after fifty years of culturally cleansing "wandering"—to a native state from which she can be recovered as an enduring Native American heroine. Such a story elevates her gender and culture in relationship to the dominant ones and proved useful to advocates for women's suffrage early in the twentieth century.[3]

The historical accuracy of these two versions of her postexpedition life has always been secondary to their mythical truth. The political agendas—sometimes acknowledged and sometimes unrecognized—of advocates for each of the stories are seen as invalidating by opponents. The two sides are both vulnerable to charges of cultural politicking and neither has a decisive evidentiary advantage.

The 1884 story is possibly more convincing than it once would have been to those who share a postmodern skepticism about the authority of written texts and post-Clintonian doubts about the veracity of great men. In addition to wondering which story is "true," we might ask why historians have found the 1812 evidence "incontrovertible" when it is weak and contradicted, and why advocates for Indian and women's rights have championed the 1884 claim in the face of its evidential flaws. What is it that leads historians to adopt the rhetoric of certainty at precisely those points where plausibility should be our highest ambition? What are the stakes, what is at risk, why has the authoritative voice become the last, unacknowledged and perhaps unconscious, refuge of the evidentially challenged? Neither question will be answered by this chapter, but the reader of the cases unfolded here will be in a position to speculate on the psychology and politics behind the historical construction of one woman's life.

The evidence for her 1812 death is indirect. Clark compiled a list of expedition members sometime between 1825 and 1828. Beside the names he noted whether each was still living. Next to her name he wrote the word "dead." The source for Clark's belief that she died is generally assumed to be John Luttig, clerk of the Missouri Fur Company, who kept a journal of his 1812–13 trip on the river. He returned to St. Louis in 1813 and is assumed to have conveyed the news of her death to Clark at that time. The journal entry for Sunday, December 20, 1812, is the text upon which the documentary link to Clark's list is forged:

> This Evening the Wife of Charbonau a Snake Squaw, died Of a putrid fever she was a good and the best Woman in the fort, aged abt 25 years she left a fine infant girl.[4]

The final piece of textual evidence for her 1812 death is the journal of Henry Marie Brackenridge, which he kept during an 1811 trip up the Mississippi River.

> We had on board a Frenchman named Charbonet, with his wife, an Indian woman of the Snake nation, both of whom had accompanied Lewis and Clark to the Pacific, and were of great service. The woman, a good creature, of a mild and gentle disposition, [is] greatly at[t]ached to the whites, whose manners and dress she tries to imitate, but she had become sickly, and longed to revisit her native country; her husband, also, who spent many years amongst the Indians, was becoming weary of a civilized life.[5]

The line of logic linking the three texts places her on the way to South Dakota with Charbonneau in late 1811 (based on Brackenridge's journal entry), dying there (based on Luttig's observation) in 1812, and Clark recording the event some fifteen years later, when he makes a list of the surviving members of the expedition.

The problems with this three-text chain include the following: (1) There is a lapse of over a decade, without intervening comment by Clark, between Luttig's journal entry and Clark's list; (2) Luttig does not name the dead wife of Charbonneau in his entry and Charbonneau is known to have had two Shoshone (Snake) wives. Perhaps it was the other wife who died in 1812 and her daughter Lizette whom he sent to St. Louis with Luttig the following year; (3) Clark's list is known to contain at least one other error. He described Patrick Gass as dead when in fact Gass was still alive and would outlive Clark and all other members of the expedition; (4) Brackenridge's journal may be evidence for her being alive in 1811, but it is certainly not proof that she was dead before 1813; (5) Brackenridge may have mistaken her identity—she is not named in the journal—or embellished his story by substituting her for Charbonneau's less famous wife;[6] (6) There is evidence directly linked to her and confirmed by multiple sources that the Shoshone woman who accompanied Lewis and Clark lived another seventy-two years.

There are several reasons for the continuing appeal of the 1812 death, despite evidential limitations. Primary among them is the traditional image of heroism that grants Clark superior standing as a source. When Clark labels her deceased, it carries more weight in historians' minds than contradictory assertions from people who have lesser standing or no standing at all in our pantheon of heroes. The hero's credibility on the subject of "his" expedition—once Lewis had killed himself—is all but sacred to those who celebrate Lewis and Clark.[7]

Historians have reasoned that Clark was also in the best position to know about the expedition's members. In other words, he is the best source not just because he is Clark but also because members of the expedition looked up to him and kept in touch. He, in turn, looked after them and kept track of their lives. In sum, according to one advocate for the 1812 death, the discovery of Clark's description of her as dead "put to rest" all contrary arguments, "settling the question of when the Indian woman died."[8]

The undisputed mistake that Clark made on the same list has not undermined his reliability in the least in the eyes of the expedition's historians. The fact that he mistakenly killed off another member of the expedition—Patrick Gass—is, they reason, an entirely different matter, which casts no doubt on Clark's description of her. After all, Gass returned to New England and she remained on the Great Plains. From St. Louis, Clark was in a better position to keep track of her than of Gass.

The most recent editor of the expedition's journals declares that the evidence for her 1812 death is "incontrovertible" and "beyond doubt." Since the evidence is both doubtful and controvertible, that is a bold misstatement of fact. His attempt to shut down debate with an authoritative labeling of the evidence for her 1884 death as "faulty" is more interesting than his conclusions. The now very old debate about whether she died in 1812 or lived to 1884 is no longer as interesting as the language and logic of Clark's defenders, whose escalation of rhetorical heat reveals a beleaguered defense against the "political" forces of modern culture arrayed against them.[9]

Stripped of its emotionality, the debate raises a general issue about the comparative value of contemporary textual evidence, however sparse and indirect, and oral sources collected postmortem, however voluminous and direct. As historians of the Lewis and Clark Expedition are prone to see it, at least there are three written accounts—from 1811, 1812, and circa 1825—upon which to base the case for her death. Their point has a defensible logic embedded in traditional historical methods and perspectives.

The evidence for her post-1812 life and 1884 death was not collected until the twentieth century. Modern historians of the Lewis and Clark Expedition dismiss oral evidence, generally without examination, on the grounds that it cannot possibly "prove" anything at all and because they find evidence for the 1812 death convincing. As Harold P. Howard summarizes the position, "documentary evidence" shows that she "died at Fort Manuel, South Dakota, in 1812 and lies buried there in some unmarked grave." According to Howard, "no written evidence or surviving objects prove" that she died anywhere else and at any other time. Therefore, as Howard and others see it, there is good evidence for the 1812 death and "no proof" at all for 1884.[10]

There are reasons to suspect that just as Clark's race, literacy, and status enhance his credibility, so, too, the gender and race of advocates for the 1884 death have undermined theirs in the same historians' eyes. The principal supporters of the 1812 death have always been white and male. The most influential advocates of the 1884 death have been, from the early twentieth century when the stories were first published, women. The sole exception, Charles Eastman, was an Indian, which discredited him in the eyes of those who contested his evidence during the 1920s and 1930s.[11]

Grace Raymond Hebard, a librarian at the University of Wyoming, was one of the earliest twentieth-century advocates for the 1884 death. Between 1905 and 1936 she transcribed testimony from whites and Indians who had known a Shoshone woman on Wyoming's Wind River Reservation between the years 1871 and 1884 who they believed "piloted" Lewis and Clark across the continent. Hebard based her book and article on the recollections of these people still alive a century and more after the Lewis and Clark Expedition.[12]

Hebard's history, Eva Emery Dye's novel *The Conquest,* suffragettes' recruitment of the Indian princess for their cause, and competing claims to the official burial site politicized the Shoshone woman's death during the first two decades of the twentieth century. A bill presented in the U.S. Senate to construct a memorial on her 1884 Wyoming grave elicited the support of local Indians, who lobbied for a bathhouse rather than a tombstone. Local boosters, tourist-minded entrepreneurs, and state historians all banged their drums in behalf of Wyoming's claim (and a monument rather than a bathhouse). South Dakotans responded in kind and the Bureau of Indian Affairs dispatched an investigator—Charles A. Eastman, a Santee Sioux M.D.—to research the "late" site in 1925. Eastman collected 441 pages of interviews and correspondence and wrote his report, which supported Wyoming's Wind River Reservation as her burial place. The bill passed, the marker was built, and the controversy continues with no significant new evidence unearthed over the ensuing eighty years.[13]

According to the stories Eastman heard, she was with Charbonneau and his other Shoshone wife in St. Louis during 1807 and 1808, up to which time there is no mention of her name. When Charbonneau returned to South Dakota in 1811, he had only one of his Shoshone wives with him. She was the one who died in 1812. During 1819 or 1820 Charbonneau took a Hidatsa wife, named Eagle, and brought her to St. Louis. Approximately one year later, in about 1821, Charbonneau "married" again, this time a young Ute woman, when he was working as a guide and translator in what is now Oklahoma and Kansas. At about this time, Charbonneau's remaining Shoshone wife, who had accompanied him on the Lewis and Clark Expedition, disappeared.[14]

Comanche oral tradition surviving into the twentieth century says that she did not get along with the new wife, that Charbonneau beat her when her two sons were away on a trip, and that she ran away from him in the early 1820s. It is possible that Clark's list, compiled several years later, reflects this disappearance rather than the assumed, but never documented, communication of her 1812 death by Luttig. Possibly Clark inferred or was actually told in the mid-1820s that she was dead when in fact she had simply run away from Charbonneau.

Perhaps because he no longer heard from or of her and Gass, Clark presumed them both dead.[15]

Comanches and Shoshones speak the same language, which is from the same Nahuatl base, so there is a cultural and linguistic link between the two peoples. The Comanche split off from the Shoshone in the early eighteenth century, sometime before 1705. The Shoshone carried no collective memory of events and places they knew before they reached the eastern Rocky Mountains at the headwaters of the Arkansas River. Other Indians called the Shoshone "Snakes," associating them with the Snake River, but they called themselves Nermenuh, or "People," which is both a claim to humanity and an assertion of cultural superiority. They believed wolves, not snakes, were their ancestors and regarded coyotes and dogs as close relatives.[16]

The Comanche stories say that she lived among them for twenty-six or twenty-seven years, until the late 1840s, during which time she married and bore five children, only one of whom—a daughter— lived to adulthood. After her husband died in battle, according to the stories, "she was not in harmony" with his relatives and therefore declared that she would no longer live among them. Then, one day, she simply disappeared and the Comanche had no idea what happened to her. When they could not find her among adjacent tribes— the Wichita and Kiowa—they gave her up for lost.[17]

If indeed she lived among the Comanche from the early 1820s through the late 1840s, she lived through turbulent times. She may have been there for the arrival of the Anglos under Stephen Austin in 1821, but would not have recognized the significance of that event for her people or of the Texans' successful revolt against Mexican authority in 1835. She would have survived the smallpox epidemic of 1839 and the vicious spread of venereal diseases among the Comanche. And she would have known of the Comanches' many military successes against the Spanish and English whites through the 1840s.

She may have heard about the arrival of the Colt revolver in 1839, a new weapon that changed Anglo military strategy against the Comanche. If she left in 1848 or so, she was in the region when Texas became a state in 1846, but it is unlikely that she knew of the event or

Showing history through Indian perspective

its significance. If she left before 1849, she missed the cholera epidemic that decimated her people and may also have gone before it was clear that the Comanche were on the defensive against Americans who would not finally defeat them until after the Civil War. No one apparently asked her, though, and no one recalled her telling stories about the battles, the diseases, the captives, and the terror that the Comanche struck among their enemies.[18]

There are other stories about her, though, which locate her in a variety of places, link her with another man, and eventually find her reuniting with her sons among the Wyoming Shoshone in 1871. Since the eastern Shoshone with Chief Washakie only signed treaties committing them to the Wind River Reservation in 1863 and 1868, she arrived soon after this dramatic transition in her people's way of life. She arrived three years after the second treaty cut the size of the original 44-million-acre grant and seven years before the Shoshone agreed to share their land with their traditional enemies, the Arapaho. She arrived after the vast herds of buffalo disappeared, but before farmers' fences cross-hatched the landscape that she had traversed with Lewis and Clark. By the time she died in 1884, the Shoshone were eating the seeds given to them for planting, having already given up the experiment to turn them into farmers on the dry and windswept valley where they lived.

Her second journey across the Plains was of great distance too, and much longer in time than the one she made with Lewis and Clark. Had we details of the sixty years between her two lives among the Shoshone, we would undoubtedly find her travels more remarkable than those of the explorers. But, of course, she kept no journals.[19]

Eastman concluded that she was approximately ninety-six years old when she died and was buried in a pine coffin, in a cemetery on the Wind River Reservation that contained only whites at the time of her death. Although she was the first Indian buried in that cemetery, she was a transitional figure in what became a predominantly Indian graveyard after her burial. Challenges to Eastman's conclusions came even before he wrote the report from those who knew of his research methods and who had a stake in the "early" death. "Some day," wrote a South Dakota historian to the Commissioner of Indian Affairs, when you have leisure and your inventive bump is functioning properly, sit down and create five original stories, about the death and burial of Sa-kaka-wea. Then at intervals of three months send out Five honest and independent investigators among the Sho-shonean tribes, the Gros Ventre and Sioux, and [take] my word for it, each one of them will return with abundant traditional testimony to support each theory you have invented.

Stories about her long life are "worthless," "contradictory," "unreliable," "a perversion of history," and inferior in every respect to "official records" and "authentic contemporary documents," according to the same correspondent. These are, of course, much the same reasons that modern historians still accept the Brackenridge, Luttig, and Clark texts as authoritative on the subject of her death.[20]

Reservations about the oral testimony should be taken seriously. Just as Clark's race, gender, status, and historical standing are no guarantee of his reliability as a source, the comparative anonymity of witnesses to the aged woman's identity has no bearing on their accuracy. There is, indeed, a cultural tradition among the Shoshone of desiring to please a guest, which includes both telling the guest what he or she wants to hear and refraining from sharing displeasing information. There are the problems of passing time, potentially garbled or mistaken memories, and motivations. Attaching oneself to a famous historical figure is an attractive prospect, and often cause enough for people to "remember" associations that distort reality.

We also know precious little about the methods used for collecting the stories. They are preserved as narratives, but without any reference to questions or prompts. We can assume that collection of the stories did not conform to modern standards of oral historians, but we cannot know how or how far the interrogators prodded their respondents.

What gives the narratives weight is their collective perspective. There are dozens of testimonials to the Shoshone woman's identity. The early stories, told before the Lewis and Clark Expedition gained fame and prior to the public celebration of their Indian "guide," are perhaps less suspect on all counts. The later ones confirm the stories told about her as much as forty years earlier, adding nuance and detail but in no obvious sense embellishing or contradicting them. The collective effect is more impressive than the case made by sources supporting the 1812 death, but that does not ensure their truth.

Indians and whites interviewed by Hebard beginning in 1905 and Eastman in 1925 were all convinced that this was the woman who had accompanied Lewis and Clark. She spoke French better than English, Shoshone with a Comanche accent, and was adept at communicating in hand signs. The Reverend John Roberts, an Episcopal missionary who conducted her funeral, recalled that her grandson often told of how she had carried his father on her back "when she showed the way to 'the first Washington' across the Crow Indian country to the big water toward the setting sun." James I. Patten, a teacher and agent among the Wind River Shoshone from 1870 to 1884, recalled that

> [t]his Indian woman not only told me that she was with Lewis and Clark on the expedition to the Pacific Ocean, but that her son Baptiste was a little papoose whom she carried on her back from the Mandan villages across the shining mountains to the great lake, as she called the Pacific Ocean.[21]

Finn G. Burnett, a teacher and agricultural adviser on the reservation from 1871 to 1932, testified that "I first knew that she was with Lewis and Clark during the winter of that first year, 1871, when she spoke of being a guide for the Lewis and Clark Expedition." Burnett had heard of the expedition, but had never read anything about it and did not know much. She "was always modest and never bragging when she spoke about being helpful to Lewis and Clark," Burnett recalled; "sometimes we had difficulty in inducing her to talk, on account of her diffidence."[22]

She told Burnett that she saved the life of either Lewis or Clark, but he could not recall which. She spoke to him about the scarcity of food, her narrow escape from drowning, and how she survived on roots when the white men were reduced to eating horses and dogs. She recalled the "people who live in the water," whom she saw but could never get close enough to speak with. She told him about a beached whale that she saw, tremendous waves, and the return trip when she guided Clark to the Yellowstone River.[23]

Geoffrey O'Gara, a recent visitor to the Wind River Shoshone, observed that the old women were enthusiastic storytellers. They age better than the men, he noted, and are often "talkative and boisterous." They still fill the hours with stories from their people's traditions. "Simply growing old confers grace and wisdom" among the Shoshone, he noted, and the stories are still listened to respectfully. The tellers still take the stories, even the humorous ones, as seriously as their listeners do. And their stories still wander, repeating phrases over and over without ever coming to the sort of aphoristic conclusion that English-speaking audiences expect.[24]

In her day, the stories were always told at night. "Always at night," one Shoshone recalled recently. "That's the way you control the sleeping end of the day." There are connections, then, between stories and dreams, with stories playing a facilitative role in achieving sought-after dream states. Because of their essential spiritual role, inventing tales was never part of Shoshone culture any more than fabricating dreams could be. "Making up a story from scratch, as we commonly do," a white visitor came to understand, "would not be art but sacrilege." Shoshone stories were true in her lifetime and remain so today.[25]

That is apparently one of the reasons why she was more hesitant in telling her stories about the Lewis and Clark Expedition to the Shoshone than to whites. She feared disbelief. When she told her stories, the Shoshone were skeptical, which was a serious threat to her standing in the tribe. They thought, for example, that her story about a beached fish that was larger than a building was preposterous. They did, however, find her stories about "people who live in the water" fascinating as there were tribal traditions of other sightings and attempts to communicate with them. Although the whites absorbed these stories as credible reports of a beached whale and seals—accounts confirmed by Lewis's and Clark's journals—the Shoshone had different contexts within which to judge their plausibility.

There are other reasons for her careful selection of audiences. Since the Shoshone had no collective recollection of Lewis and Clark, they lacked the curiosity about the trip that whites had. According to her great-grandson, Indians

> never thought much about her work with the white men out to the coast, because the importance of that expedition had never been brought to the attention and the minds of the Shoshone.

Their memory of her journey was vague by the early twentieth century, but it probably had never been precise. As Quantan Quay explained, "the tradition was generally known by every Shoshone . . . that she led a large body of people in the early days to the waters in the west."[26]

This recollection mentions neither the race of the people she "led" nor the purpose of the journey. The story harks back to an almost timeless "early days." It is a trip without an obvious point, but one that was important to the people who made it and in which she was, in every variant of the memory, a leader and savior of the group.

The Shoshone "generally" believed her claim to have traveled to the coast with a large number of white men. She was old, the Shoshone listened politely, they knew that the whites valued her stories, and some of the stories were memorable. A number of people recalled her telling about the white men eating horses and dogs. The Shoshone considered dogs their relatives and did not eat them. She and other Shoshone would hungrily consume the warm blood and the raw steaming livers and entrails of a buffalo, all of which Lewis and Clark found unappetizing. The thought of eating dogs prepared in any fashion, though, turned her stomach and those of her Shoshone listeners.[27]

Such stories about Lewis and Clark, which demeaned whites and elevated her by comparison, continued to be retold after her death. So the stories about her feeding the men, leading them when they were lost, and saving the life of a white chief survived her by over fifty years. They were culturally uplifting to a people whose numbers and self-respect were in decline since the days when Lewis and Clark met them.[28]

As advocates of the 1812 death rightly observe, such stories also fed the mythic hunger and political needs of twentieth-century whites who made her into a leader of men. For Hebard,

> the most hazardous and the most significant journey ever made on the western continent—a journey that rivals in daring and exceeds in importance the expeditions of Stanley and Livingston in the wilds of Africa—a journey that resulted in the greatest real estate transaction ever recorded in history, and gave to the world . . . riches beyond comprehension—was piloted by a woman.

To the novelist Eva Emery Dye, she was a "madonna of her race, she had led the way to a new time. To the hands of this girl, not yet eighteen, had been entrusted the key that unlocked the road to Asia." To the Woman's Club of Portland, Oregon, which raised money to build the first of many statues in her honor, she was "the brave Shoshone princess who led the way across the continent." Such characterizations linked supporters of the woman suffrage movement to Portland's hosting of the 1905 meeting of the National American Woman Suffrage Association and contributed greatly, in supporters' estimation, to Oregon's endorsement of woman suffrage in 1912.[29]

So, just as supporters of her "early" death argue, the genesis of interest in the story of her "late" death was political. Such interest was intimately connected to the woman suffrage movement and the perceived need for gender-uniting heroines to help convince male voters of women's capacity for independence and leadership. Accurately identifying political motives among those who recorded or believed stories about the Shoshone woman who died in 1884 does not prove, however, that the stories are untrue.

There are political implications to the claim that she died in 1812, too, which is why it matters so much to those who support it. Clark's credibility is at stake, as is his standing as "leader" of the expedition.

Sacajawea statue. State Archives and Historical Research Library,
State Historical Society of North Dakota. Negative number A4264.
Photograph by R. Reid.

The competing claims to the locations and dates of her death are both embedded in the mythic politics of this nation's origins. Neither has the "historical" high ground.

As such cultural uses of her life demonstrate, modern Americans need her as much as Lewis and Clark did. There are more monuments to her in the United States than to any other woman. She replaced Susan B. Anthony on the one-dollar coin—a dubious distinction to be sure, given the unpopularity of the Anthony dollar. All of this came in the twentieth century because we did not need her at all for a century after she traveled with Lewis and Clark.

Her visage on statues, paintings, and a coin is a fiction which perfectly represents her standing in our mythology. She is the epitome of a heroic Indian woman. She is a madonna with child, a princess saving white men from savages, and an ageless beauty who is always portrayed as the teenage mother she was on her journey with Lewis and Clark. She is strong, tender, angelic, and seductive. She is an idealized racial and gender Other.

Ideally, from a myth-sustaining perspective, we have no actual knowledge of her beyond what the Lewis and Clark journals provide. That is another of the reasons why the stories collected by Hebard and Eastman are so threatening and why the "early" death has such appeal. In the absence of information beyond the journals, she is a creation of the explorers. They give her life. They name her. They define her. They tell her story. They leave her underdescribed and thus a nearly empty vessel into which the makers of our national myths can pour what we need to cast the Lewis and Clark Expedition as a multicultural, multiracial, gender-integrated success. In this sense, we may need her even more in the century to come than we did in the one that just ended, as our "melting pot" becomes even more of a polyglot stew than it now is.

Stories about the Shoshone woman who died in 1884 were not created in 1905; that is simply when attempts to record them began. As early as 1871 the Shoshone knew that she had papers with writing on them that she carried in a leather purse, and which she had received from "some great white chiefs." People also remembered that she wore a medal, which she said the chiefs had given her, and which some of her descendants considered "bad medicine" because every-one who wore it eventually died.[30]

The Shoshone respected her because she was the mother of sub-chief Basil, because she was old, because she told good stories, and because the whites valued her. One of them remembered an elder remarking that she would someday be valuable to the tribe. And, indeed, after her death, when the whites began to value the Lewis and Clark Expedition more highly, her fame and their association with her in life and death did bring the Shoshone federal money, tourists, and jobs.[31]

For all this desire to know her, to use her, to share her, and ulti-mately to possess her, it is still not clear after a century of quarreling about her that we know who she was. She remains an enigma. Even the spelling, pronunciation, and meaning of her most famous name is a political act. Her larger identity and historical significance in her own time is still harder to assess.

As is the Shoshone custom, she did not introduce herself by name. She referred to herself indirectly. She had more than one name when Lewis and Clark met her, but we do not know what they were. Refer-ences to her in the expedition's journals usually do not name her at all. "Our squaw," "our Indian woman," "our translator's wife," "Char-bonneau's squaw," "the Frenchman's squaw," "one of his [Charbon-neau's] wives," and "his woman" are some of the most common variations.

She is, then, most often identified as a possession, as "Charbon-neau's" or "ours." By far most of the time, she lacks the independent standing conferred by a role or a name. Of about 130 references to her in the journals, only 11 are by name—ten times by one of the variant spellings of Sacajawea and once as Janey. Only Lewis and Clark, among the five journalists, ever name her. Lewis names her six times. Clark names her four times plus once by the nickname Janey. Joseph Whitehouse refers to her eighteen times and John Ordway nineteen without ever giving her a name. Even York and Seaman are usually named, when they are mentioned in the journals, so her identity is personalized less frequently than those of Clark's slave and Lewis's dog.

The journalists refer to her more often as "the squaw," "the Indian woman," or even "the woman who is with us" than they do by name. Once Clark calls her "the squaw interpretress," which acknowledges a role rather than just a status. These less possessive labels acknowledge her gender. Some also highlight her race. Each grants her a generic identity exchangeable with many others. They imply her insignificance and suggest that she is indistinguishable from others of her gender and race.

Such descriptions naturalize her. Like rattlesnakes, she is defined by genus—"Indian." Like buffalo and bears, she is identified by gender. Such identities are enough for the journal writers, who find little else remarkable about her. They point out her significant differences from the writers and imply her inferiority as well.[32]

Wife, mother, and translator are the identities generally ascribed to her by the journal writers. Her status as wife is not even unique, since Toussaint Charbonneau claimed two at the time. She was the only "wife" he brought along on the expedition, though, so perhaps he spoke to and about her only generically—"wife," "squaw," or "woman" would have identified her clearly enough among the men.

Whatever he called her, "wife" is an imperfect description of her status. As a child, she was captured by a Hidatsa man during a raid on her Shoshone village. She was his slave. Her master sold her to Charbonneau, which makes her Charbonneau's slave. The distinction between "wife" and "slave" may have been insignificant to the journal writers, who would have accepted Charbonneau's possession of her in either status.

This financial transaction between one owner and another did not conform to marriage *à la façon du pays* (by the custom of the country) as it was practiced in fur-trade society. Indian women often initiated relationships with white fur traders and marriages were generally consensual. Such marriages were a product of parental consent followed by the payment of a bride price. The marriage was then solemnized by tribal rituals.[33]

The relationship between her and Charbonneau did conform to normal slave-trading practices in the Indian societies of North America. Most of the slaves traded were women and they were commodities exchanged between tribes and traded with Europeans. Her status as a slave, her family's obvious lack of involvement in the transaction, and the absence of a solemnizing ritual better define her status as "slave" than as "wife," whatever the journal writers chose and historians decide to call it. The story works better mythically, though, if a slave turns into a wife and an Indian maid into a princess, so that is what our history does.[34]

"Wife" may have been Charbonneau's term as well. Indeed, as her master he had the power to alter her status at will. Lack of choice in the selection of a marriage partner did not make her a slave. Neither was his possession of more than one "wife" a disqualifying marital trait. Since such relationships existed outside of Euro-American law, the more critical determinant was cultural practice.

If Charbonneau acknowledged her son as his kin, that could alter her status from slave to wife. "A slave stops being a slave," James L. Watson argues, "precisely at the moment when he or she begins to play a role in the dominant kinship system." Whether Charbonneau accepted Baptiste as his son, rather than simply as his property, is unclear.[35]

In these regards, it is possible to speculate on why she did not remain with the Shoshone when Lewis and Clark found them. At first glance, it seems logical that she would want to abandon the expedition and stay with her tribe. (1) Charbonneau beat her. "I checked our interpreter for striking his woman at their dinner," Clark wrote.[36] And this was not the only time Clark noted such violence. What better way to escape an abusive master than to remain with the Shoshone? (2) Her brother had high standing in the tribe. As Clark told it, "the great chief of this nation proved to be the brother of the woman with us and is a man [of] influence."[37] What better way to return to her people than as the sister of a "great chief"? (3) She had emotional reunions, which Lewis described as "really affecting," especially with a woman who had been taken prisoner with her and later escaped from the Hidatsa. So she had attachments to individuals and immediately accepted responsibility, too, because (4) she adopted her late sister's son. Why not stay to raise both her sons among the Shoshone, with her friends and under the protection of her brother?

Myth-supporting accounts of the expedition attribute her decision to a higher loyalty to Lewis and Clark. Some argue that the Corps of Discovery was now her "tribe," that she honored the contract Charbonneau made for her services as translator, and that she shared the sense of mission and ambition that motivated the explorers. Such speculation creates a modern white male logic for her; not surprisingly, such are the musings of male historians, who provide no particular authority for their views. They simply admire her "good judgment" in valuing her association with Lewis and Clark more highly than her tribal relationships.

he's being sarcastic again

The journals suggest, though, that however "natural" it might have been for her to stay, there were barriers keeping her from returning at this time. Lewis, for one, was perplexed by her reaction to the site of her capture by the Hidatsa: "I cannot discover that she shows any emotion of sorrow in recollecting this event or of joy in being again restored to her native country."[38] Her lack of emotional display could reflect any number of things, including her emotional inaccessibility to Lewis. We know she was more emotive around Clark and displayed great joy upon meeting her brother and a fellow captive. Certainly, though, she had nightmarish memories of her own capture and the violent deaths of her family members.

Even beyond those traumatic memories, her place in the tribe should she stay, could she stay, was not obviously enviable. A woman's life with the Shoshone was a product of decisions made by her father during her infancy. At that time an exchange of horses or mules would make the baby the wife of a man. She would continue to live with her parents until she reached puberty, at which point she would take her place as a wife. In the case of the Shoshone woman who accompanied Lewis and Clark, she was captured by the Hidatsa shortly before the transfer would have occurred.

Her husband was still living among the Shoshone when she returned with Lewis and Clark. In 1805, though, he was over forty years old and had two other wives. According to Lewis, "he claimed her as his wife but said that as she had had a child by another man, who was Charbonneau, that he did not want her." By rejecting her as tainted by bearing another man's son, her husband cut her adrift in the tribe. Her mother's line was dead. Her father was dead, too, as were her sisters. She might quite reasonably have decided that it was risky for her to live among the Shoshone with her sons, and it may have been particularly dangerous for her métis son Baptiste. However undesirable her life with Charbonneau, there was no clearly preferable alternative for her at that time. She was a marginal figure in Shoshone culture, and her association with Lewis and Clark may have alienated her even more. Sixty years later, after her Shoshone husband and memories of Lewis and Clark were dead, the danger for her and her sons was past.[39]

There is also some evidence of positive reasons for her to continue associating with the explorers. Much has been made of her relationship with Clark, with white male historians explaining that his paternalism was based on the explorer's admiration for her courage, competence, and helpfulness in several critical situations. Some women novelists have pushed the journal evidence in more romantic directions, which historians dismiss out of hand as (1) unproven and (2) inconsistent with Clark's character.

[handwritten margin note: historians tend to be the bad guys]

It is important to the expedition's historians that Lewis and Clark practiced sexual restraint during the journey. Again, this seems more a mythically based need than a weighing of evidence that is largely silent when it is not self-serving on the subject. Abstinence, at least from relations with racially darker women, is also a defining characteristic of the heroic type of which Lewis and Clark are ideals. Such historiographic racism and prudery continue to inform the analysis of modern male historians, who really have not come all that far from Natty Bumppo's and Thomas Jefferson's lust for dark-skinned women. In any event, there is a striking need displayed in the Lewis and Clark literature to make an authoritative declaration on a subject for which there is no credible authority.

The journal evidence suggests a special relationship between her and Clark that goes beyond anything he had with the expedition's men. Clark, alone among the journalists, gives her a nickname—"Janey"—in the context of noting her preference for a winter campsite. "Janey in favour of a place where there is plenty of Potas," he wrote. Although he is capable of telling us his preferences or Lewis's,

[handwritten margin note: How do we know Janey = Sacajawea / Which are slips / inentional?]

this entry reflects a solicitation of her views that is exceptional among Clark's entries. He never uses the name again in the journals and returns more often than not to nameless references, so the act in this context has a tender quality about it and seems to reflect a slip from the professional voice the explorers intended for the journals.[40]

There are other journal entries that reflect the special relationship between her and Clark, including the gift of a simple piece of bread, "which she had reserved for her child" and which Clark greatly appreciated, "it being the only mouthful I had tasted for several months past." Clark also records that she gave him a present of "2 doz. Weasel tales [*sic*]" at Christmas, but neglects to mention what he gave her. Within the context of other gifts exchanged among expedition members, this one seems extravagant.[41]

Clark was apparently sensitive to her full emotional range. He cared enough about her anger at him to make a note of it, at least parenthetically: "(Squaw displeased with me for not [Sin?] &c. &)." Although it is unclear why she was upset with him, Clark seems to be wallowing in self-pity about a bad day—"I am wet &c. &c . . . (Squaw displeased with me for not [Sin?] &c &) . . . I cut my hand." She had an emotional freedom with Clark that transcended the military camaraderie he enjoyed with the men. She could express affection within the limits imposed by her "marriage." Clark repeatedly described her as "Charbonneau's," either as a reminder to himself or as a simple statement of her most obvious trait.[42]

She could be mutinous, too, in ways that would have gotten the men whipped. Lewis may not have approved of Clark's "indulgence" of her, but there is no evidence that he challenged the relationship. He, too, granted her a dispensation from military discipline that he denied to the men. When they determined to split up the party, with only one contingent under Clark continuing all the way to the Pacific from their camp on the Columbia River, she objected to being left out. As Lewis recounted the event,

> Capt. Clark set out after an early breakfast with the party in two canoes as had been concerted the last evening; Chabono and his Indian woman were also of the party. The Indian woman was very

importunate to be permitted to go, and was therefore indulged; she observed that she had traveled a long way with us to see the great waters, and that now that monstrous fish was also to be seen, she thought it very hard she could not be permitted to see either (she had never yet been to the Ocean).

Her status as a woman undoubtedly mattered here. So, too, did her special relationship to Clark, which gave her the emotional freedom to challenge the captains' command of her.[43]

This is not to say that, although she was independent-minded, she enjoyed independence, either from her husband or the captains. When Charbonneau needed a horse, he traded one of his shirts and two of her leather dresses. There is no mention of whether he consulted her about the transaction. When Lewis and Clark admired a robe made of sea otter skins, they traded the belt of blue beads that she wore. The next day they gave her a blue coat as compensation, but there is no way to know whether she found the coat of comparable value.[44]

She did enjoy the patronage and protection of Clark, though, which shielded her from some of her husband's violence and apparently limited his ability to sell her body during the expedition. The basis for this special relationship was possibly Clark's tender nursing when she became ill during the journey. As her fever rose, her pain increased, and her overall condition worsened, Clark grew more attached to his patient. He ministered to her through the night, prepared a special shaded place for her in his boat, and made bark poultices and applied them himself. She, in turn, may have felt gratitude for his care. "If she dies," Clark wrote in the depths of his concern, "it will be the fault of her husband as I am now convinced." This passage is often interpreted as Clark's diagnosis of a venereal disease, which is consistent with the symptoms as he described them and the treatments he gave. The blame has also been interpreted by romantic readers as the jealous judgment of a competitor for her affections.[45]

There is also the story recounted to Hebard and Eastman that she saved one of the captains' lives. There is no mention of such an event in the journals and the story may simply have been untrue. Even if it was accurate, though, there is no telling whether it was Lewis, whose embarrassment complicated their relations, or Clark, whose affection for her was at least partly based on his gratitude.

Some would label such a story "worthless" because it is "unverifiable" by the "official" written record of the expedition. However, an alternative vision suggests that it is precisely in the stories that she told and Lewis and Clark did not that she made the strongest case for her identity. This was not simply an old Indian woman relating "white" tales to a white audience. These were her stories, which parallel, intersect, and potentially contradict others' perspectives. Perhaps, then, her stories' greatest claim to truth is precisely in those passages where they are uniquely hers.

Stories about Clark protecting her from Charbonneau, though, have their basis both in the journals and in stories told to Hebard and Eastman. Finn Burnett, among others, remembered the Shoshone woman's responses to questions about her "husband"; she "rarely spoke of Charbonneau. When she did mention his name, it was with bitterness and in remembrance of his temper and abuse." She described him as "a bad man, who would strike her on the least provocation." She recalled how Clark defended her from Charbonneau's violence during the expedition. Burnett also believed that some of the tension between her and Charbonneau was a result of his desire to prostitute her to Lewis's and Clark's men. "Captain Clark evidently protected her from the advances of white men," Burnett testified;

> some tribes might commercialize their women, but the Shoshones never did. . . . Infidelity was a disgrace. If Sacajawea had allowed her body to be commercialized, she would not have been honored and loved by Chief Washakie and all of her people. She would have been ostracized and banished from the tribe.[46]

The explorers admired her courage, fortitude, and competence— qualities they usually associated with men. She could take care of herself and her child and still handle her share of the expedition's work. Lewis admired her quick thinking when one of their boats capsized with her and her baby on board: "[T]he Indian woman to whom I ascribe equal fortitude and resolution with any person on board at the time of the accident, caught and preserved most of the light articles which were washed overboard." Clark also appreciated her skills as a guide on their return trip through the Bozeman Pass: "[T]he Indian woman . . . has been of great service to me as a pilot through this country."[47]

We must remember, though, that the journals neither record everything she did nor necessarily report what she would have considered the most significant events of her journey. There is no reason to believe that she ordered experiences chronologically, as the journals do, or that she told them as stories about motion, time, and the accomplishment of set goals. The stories of hers that come down to us are more snapshots than the panoramas that the journals try to be.

Both the journals and the stories told to Hebard and Eastman confirm that the Pacific Ocean and the beached whale were memorable to her. Both confirm her closeness to Clark, her troubling relationship with Charbonneau, and her joy when they "found" the Shoshone. Beyond those events and the qualities that all ascribe to her—courage, kindness, fortitude, independence, and competence—it is difficult to know her.

Those who testified in the twentieth century to her identity as the Shoshone woman who accompanied Lewis and Clark apparently never addressed her by any of the variants of her most famous name. According to Atsie McGhee, a Wind River Shoshone,

> She had three Indian names, Porivo, Wadze-wipe or Lost Woman, Pohe-nive or Grass Woman. The first two names were given to her by the Commanches when she lived among them. The last name was given to her by the Shoshones after she came back here. The white people often called her Basil's mother and also since she died the white people call her Sacajawea.

Some people also remembered her as Bah-ribo, "Water-white-man" or "Guide to White Man up the River." The Shoshone called her Yang-he-be-joe, "Old Comanche Woman," when she first arrived among them, but later more often called her "Basil's Mother" or Porivo. It was the Comanche who named her Porivo (Chief) and who referred to her as Wadze-wipe (Lost Woman) when they could not find her.[48]

Since the Shoshone and Comanche never knew her as Sacajawea during her lifetime, they could only speculate on its pronunciation and meaning. Historians have speculated, too, in endless debates that focus on two variants with several different spellings. The issue is whether Lewis and Clark called her "Sacajawea" or "Sacagawea." The arguments hinge on whether it is a Shoshone or Hidatsa name, whether Lewis's and Clark's phonetic spellings suggest a hard *g* rather than a soft *g* or *j* sound in the middle of the word, and whether it means "Boat Launcher" or "Bird Woman." As with all battles over the Lewis and Clark Expedition, this one has been fought as much with the hearts as the heads of advocates for all positions and is irresolvable based on the evidence that has survived.

Given the difficulty of establishing the linguistic provenance of her most famous name, it possibly reflects a garbled hearing by Clark, who first used it in his entry for April 7, 1805. It is also possible that members of the expedition seldom, if ever, called her by that name. Only Lewis and Clark took rare stabs at writing the name down; we have no reason to suspect that the explorers found it any easier to say than to write. "Janey" may have been an attempt to shorten it. It is possible, though, that nobody called her Sacajawea or any of its variants during the expedition.

There is no record of the name's use by anyone except Lewis and Clark at any time during her life. It has even been suggested that the journal entries naming her were added retrospectively, when they were revised from field notes and rough drafts. Although there is no evidence to support that theory or any convincing explanation for the amendments, it is odd that all ten recordings of "Sacagawea" in the journals fall between April 7, 1805, and May 16, 1806, and that eight of the ten named references are in a four-month period from April through August 1805. Before and after that the journals describe her as a possession or generic Indian woman.[49]

Her name matters now, as does the date of her death, because she is important to us. She had several names and the most famous one she had only in passing until the twentieth century, when her name became contested terrain. Whatever her name was, however it was pronounced, and whoever gave it to her, it was not the one that mattered during most of her life.

It was not a name that the Shoshone or Hidatsa recalled. Indeed, she was not remembered in Hidatsa tradition at all. She was an unremarkable slave sold to a métis fur trader. Had she not returned to the Shoshone as an old woman, they would not have known her by any name.

Had not the whites begun calling her "Sacajawea" in the twentieth century, the Shoshone would have remembered her as Porivo and told her stories for several generations after her death. Then her stories would have died too. Instead we have "Sacajawea Straits," a smooth stretch of river through the Wind River Valley named for her by whites who now own the hot springs, lead rafting expeditions, and control precious water rights.[50]

"Sacajawea" is a creation of twentieth-century American culture. Our history made her up. She is our national Indian, our founding princess, and a symbol of what our interracial history might have been. By turning her from a slave into a leader of the Lewis and Clark Expedition, we have fabricated heroic qualities that our culture needs. By killing her off seventy-two years before she may have died, we have denied her a life apart from the explorers and a voice that could in any sense be recognizably hers.

The Lewis and Clark Expedition freed her imagination even though she remained a slave. What she saw, the people she met, the contributions she made, and the sense of triumph that came from conquering the physical challenges of the journey changed her, as they changed the men, in ways that we can only imagine. According to oral testimony, the captains gave her a "chief's" medal and papers that honored her, which led her to value herself more highly.

Climbing through mountains, paddling long and sometimes rough rivers, and seeing the ocean and whale were thrilling experiences. By making it back she was also part of an amazing collective accomplishment. Nonetheless, her most remarkable achievements may have come after she left Lewis and Clark. According to oral tradition, she gave birth six times, raised a daughter and two sons, escaped slavery, chose her own Comanche husband, made her own trip, told her own stories, and lived to age ninety-six in a century when disease, liquor, and violence took a heavy toll on people of her race. Returning to the Shoshone in her early eighties would have been more amazing than anything she did in her teens.

We have mythologized our history by denying her enslavement, her life, and her voice. By creating the beautiful Indian princess "Sacajawea" from the recoverable shards of her life, we ignore the violence done to her and upon which our nation is based. We would honor her and be truer to our history by celebrating her accomplishments as a slave who transcended and eventually escaped her condition. She earned the name "Chief" and history should respect her name.

CHAPTER SIX

York's Mystery

Y ORK WAS WILLIAM CLARK'S SLAVE and was about the same age as
his master, which would make him in his thirties at the time of
the Lewis and Clark Expedition, perhaps thirty-five at its end. His first
master was John Clark, William's father, who may have named him
after the York River near where he was born or for the slave's father,
who bore the same name. His parents may have been the slaves
referred to as Old York and Rose in John's will, who were among the
eight slaves bequeathed to William by his father, or his mother might
have been a slave named Nancy, as another source claims. It is likely
that York became William's personal slave at the age of fourteen,
about when the family moved to Kentucky.[1]

York joined the expedition with Clark in 1803. The first reference
to him in the journals is by his master, who noted in passing that
"Corporal Whitehouse and York commenced sawing with the whip
saws" on December 26, 1803. There are, altogether, about thirty references to York in the journals, most of which are, in isolation from the
others, no more revealing than the first one.[2]

We do learn, though, that York nursed Charles Floyd, the one man
who sickened and died on the expedition. He also swam to an island
on another occasion to pick medicinal greens for his master, who had
a fever. York himself became ill at least twice during the expedition
and also suffered from "a little" frostbite on his toes and penis. He
danced for Indians on the command of his master more than once
and perhaps of his own volition on other occasions as well. He hunted

successfully, which means that he carried a gun. And he generally traveled with his master, which is not a surprise, although he also went off in small hunting parties without Clark.[3]

In other words, the journals do not tell York's story any more than they tell the Shoshone woman's. They both are treated as possessions in the expedition's narratives. Just as in her case, though, there is enough in the journals to heighten the mystery and to make York into a culturally emblematic figure. Reflecting white culture's greater fear of black men than Indian women, York has not achieved a place comparable to Sacajawea's in our nation's origin myths. He has served as comic relief, a fool, a braggart, a drunk, and a failure, reflecting racial stereotyping typical of the nineteenth and twentieth centuries. He was also resurrected in the 1960s by those seeking heroic figures from the African-American past. Interestingly, portrayals reflecting both white stereotyping and "Black Pride" focused on York's sexuality, so he became either "the black bull" or an "Adonis sculptured in ebony" in creations from the 1950s and 1960s. More recently York has continued to play cameo roles in support of the expedition's main characters. Although depictions of York remain far less significant in our culture than those of Sacajawea, they are no less revealing.[4]

The York of the journals is literally subsumed under the identity of his master. When Clark listed expedition members, he counted himself as two: "[T]he party consisted of 2, self, one Frenchman, and 22 men in the boat of 20 oars." This characterization of two as one is typical of the way Clark identified with his slave. References to York reflect either recordings of the commonplace from which he was not excluded, such as Clark's tallies of hunting trophies, or exceptional news.[5]

Recent accounts of the expedition have emphasized its "democracy" and have made much of its West Coast ballot on the winter camp for 1805–6. The captains permitted the men to choose between locations on opposite banks of the Columbia River and recorded the decision as a vote. Historians typically portray York's "vote" as a reflection of Clark's liberalism and of the democratizing influence of wilderness travel. They interpret it as both a foreshadowing of better racial times two centuries ahead and as evidence that York stood shoulder to shoulder with the other men, none of whom was black or a slave, as a virtual equal.[6]

This interpretation makes too much of a shrewd leadership device which was not unprecedented in American military history. Apparently Lewis and Clark did not care which of the locations the men chose. Quite possibly York either expressed his own view on a matter of no consequence to the captains or Clark knew he could count on York to vote the "right" way. We do not know, but speculation should include those less sanguine theories. More important, though, there is evidence both from within the journals and of York's relationship with Clark after the expedition that contradicts idealizations of Lewis, Clark, and their men as racial liberals for their times.

There are two events mentioned in the journals suggesting that York's relationship with the other men was not as an equal. In the first, Clark wrote, "York very near losing his eyes, by one of the men throwing sand at him in fun and received into his eyes." Some have read this as evidence that York participated in the "fun" as an equal and was simply injured in some good-natured roughhousing. There is no reason to believe, though, that York was enjoying himself. It seems more likely, given what we know about the state of race relations at the time, that York was the butt of a joke rather than an active participant in rough play. In the second surviving draft of this same entry, the one that Clark meant for publication, there is no mention of "fun." "My servant York nearly losing an eye," Clark revised, "by a man throwing sand in it."[7]

The meaning of another incident is even more elusive, but again suggests that York was not simply one of the men. Clark reported the return of a party sent to retrieve game abandoned by the expedition's hunters because it was too heavy to carry back to camp. York was a member of the group, but did not return with the rest of the men. According to Clark,

they informed me that they found the elk after being lost in the woods for one day and part of another. The most of the meat was spoiled. The distance was so great and uncertain and the way bad. They brought only the skins. York left behind by some accident which detained us some time eer [until] he came up.

Perhaps it was an "accident." Possibly it was more "fun" at York's expense. In any event, leaving him alone in the wilderness was thoughtless, unkind, and dangerous. It also delayed the expedition's departure. At a minimum, the incident suggests that York was peripheral to the search party and less quickly missed than he might have been. Whether these two stories together reflect a general pattern of distance between York and the other men is unclear, but they do imply York's solitary status rather than the integration asserted by recent idealized accounts.[8]

York's role in the expedition amplified his role in Clark's life. He danced when Clark told him to dance, shot a buffalo when Clark dictated it, fetched herbs, carried dead animals and heavy logs, and nursed a sick man. A jack of many trades, York performed tasks that ran the gamut of enlisted men's chores in addition to rendering personal service to Clark.

When Lewis listed expedition members by their function—translator, hunter, etc.—he described York as Clark's "servant," which was a Southern euphemism for "slave." Since the party identified the Shoshone woman as Charbonneau's "wife" rather than as his slave, they distinguished York as unique in the party both by his race and by his status. "A black man by the name of York, servant to Capt. Clark," was the way Lewis identified him. His identity as a slave was clear and we should expect that York's treatment by Clark, Lewis, and the rest of the party never left that in doubt.[9]

Clark made the distinction more systematically in his entries. "I set out with ten men and my man York to the ocean by land," he wrote at one point. Both the possessive "my" and the distinction from the unmodified "men" clarify the difference. "My black servant," "my boy York," and "my man York" all made the point. Clark seldom took York's status for granted in the sense that he documented his possession time and again in journal entries that mentioned the man. This may be simply a habit, a distinction without real significance, or it may be a function of challenges to the status that raised doubts in Clark's mind.[10]

There are reasons that Clark may have felt his mastery of York threatened. However constraining York's status was on the expedition, it was also liberating by comparison with his past life. The sheer magnitude of travel, the contrasts and challenges of landscape, the awesome sights from the rivers and Plains to the buttes, Rockies, Pacific Ocean, and beached whale, were York's vistas and experiences as much as anyone's. Participation alone changed York, brought his status into play, and eventually led to a questioning of his former relationship with Clark. There were now days when they were not together, when York enjoyed the comparative freedom of solitude, and that led York to imagine, and likely to yearn, for more freedom.

York also found himself valued by others in new ways that undoubtedly led him to value himself more highly than ever before. "[T]he [Arikara] Indians much astonished at my black servant," Clark noted in surprise, "and call him the big medicine. This nation never saw a black man before." The Indians were "much astonished at my black servant," Clark repeated, "who did not lose the opportunity of his powers, strength, &c." There was the rub, albeit a bit garbled in the recounting. The Indians were astonished, which was harmless enough, but York "did not lose the opportunity" to display his "big medicine."[11]

Quickly Clark felt his power over York diminishing as the slave played to another audience. "The Indians much astonished at my black servant," Clark wrote yet again, "who made himself more terrible in their view than I wished him to do." York growled, made ferocious faces, rose up in a bearlike posture, proclaimed to his audience that he was a cannibal, and described young children as particularly tasty morsels.[12]

Sure, it was a joke, which perhaps even the screaming children recognized. The problem for Clark was not the screeching children or laughing adult Arikaras; the issue was that York "carried on the joke and made himself more terrible than we wished him to do." Perhaps Clark worried about the consequences of York's behavior for the expedition's Indian diplomacy. More obviously, he resented York becoming the center of attention and slipping from his master's control.[13]

York was irrepressible. He hammed it up; he flexed his muscles, rolled his eyes, growled, and displayed himself to the curious bystanders. The Arikaras "all flocked around him and examined him from top to toe." They touched him, marveled at his skin color and hair; they obviously found York more mysterious than the leaders of the expedition. Clark and Lewis resented their secondary role in the eyes of the Indians. They quite possibly also felt disgust born of their racism that the Arikaras deemed a black man more physically attractive than either of them.[14]

Clark reiterated that "those people are much pleased with my black servant." He also observed without comment that "their women [are] very fond of caressing our men &c." Given the juxtaposition of those successive comments, we can be sure that although York was not the only man fondled, Clark found his slave's attractiveness to the Arikara, especially the women, remarkable. If we take seriously Clark's implication that he and Lewis were somehow above or, at least, outside the caressing, then we might wonder as well how the two Southerners from slaveholding families felt about their comparative unattractiveness to Arikara women.[15]

The broader issue here, though, is the Arikara's estimation that York was a man of greater "mystery" or "medicine" than the white members of the expedition. Clark recognized that this was an insult on a more comprehensive scale than Indians finding a slave more sexually appealing than the master. He knew that when the Arikara repeatedly proclaimed York "great medicine," they elevated him to a spiritual plane above the captains and the other men. "Whatever is mysterious or unintelligible is called great medicine," Clark explained in his journal.[16]

Even with Clark's weaponry and trickery—magnifying glasses to start fires and magnets to manipulate a compass needle—he was no competition for York. The handy diagnosis was that the Indians were simple, superstitious folk whose inversion of respect—finding the slave more impressive than the master—was additional evidence of their savagery. But the problem could not be so easily dismissed as this, both because it challenged Clark's mastery of York and because it threatened the white race's potential mastery of Indians as well. The supposition of the captains was that they could capture the loyalties of "primitive" peoples with the baubles they brought on the trip. They expected the Indians to be awestruck by their weaponry, science, and "gifts." It never occurred to them that Indians would find persons, and the wrong people, more impressive than things.

By the time Lewis and Clark crossed the Rockies, York had practiced his bear act time and again. Not all groups reacted the same, though; and not all found York an appealing figure. For the Nez Perce, all of the expedition's men were remarkable, but York was the most alien of all. "Why was that one man painted black as if for night work?" some wondered. "Must mean something evil," some reasoned. "Look at that big man, black all over! Covered from head to foot with charcoal. Maybe painted that way for night work. He could bring much harm to us. Look at his hair, not long and straight like ours. Look at his eyes! He rolls them around! Much white shows like in eyes of [a] mean horse." "A—a-a-a-a," others agreed. "Have to watch out for him. May be dangerous."[17]

The initial assumption that York painted himself black led the Nez Perce to think of him as a warrior and of the expedition as a war party. The presence of two Shoshone Indians—Sacajawea and a guide—inspired further distrust as the Shoshone were their traditional enemies. The fact that one of them was a woman simply confused, and thus unsettled, the Nez Perce more. A group of about ten teenage boys decided to resolve the mystery of the blackened man for themselves. When they caught York alone, they pinned him to the ground and tried to rub the black off with coarse sand. When they discovered that the black was skin deep, as blood oozed from a spot rubbed raw, they ran from their victim in even greater fear. York's blackness was, to the Nez Perce, no joke.[18]

Although this may have been the most painful attempt to discern the meaning of York's skin color and hair texture, it was not the only one. The symbolic significance of black and of blackening made York a curious figure wherever Lewis and Clark went after they left St. Louis. From the perspective of most Indians they met, York was the expedition member in the best position to claim to be "first." York was the first black man ever imagined by many of the Indians. They had never even heard stories about men with black skin and short curly hair. Most tribes had firsthand experience with whites, virtually all had individual members who had met Europeans, and all the tribes had integrated whites into their myths. But a black man required some mythical reconsideration and inspired awe.[19]

Although we are left to imagine York's reaction to all this attention, we can surmise that he relished the adulation that Lewis and Clark resented, that he enjoyed the performances that he continued to give after they left the Arikara, and that he experienced the attack of the Nez Perce teenagers as painful and scary. On balance, though, surviving sources suggest that by far most Indian reactions to York were admiring. Indians treated York as a great man and sometimes as *the* great man of the expedition. It does not take a flight of imagination from these sources to surmise that York's expedition was personally transforming and empowering. It was the time of his life.

For good or for ill, as nearly as we can tell from surviving oral traditions and the journals' sparse comments, Indian reactions to York were always extreme. In the Northwest, Indian memories of York survived into the twentieth century. There, too, they remembered trying to wash the black off. They called him "Raven's Son" for his color and the "mystery" he embodied. He was the most impressive, attractive, scary, funny, and outrageous of all the expedition's members. He was the focus of attention that Lewis and Clark expected to be on them. Lewis and Clark sought to demean York by equating the Indians' curiosity about him with their interest in animals. Of the Shoshone, Lewis wrote, "the black man York and the sagacity of my dog were equally objects of admiration." According to Clark, "York made Indians believe that he had been wild like [a] bear and tamed."[20]

From Indian perspectives, the equation of York with an animal was an expression of respect. Where Lewis and Clark diminished him by association with animals, Indians elevated him above the expedition's leaders by such comparisons. The particular animal identity York adopted was that of a bear, which was an association that made him a man of even greater mystery in the eyes of Indians who were already impressed by his powers.

Mandan and Arikara Indians believed that spiritual power is a constituent of sperm. They believed that just as a father's seed carried his character through a mother to their son, so, too, the mystery of a great warrior passed through a wife to her husband. In order to secure York's mystery for himself, an Arikara man offered his wife to the black man for sexual intercourse. According to Clark in interviews with Nicholas Biddle in 1810, York retired to the man's home and completed the act while the man stood outside his door to prevent any interruption. How often men approached York with such offers remains a matter of prurient speculation among historians and novelists, but Clark mentioned only one specific case recorded by Biddle, who was editing the expedition's journals for publication.[21]

Whether York was a more sought-after sexual partner by Indian women than the other men of the expedition is unknowable, but from what we do know of the comparatively greater curiosity about York and of the spiritual (as well as recreational) functions of sexuality among Northern Plains tribes it seems likely that York enjoyed at least equal standing among the explorers in this regard. The offer of sexual intercourse was also an expression of hospitality among tribes visited by the explorers. Clark told Nicholas Biddle in 1810 that "two very handsome young squaws," also Arikara, made themselves sexually available to York and other men of the expedition. In Biddle's recounting,

> the black man York participated largely in these favors; for, instead of inspiring any prejudice, his color seemed to procure him additional advantages from the Indians, who desired to preserve among them some memorial of this wonderful stranger.

Since sexual intercourse among Plains Indians and fur traders was so frequent that it affected the gene pool, there is some basis for assuming that recreational and spiritually motivated sexual intercourse were a significant part of York's experience during the expedition. There are also oral traditions among the Shoshone, Nez Perce, and Mandan that York fathered children among them.[22]

The information about York gleaned from the journals and Indian oral traditions is significant in its own right for what it reveals about him, about attitudes toward him, about the tribes that are part of the stories, about the expedition, and about Lewis and Clark. It is also contextually relevant to imagining York's state of mind upon his return to St. Louis and for the two stories told about his postexpedition life.

Traditions that Clark freed York upon their return to St. Louis in 1806 are untrue. It is revealing, though, that celebrations of Lewis and Clark dating back to Elliott Coues's 1893 edition of Biddle's history of the expedition record this "fact" as part of the documentary record. Clark's family, novelists, editors, and historians have always agreed that Clark should have freed York, thereby erasing slavery's morally troubling blot on the expedition's record. The continued enslavement of York for about thirteen years after the expedition's return is a mythically unattractive historical fact.

York married sometime before the expedition and left his wife behind in Louisville when he and his master embarked in 1803. We do not know her name. She was a slave, but not owned by Clark. York included a buffalo robe for her when Clark sent specimens back east in May 1805. That is all we know about her until after the expedition's end.[23]

York traveled with Clark to St. Louis, Kentucky, and Virginia after their return. Clark purchased tailor-made clothes and boots for York, of much better quality than was usual for slaves, reflecting York's status as companion and body slave to his master. These travels brought York both reunion with his wife and further separations from her. They also contributed to tensions between Clark and York.[24]

The earliest evidence of this tension appears in a letter from Clark to his brother Jonathan dated November 9, 1808, which refers to issues dating back at least five months. On June 2, 1808, Clark and York had left for St. Louis, where Clark was to take up his official duties as territorial governor, representing a permanent move for Clark and thus an indefinite separation of York from his wife. In the letter, Clark acknowledged York's unhappiness with the situation. Clark also proclaimed his willingness to sell York to a Kentuckian to satisfy the slave's desire to be near his wife. Clark resented the suggestion that he bend his will to accommodate a slave's desire. He may also have wanted to avoid such a precedent lest his other slaves request reunion of their family groups.

There was no question of emancipation. Clark granted York leave to visit his wife for a few weeks, but the slave was ungrateful even for that magnanimous (in Clark's eyes) gesture. "He wishes to stay there altogether," Clark explained to his brother, "and hire himself, which I have refused. He prefers being sold to return[ing] here. He is serviceable to me at this place and I am determined not to sell him to gratify him."

Their relationship had so deteriorated that Clark imagined York fleeing his enslavement. "If any attempt is made by York to run off," Clark confided to his brother, "or refuse[s] to perform his duty as a slave, I wish him sent to New Orleans and sold or hired out to some severe master until he thinks better of such conduct."[25] One month later, Clark sounded even more determined, less tolerant, and less hopeful that York would ever again be "useful." Clark took particular offense at York's insistence that he was owed freedom for the past services he had performed for his master.

> I did wish to do well by him, but as he has got such a notion about freedom and his immense services that I do not expect he will be of much service to me again. I do not think with him that his services have been so great or my situation would permit me to liberate him.[26]

At some point Clark shared with Lewis both his displeasure and his plans for selling York to harsher enslavement. Clark wanted both to teach York a lesson and to receive some financial benefit from his ownership of York. "I do not care for York being in this country," Clark wrote to his brother.

I have got a little displeased with him and intended to have pun-
ished him but Govr. Lewis has insisted on my only hiring him out
in Kentucky which perhaps will be best. This I leave entirely to you.
Perhaps if he has a severe master a while he may do some service. I
do not wish him again in this country until he applies himself to
come and give over that wife of his. I wished him to stay with his
family four or five weeks only, and not four or five months.[27]

Clark expressed no sympathy for York's "family" attachments, which
suggests that there may have been children in addition to a wife. In
any event, Lewis apparently persuaded Clark to back off from his
most retributive ideas about teaching York a lesson.

Whether Lewis's perspective reflected a personal attachment to
York is unclear. There is no reason to believe, though, that Lewis suggested freeing York. The two captains apparently agreed that York
had not earned manumission by his services on their expedition. It is
possible, though, that Lewis perceived a public relations problem
with potentially serious political consequences should Clark sell York
into plantation slavery in the Deep South.

By the spring of 1809, York was back in St. Louis and not happy
about it. Whether he fully appreciated the danger he was in, knew
that his master contemplated a retributive sale, or resolutely stood
his ground in the face of full knowledge of the possible consequences
we cannot know. We can see York's point of view only through the
eyes of his master. Clark was fed up. "He is here but of very little service to me," Clark wrote to his brother. "[He is] insolent and sulky. I
gave him a severe trouncing the other day and he has much mended
since." Whether what "mended" was wounds or behavior is unclear.[28]

In any event, Clark was still contemplating selling or hiring York's
labor to anyone in Louisville who would pay a fair price. In July 1809
Clark reported that he had "taken York out of the calaboose and he
has for two or three weeks been the finest Negro I ever had." We do
not know why York was imprisoned or how long he had been there.
Only one month later, though, Clark was again resigned to hiring out
or selling York. By September, York was on his way back to Louisville,
perhaps to one of Clark's brothers until someone purchased the

slave's labor. That would not be easy, Edmund Clark informed his brother, because "I don't like him. Nor does any other person in this country and was it not for their friendship for you, I believe he would have been roughly used when he was up last."[29]

By early 1810 York was working as a teamster, making deliveries. We know this from an account book reference to repairs made to his cart. The next evidence of York's ongoing enslavement is a letter to Clark from his nineteen-year-old nephew, John O'Fallon, which was posted from Louisville on May 13, 1811. That was about four months shy of five years after the expedition's return to St. Louis. O'Fallon's letter reported that the contract for York's labor had just come to an end. The letter also explained that the owner of York's wife was about to sever the relationship by moving with her to Mississippi. The letter goes on to assess York's state of mind as a plea in the slave's behalf.

> I apprehend that he has been indifferently clothed if at all by Young [York's contracted master] as appearance satisfactorily prove[s]. He appears wretched under the fear that he has incurred your displeasure and which he despairs he will ever remove. I am confident he sorely repents of whatever misconduct of his that might have led to such a breach and moreover has considerably amended and in fine deems it not unreasonable to recommend his situation to your consideration.

York was about to lose his wife in one of the many cruelties of slavery. He lived in abject poverty, was despondent, and had lost his master's goodwill. Clearly York's circumstances had plummeted, not just from the comparative freedom he had enjoyed on the expedition but from his preexpedition status as Clark's body servant. He had gone from the best to the worst situation of his enslaved life.[30]

It is peculiar that York surmised Clark's displeasure with him but claimed not to know its source. Clark's low regard for York may have reflected the general change in their relationship rather than a particular incident. York was less satisfied by his condition upon their return, made demands for freedom, and expressed his opinion of slavery's injustice to him. Clark, in turn, resented having his mastery called into question. York was unappreciative of his favored status as a body servant rather than a field hand. Clark aimed to teach him that things could be worse. York had confronted Clark with the issue of his freedom, thereby revealing his "ingratitude" and challenging both Clark's mastery and his conscience.

We do not know how Clark reacted to O'Fallon's missive. We do know that Clark traveled east with his new wife and a new body servant in the fall of 1809, because York was no longer part of his household three years after the expedition ended. Clark's grandson mentioned in his memoir that York was Clark's body servant in 1819. Perhaps York returned to St. Louis and to Clark after his wife's master took her to New Orleans.[31]

York is the only expedition member whose name is not on Clark's list drafted between 1825 and 1828, the one in which he lists Sacajawea as dead. This may reflect Clark's taking York for granted. It may reveal a personal hostility. If York was by this time free, Clark may have wanted the "ungrateful" slave out of his mind as he was out of his life.

Here the evidence splits down two paths. The first story is Clark's, albeit secondhand. Washington Irving visited Clark in St. Louis in 1832. In his notes on that visit, Irving summarized for his journal comments Clark had made about his slaves.

> His slaves—set them free—one he placed at a ferry—another on a farm, giving him land, horses, &c.—a third he gave a large wagon & team of 6 horses to ply between Nashville and Richmond. They all repented & wanted to come back.[32]

Nonsense. This story tells us more about Clark than about his slaves. It drips with Clark's self-justification, of a master's rationalization for continuing to own slaves, which the story seems both to explain and to deny. Clark freed his slaves, but he still had slaves, and the slaves he freed were better off under his mastery than on their own. Every one of them knew this and "repented" of his desire for freedom. They "wanted to come back." What could he do?

As a master perhaps too kind for his own good, but a responsible man who knew his duty to these people, Clark still had slaves when Irving visited because, the story implied, they wanted to be slaves, not because he want to be a slave owner. Clark, not the slaves, was the victim. Clark, through Irving, parodied the self-righteous slave owner's rationalization for slavery. It was his duty, not his vice. It was his virtue, not his sin, that accounted for what Irving saw. <u>No one should believe a word of this story</u>, but it probably reflects accurately what Clark or other men in his position might have claimed at the time.

Motives twist the truth

There is more to Irving's account, though, and the rest is specifically about York.

> The waggoner was York, the hero of the Missouri expedition & adviser of the Indians. He could not get up early enough in the morning—his horses were ill kept—two died—the others grew poor. He sold them, was cheated—entered into service—fared ill. Damn this freedom, said York, I have never had a happy day since I got it. He determined to go back to his old master—set off for St. Louis, but was taken with the cholera in Tennessee & died. Some of the traders think they have met traces of York's crowd, on the Missouri.

Given the incredible nature of the first part of the story, why should we believe this part either? Well, it does have details that lend it credibility. It counts the number of horses and describes separate fates for two pairs, refers to a specific incident that led to York's fall, quotes York, diagnoses his last illness, and names where his body fell. The story seems possible, and yet the quotation harks back to the first part of the story and draws the same moral from the slave's mouth. " 'Damn this freedom,' said York," but to whom? Not to Clark, because York never made it back to St. Louis in this telling.[33]

Slaughter has complete control of his rhetoric

Maybe the quotation is merely some storyteller's license for a tale that is basically accurate in other ways. What was York doing in Tennessee, a freed black man living by choice in the Deep South during the 1830s? From where was York headed to St. Louis that Tennessee would be on his route? Even deeper south, it would seem. That is less likely, for sure, but there is the romantic possibility that he traveled south into the jaws of slavery, at great personal risk to himself, to search for his wife. That would be quite a story, and a sad one, if true.

The story's details are pretty deep in improbabilities, though, and self-justifying rot, just as the first paragraph of Irving's notes is. Perhaps York's fate, as described in the second paragraph, was simply specific evidence for the general conclusions that the first paragraph drew. At least that may be how the slave owner gave York's end a meaning that we have no reason to believe, and good reasons to doubt, that York would have shared.

Here is the other story, which is also improbable. On the other hand, it is no less likely than Clark's story, and maybe it is true. The problem is that this story gives York a happier postexpedition, post-slavery life, which may make us want it to be true so much that it throws our judgment off about whether we should believe it.

In 1832, the same year Washington Irving visited William Clark, a fur trader by the name of Zenas Leonard traveled through what is today northern Wyoming. In a Crow Indian village on the Shoshone River, Leonard met a black man who lived with the Indians. Yes, the man introduced himself as York.

> In this village we found a Negro man, who informed us that he first came to this country with Lewis and Clark—with who he also returned to the state of Missouri, and in a few years returned again with a Mr. Mackinney, a trader on the Missouri river, and has remained here ever since—which is about ten or twelve years. He has acquired a correct knowledge of their manner of living, and speaks their language fluently. He has rose to be quite a considerable character, or chief, in their village; at least he assumes all the dignities of a chief, for he has four wives with whom he lives alternately. This is the custom of many of the chiefs.

William Clark Kennerly recalled York being in St. Louis in 1819. If true, that would make York's 1832 estimation that he had been with the Crow for ten to twelve years possible. Of course, Clark told Irving that York was dead by that time.[34]

Leonard's story has more details about York. The traders asked him about horses of theirs that had been stolen. York explained that his tribe had them and that the Indians had taken the horses because they found the animals in an enemy's territory and the Crow assumed that the traders were going to trade guns and ammunition to their enemies. York suggested that the traders bestow gifts on the chiefs and they did so. The Crow returned the horses unharmed.[35]

Leonard went on to describe York as fluent not only in the Indians' language but also in their culture, and thus of great value to the Indians and to the traders as a facilitator of transactions between the groups. "He enjoys perfect peace and satisfaction," Leonard reported, "and has everything that he desires at his own command." York was a tribal wise man who understood the ways of the whites—a man of mystery whose presence among the Crow was a gift.[36]

Two years later, in 1834, there was a great battle between the Crow and the Blackfeet, which Leonard watched. The Crow suffered considerable losses, were in disarray, and showed signs of despair.

> The whole Crow nation was about to retreat from the field, when the Negro, who has been heretofore mentioned, and who had been in company with us, advanced a few steps toward the Crows and ascended a rock from which he addressed the Crow warriors in the most earnest and impressive manner. . . . He told them that their hearts were small, and that they were cowardly—that they acted more like squaws than men, and were not fit to defend their hunting ground. He told them that the white men were ashamed of them and would refuse to trade with such a nation of cowards. . . . The Negro continued in this strain until they became greatly animated, and told them that if the red man was afraid to go among his enemy, he would show them that a black man was not, and he leaped from the rock on which he had been standing, and looking neither to the right nor to the left, made for the fort as fast as he could run. The Indians guessing his purpose, and inspired by his words and fearless example, followed close to his heels, and were in the fort dealing destruction to the right and left nearly as soon as the old man.

According to Leonard, the Crow lost about thirty men that day, a devastating toll. They left the field in victory, though, inspired by

York to avenge their losses and reclaim their honor as Crow and as men.[37]

Eloquent, courageous, and a formidable foe, York carried the day. He also lived to dance in victory. "The person who struck the first blow at their late battle with the Blackfeet," according to Leonard, "now commenced dancing and was immediately followed by every young man and woman belonging to the tribe (except the mourners, who stood silent, melancholy spectators)."[38]

As I said, the problem with this story is that it is too good. It invites cynicism while repelling it at the same time. York was indeed an "old man" by 1834, when the battle occurred—if, that is, he was still alive and Leonard's "York" was him. Clark was sixty-four and York was about the same age, possibly a few years younger, but no more. So York would have been at least sixty when he ran ahead of the Crow, fearlessly leading them in battle against the Blackfeet. Perhaps it was somebody else who accepted the identity bestowed upon him by people who knew of only one black man, who made space for one "York" in their mythology. And yet if it was someone else, how did he dare to make the trek west? Why did he expect that there was a life for him there? Maybe York inspired him.

Skeptical of almost everything

What reason has York given us to doubt his word about his identity? Unlike Clark, we catch him in no lie. Two other men have been offered as candidates for York's place among the Crow. We now know that one of them died over a year before the battle Leonard described. The other was thirty-four, not "old," and, although of mixed racial ancestry, neither appeared nor self-identified as "black."[39]

York earned a reputation as a storyteller upon his return to St. Louis in 1806. Whether it was the influence of liquor, as nineteenth-century sources attest, or simply enthusiasm given free rein by a few drinks, York told his stories well. Enraptured audiences of fur traders had to defer to York's authority since he had traveled farther west, seen more, done more, and met more Indians than they. We might suspect that his stories were of sexual exploits, as well as tall mountains, heroic deeds, and great waves, but we cannot know. "York was much given to romance," local people recalled, by which they apparently meant that his stories were unbelievable. He was prone to "flights of erratic fancy," recalled those who bought him drinks in return for his tales.[40]

Perhaps much of what York said in St. Louis's taverns was true. Possibly his stories seemed incredible to a white audience because they were told by a black man. Maybe the disbelief York saw in the white faces helped him to understand that the freedom he longed for more passionately after the expedition could not be realized east of the Missouri breaks. York had to go west to escape slavery, to be free, to be wise, powerful, brave, and heroic.

What a strange choice it would have been for York to head south, to end his days in Tennessee, when an alternative life beckoned. After Clark berated him, fought for a decade and more York's insistence that he had earned his freedom, and hired out his enslaved labor to Young, who abused him further, why would York head south? After the cruelties of slavery tore his wife away and sent her to Mississippi, where he could not follow and live, how could York deny the life that lay ahead of him?

York could aspire to no greater standing in a culture dominated by whites than that of the libidinous drunken fool that Clark and historians made him during his life and after his death. What remnants of traditional bigotries lead us still to believe Clark despite the incredible holes in his stories and to disbelieve Zenas Leonard, whose account lacks Clark's need for self-vindication? When will we stop believing great men because they are great when there are good reasons not to believe them? When will we acknowledge that great men lie no less, and sometimes fabricate more, than the rest of us?

including Bush & Cheney

We have known for two centuries how York's story should end. That is why folk traditions associated with the Lewis and Clark Expedition have claimed all along that Clark freed York upon their return. That is not true. York fought his slavery and his master's stubborn resistance to letting him go. It is a tribute to York, not to Clark, that York ever got free.

We should want York and Sacajawea to escape slavery and we must admit that their very presence on the expedition reflected slavery's cruelty. We need to acknowledge that the Shoshone woman was a slave; there has never been any doubt about the black man's condition. Neither York's "vote" on the expedition's winter camp nor the Shoshone woman's insistence that she see the Pacific coast redeem the expedition or our culture from the horrors of slavery. Finding democracy within slavery is not history; it is racist romance.

The irony is that York and Porivo did escape slavery and we have been unable to let them go. We know that York and Porivo should have returned to the West. We have good evidence—better than the evidence against it—that they both did. To let them go, though, is tantamount to admitting that Lewis and Clark failed. It requires us to face the interracial cruelties of our nation, and to admit that our origin myth is a lie. It leads us to believe Indians over whites, oral traditions over documents, and people we have never heard of over the written words of great white men.

We do not know when York died or where. We can celebrate both York and Clark, but not in the same ways we once did. Both were human; both were great men. Both undoubtedly lied when it suited their ends. Only one of them, though, was a bear. Only York achieved that status among the people whom the expedition met on the Plains. Pierre Antoine Tabeau, a fur trader who was with the Mandan when Lewis and Clark passed through, recalled how the Indians reacted to the explorers. Lewis's and Clark's quadrant, phosphorus, and magnet impressed them as "medicine: that is to say, as supernatural and powerful." The "most marvelous" of all, though, according to Tabeau, was "a large, fine man, black as a bear, who spoke and acted as one."[41]

CHAPTER SEVEN

Hunting Themselves

Euuropean and American culture traditionally took a view of the wilderness opposite from that of Plains Indians. Judeo-Christians saw the wilderness as hellish, wild animals as evil, and mankind as both fallen from Eden and threatened by nature. Hunting was, therefore, a war against aggressive, threatening, and devilish enemies which took place on a hostile battlefield.[1]

These cultural traditions influenced Lewis and Clark, who sought Eden but often found hell in the wilderness. They brought with them assumptions about the symbolic significance of hunting, and about themselves, which they were not very self-conscious about. They were also so secularized that the spiritual implications of hunting were outside of their ken; they denied the existence of animal spirits, only glimpsing them in experiences they did not fully comprehend.

"As usual," Lewis wrote in his entry for May 5, 1805, "saw great quantity of game today." Who saw? The imprecision of the subject— I/we?—elides the personal or collective relationship that he described. He/they saw "game"—not animals but game. Lewis envisioned beef on the hoof, imagined the creatures dead and cooked, appreciated them for their potential use—their succulence and as sustenance. So did the rest of the expedition's men. Other journalists shared Lewis's imaginative consumption of nature when they measured forests in board feet and imagined the Plains as demarcated fields for grazing domestic cattle and growing crops.

Captain Meriwether Lewis, watercolor on paper by Charles B. J. F. de Saint-Mémin,
accession no. 1971.125, negative number 51322.
Collection of the New-York Historical Society.

"Buffalo, elk, and goats or antelopes feeding in every direction," Lewis reported. "We kill whatever we wish"—a hunter's dream foretelling the obliteration of whole species by men who killed because they "wished" to kill, not to eat, not to live, but to shoot. "We killed two buffalo," Clark explained, meaning that someone other than himself shot the animals, "and took as much of their flesh as I wished." "We" shot; "I" took; they killed more meat than they could eat. "Some men went for meat," Joseph Whitehouse reported in his journal. The hunters "killed six buffalo and saved only the brains and tongues." The meat sated their hunger, but not their appetites; they continued to shoot for delicacies.[2]

"The buffalo furnish us with fine veal and fat beef." "Furnish" is an interesting choice of words, deceptively close to the Indians' sense of game as gifts from the animals themselves, but more utilitarian, not spiritual, in its intended meaning. "We also have venison and beaver tales when we wish them," Lewis concluded the passage. "Tales," not "tails"—surely a slip, but again a tantalizing one, because the beavers told tales to the Indians that Lewis and Clark never heard.[3]

Not only did the buffalo "furnish" themselves, but the hunters also "harvested" them. Not only were the buffalo plentiful, but they were "gentle" as well. Indeed, they were "so gentle that the men frequently throw sticks and stones at them in order to drive them out of the way." The language of crops and gentility was a linguistic domestication of wild animals. The words implied rightful possession and the "dominion" over beasts that Genesis granted the explorers' culture. The hunters felt entitled to the animals and whatever use they made of them. They took their "right" to kill for granted and thus secularized the relationship in the language of politics and nationhood.[4]

In other words, killing animals was not a spiritual act for Lewis and Clark. To the explorers, hunting was a creative extension of themselves which gave hunters the right to possess their prey. Although such rights were subject to dispute in civilized society, where property and hunting laws intervened, the wilderness hunt had different constraints. The explorers shot what they wanted, much more than they could use, and celebrated their creation of meat from living animals. "We discovered two deer at feed some distance near the river,"

Lewis wrote in his journal. "I here halted the party and sent Drouillard to kill one of them for breakfast. This excellent hunter soon exceeded his orders by killing of them both."[5]

The excess excited Lewis. The hunter's skill impressed him. Enthusiasm for the ability to kill transcended any sense of responsible husbandry, morality, or spiritual consequences.

In their entries for April 27, 1805, Lewis and Clark explained the rule that guided their hunting. "Although game is very abundant and gentle," wrote Lewis, "we only kill as much as is necessary for food." Clark essentially repeated the message of Lewis's entry, writing that "although the game of different kinds are in abundance we kill nothing but what we can make use of." The entries fascinate because the language is not identical. Although they talked about the issue with each other and perhaps with the men on that day, they recorded the sentiment in different words. These were thoughtful, purposeful entries which are all the more interesting because what they say was untrue.[6]

Who were the captains fooling? What was their game? They shot the heads off of ducks, nesting geese, buffalo for only their tongues, bear cubs in their mothers' dens, bald eagles from the sky, and prairie dogs to practice their aim. Why claim otherwise in the face of counterevidence they continued to provide?

Perhaps the explorers expressed a resolve, an intention, to do better than they had in the past. Possibly they worried about exhausting their ammunition if they fired at their current pace. Maybe they knew that they were doing something wrong, despoiling this hunter's paradise, betraying the injunction of Genesis to "have dominion over the fish of the sea, and over the fowl of the air, and over the cattle, and over all the earth, and over every creeping thing that creepeth upon the earth." Perhaps they felt like despots and knew in their hearts that wanton killing is wrong. They did not say and they did not mend their ways, so the guilt and the consequences of undisciplined kills endure.[7]

"One of the Indians pointed to a flock of brant sitting in the creek at [a] short distance below and requested me to shoot one," Clark explained. "I walked down with my small rifle and killed two at about forty yards distance." He reported the Indians' amazement, implied that they were impressed, and asserted that when he proceeded to blow the head off a duck, the Indians described his rifle as "good." Clark also recorded the Indians' disbelief, however, which could be interpreted differently than he did. They "said in their own language," according to Clark, "do not understand this musket &c," which even without an explanation of the et cetera is not necessarily a compliment.[8]

"Drouillard fired at a large brown bear across the river," according to Lewis, "and wounded him badly, but it was too late to pursue him." The bear posed no threat. The explorers would have been unable to pursue and bring the animal down had it fallen. It was not fear or hunger that led Drouillard to shoot and Lewis to encourage him. Sometimes they tried to kill just to prove that they could.[9]

The hunters' motives are not always discernible from the journal entries. "I killed four plover this evening of a different species from any I have yet seen," wrote Lewis. Scientific curiosity may have been the cause. The birds were new to Lewis and perhaps the species would also be new to ornithologists. "We could not kill it," Lewis lamented on another occasion, "therefore I can not describe it more particularly." Plover are easier to observe at close hand when they are dead, but he did not need four to write a description for the journals. Perhaps he wanted specimens, but the explorers were not preserving birds on the expedition and Lewis did not return even feathers from these birds to the East Coast.[10]

Clark shot four prairie dogs in one outing; the motive was to have their skins stuffed. When Lewis saw "the most beautiful fox that I ever beheld," his reaction was to kill it. When he shot at an antelope, Lewis's "object was if possible to kill a female . . . having already procured a male."[11]

Ornithology was a brutal science, as we know from John James Audubon's executions of birds. Lewis did not just shoot specimens; like Audubon, he experimented with extracting their life force. "This day," Lewis explained, "took a small bird alive of the order of the . . . goat suckers. It appeared to be passing into the dormant state." No need for Lewis to kill this one to observe it closely in the palm of his hand. Nonetheless, "I run my penknife into its body under the wing and completely destroyed its lungs and heart, yet it lived for upwards of two hours." The goal was to see how slowly the poorwill (a relative of the whippoorwill) died when in hibernation.[12]

Why Clark shot a goose which was sitting on an egg in her nest is unclear, but maybe he ate her. There is no description of the goose, the egg, or the nest in the journals. Someone did climb the "high" cottonwood tree to examine the nest and fetch the egg, but there was nothing remarkable about them. Still, Clark commemorated the event by naming "Goose Egg Lake," so there was something about the killing that he wanted to recall. Perhaps it was a difficult shot that brought the sitting goose down. Possibly it was a beautiful setting that warranted a name. Maybe the goose and/or the egg just tasted good. Clark associated the discovery with the kill, and took credit for both with pride.[13]

The hunters did not kill everything that breathed, though, so the rare exceptions to their de facto hunting rule define their sense of fair game. There was a dog that followed them for miles before they killed it. "This morning," Lewis wrote, "one of the men shot the Indian dog that had followed us for several days; he would steal their cooked provision." Their instinct was not to kill the dog; its domesticity, fawning behavior, and emaciated state led them to think of it as pathetic rather than as food. Only when it became an annoyance did a hungry explorer eliminate the nuisance in a pique of rage.[14]

Lewis refrained from killing a buffalo calf that also presented itself in the manner of a stray dog. "Walking on shore this evening," he explained, "I met with a buffalo calf which attached itself to me." Lewis eventually abandoned the calf, which was afraid of his dog, without a shot. Since Clark killed a buffalo calf the next morning for meat, it seems that sparing the life of one was an exceptional act of compassion by Lewis.[15]

The immaturity of an animal affected the hunters on other occasions too. Lewis recorded that "the hunters brought in a living young sandhill crane." The qualifier "living" was necessary because it was their custom to return with dead game. "It has nearly obtained its growth, but cannot fly." This was a vulnerable creature, but far from "gentle." "This young animal is very fierce," Lewis wrote, "and strikes a severe blow with his beak. After amusing myself with it I had it set at liberty and it moved off apparently much pleased with being relieved from its captivity." Lewis made no claim for scientific inquiry. He "amused" himself and then let the animal go.

Again, as in the case of the buffalo calf, the animal's age affected the explorers. This time gentleness or domesticity did not play a role, but perhaps the immature crane was also unappetizing. Since the crane's ferocity entertained rather than hurt Lewis, it is likely that this animal escaped, at least in part, because it was cute. The crane "amused" the men.[16]

So although cuteness or immaturity could lead to compassion, and although domesticity appealed to the hunters, neither kept them from killing game. In combination, though, they prevented the explorers from feeling manly about killing cute, friendly young animals, even when they shot them just the same. They may even have experienced guilt when they killed fledglings and cubs.

An incident involving a puppy reveals some of the cultural complexity surrounding the consumption of animals generally considered pets rather than food. It also suggests the complications presented by an animal's immaturity for the men whose hunger led them to see dogs as game. In the spring of 1806, the explorers were starved, not starving but extremely hungry, as were the Nez Perce, whose hospitality they taxed for a second time. It was a time of year when the winter supplies were exhausted, the salmon had yet to run, and game on the hoof was "inadequate." The explorers were reduced to purchasing dogs and horses from the Indians, who were reluctant to part with valuable steeds at any price.

The Nez Perce did not eat dogs, and they had a revulsion against the practice which led them to judge the explorers harshly for this cultural difference. Indeed, dogs were not the explorers' preference either, but they required meat and settled for horses and dogs (in that order) when there was none other to satiate their hunger. You will recall that Sacajawea declined to eat the dogs even though she shared the explorers' hunger. Porivo long remembered her revulsion, which

Shoshone listeners shared at her story of Lewis and Clark eating the animals.

In early May 1806, the explorers' nerves were on edge and their hunger overwhelmed them. They were able to purchase two dogs and one horse on May 5, along with some root bread and dried roots, in exchange for some eye medicine. While they dined with some Nez Perce Indians, which you may remember is a tribe that considered killing the white men during their previous visit, an Indian teased Lewis about his diet. "While at dinner," Lewis explained, "an Indian fellow very impertinently threw a poor half-starved puppy nearly into my plate by way of derision for our eating dogs and laughed very heartily at his own impertinence." There was no communication problem here despite the language difference. Lewis understood the symbolism of the "poor half-starved puppy" and felt the sting of self-recognition that the Indian intended to evoke. "I was so provoked at this insolence," Lewis continued, "that I caught the puppy and threw it with great violence at him and struck him in the breast and face, seized my tomahawk and showed him by signs if he repeated his insolence I would tomahawk him."

Lewis's violent use of the puppy proved the Indian's point, but the journal entry lacks such introspection. "The fellow withdrew apparently much mortified and I continued my repast *on dog* without further molestation," Lewis concluded. The italics are defiant; they protest too much. Lewis's victory over his adversary was Pyrrhic, but Lewis had not a clue how close he came to paying with his life for this fit of temper. Clark understood better, or, at least, admitted his concern by attaching the qualifier "apparently" to his description of Lewis's triumph. Clark was not so sure whether some form of retaliation—theft, the withholding of food or other critical support, or violence—would yet be the consequence.[17]

This was not a case of miscommunication. The Nez Perce man and Lewis understood each other perfectly well. Lewis and Clark comprehended precisely how insulting the gesture was to Lewis's status as a hunter and hence as a man. Such comprehension eluded the puppy, whose fate we can only imagine.

Not only did the explorers self-identify as hunters and read their own masculinity through their hunting skills, they saw surrogates as extensions of themselves, thereby identifying personally with what others did. That is why so many of the attributions are either vague or misleading. "I" and "we" were interchangeable, indistinguishable sometimes for men who identified so closely with the group. "Shot a bear" could mean that any one of them pulled the trigger, but generally meant that someone else did. "We shot" meant that someone else did the shooting, but that the journalist identified with the accomplishment, which he was proud to share.

The expedition's hunters, whom Lewis and Clark honored by that status, were one class of surrogates. Clark's slave York and Lewis's dog Seaman had other statuses even closer to the captains. "I made my dog take as many [squirrels] each day as I had occasion for," Lewis explained early on. "They were fat and I thought them when fried a pleasant food." "Caught several by means of my dog," he wrote on another day. Lewis "made" his dog hunt and "caught . . . by means of my dog," suggesting that the action belonged as much to the master as the dog, who was an agent of Lewis's will. Rifles and dogs were "means" of hunting. Lewis was the hunter.[18]

Likewise, York was a "means" by which his master hunted. Most of the entries that mention the slave describe hunting that Clark ordered him to do. "Directed my servant York with me to kill a buffalo near the boat from a number then scattered in the plains," Clark explained. He "directed" his slave; Lewis "made" his dog. The agency was the masters'. Clark describes York's hunting with a possessive qualifier—"my servant killed a buck"; "my man York killed two geese and eight brant." The point was to tally those in Clark's column.[19]

The men of the Lewis and Clark Expedition considered hunting their most essential survival skill. They competed against each other as well as their prey. The journals read as scorecards lacking only the final tally to determine who won. "We sent out some hunters," Lewis wrote in a typical entry, "who killed a buffalo, an elk, a goat, and two beavers." Size, number, elusiveness, and danger were the standards journalists set for their kills. Comparisons to previous bests, stories about those that got away and animals that hunted the hunters, and claims to individual achievement run through the texts. The journals are, in sum, hunting logs in which we can see the journalists' triangulation of self against animals and other men.[20]

Clark's competitiveness shows through in a series of early entries about wolves, which along with snakes and bears were among the animals most feared by the explorers. "Killed a wolf on the bank," Clark reported. From Joseph Whitehouse's journal we learn that Lewis wounded the animal and Colter killed it, so we cannot take Clark's statement literally. In an entry for three weeks later, it becomes even clearer that Clark was not claiming that he shot the wolf himself. "I killed an immense large yellow wolf," Clark bragged. When the kill was his, Clark both said so explicitly and compared the carcass favorably with others. "Immense large" may seem redundant, but only if you see the entry outside a context in which others claimed to have killed either an "immense" or a "large" wolf. Clark thought that his was bigger than any of those.[21]

When Lewis killed a buck elk, he documented its size to establish precedence over others shot by expedition members. "It appeared to me to be the largest I had seen," he wrote, "and was therefore induced to measure it; found it five feet three inches from the point to the hoof, to the top of the shoulders." Any subsequent claims based on size would have to measure up to this one. Very late in the expedition Clark claimed to have bested him. "I landed opposite to a high plain on the S.E. side late in the evening," Clark recorded in his entry for August 9, 1806, "and walked in a grove of timber where I met with an elk which I killed. This elk was the largest buck I ever saw and the fattest animal which has been killed on the route." What made the accomplishment even more satisfying was that "the hunters killed nothing this evening." Clark won both for the day and the journey.[22]

More often the explorers scored their hunts according to the quantity of animals they shot, although even in those cases size and quality created room for disputing opponents' victories. In his entry for December 7, 1804, for example, Clark noted that he and a hunting party killed eight buffalo and a deer. Lewis went out the next day with another party and stayed away overnight until he got nine buffalo, one more than Clark. Reluctant to admit defeat, Clark labeled Lewis's buffalo inferior: "[M]any . . . were so meager that they [were] not fit for use."[23]

The competition was friendly but personal between Lewis and Clark. "We killed a small black pheasant," Lewis wrote. The "we" who killed the pheasant was Clark, but Lewis could not bear to single out his competitor's accomplishment. They competed both as heads of hunting parties and individually. "Capt. Clark was hunting the buffalo this day," Lewis wrote; "killed three buffalo himself and the party killed five others." John Colter and George Drouillard were better hunters than either of the expedition's leaders, so the ongoing tally was not for the expedition's top spot. It is possible, though, that neither Lewis nor Clark admitted that he was not the best shot. They may simply have seen themselves as too busy with other leadership demands to hunt on a daily basis. Theirs was more like a side bet on a serious enterprise in which the professional hunters did the hard work of providing meat for the expedition, and the rest of the men hunted for fun.[24]

When the explorers reached huge buffalo herds, the body counts rose and the competition accelerated. With meticulous care, which had nothing to do with the science or diplomacy that the explorers intended the journals to report, Clark and Lewis kept track of the animals they felled. "I set out with about sixteen men, three horses, and two sleighs, descended nearly sixty miles, killed and loaded the horses back. . . . We killed forty deer, three bulls, [and] nineteen elk," Clark reported. He could not be precise about the number of men in his party ("about sixteen") or how far they traveled ("nearly sixty miles") but he claimed to know the number of carcasses by gender and species with precision. Two days later, Clark reported that Lewis's hunting party had failed to best his in numbers but brought back a heavier load. "Capt. Lewis returned the twenty-first with 2,400 lbs. of meat, having killed thirty-six deer and fourteen elk." Lewis won for two reasons, according to Clark: many of the animals Clark's party shot "were so meager that they were unfit for use," and the Sioux destroyed one of his meat houses.[25]

It is likely that other expedition members also kept score. "We Labiech killed fourteen geese and a brant, Collins one, Jos[eph] Fields and R[euben] three," Clark tallied. The "we" is another one of those fascinating elisions which both connect the writer with those he is writing about and personalize the events. The journals have many such daily tallies, which take on meaning from the regimen of keeping score. From John Ordway's journal we learn that the explorers shot a large beaver, a white rabbit, a deer, and a bald eagle all in one day. This was quite a range of animals, but far from their largest haul. Two days later they added an otter and a muskrat to their list of animals killed.[26]

For whom were they counting? Did they look back periodically to refresh their recollections? Possibly the entries reflected more what was on their minds than what they had any conscious reason to recall. Tallying the day's kill and entering it "officially" into the journals brought its own satisfactions, short-term boosts of morale for those who did well and spurs to greater accomplishment for those who shot less.

Although other journalists were even more focused on body counts than the two captains, it is only possible to follow the competition between Lewis and Clark. The enlisted men lacked the time and energy to do as much sport hunting as the two captains; and their entries of dead animals lack the self-referential focus that Lewis's and Clark's have. "Having for many days past confined myself to the boat," Lewis explained, "I determined to devote this day to amuse myself on shore with my gun and view the interior of the country. . . . My object was if possible to kill a female antelope, having already procured a male." Lewis was not hunting for food and he would even spare an elk of the wrong gender, however meaty, in order to add to his list of hunting accomplishments.[27]

When there was work to be done and others were doing it, leadership had its perquisites in the leisurely pursuit of small and large game. "While they were getting the boat through this long riffle," Lewis explained, "I went on shore and shot some squirrels. My men were very much fatigued with this day's labor, however I continued until nearly dark." Surely squirrels could be eaten, but that was not the motive or even the excuse Lewis offered. The hunting was his amusement while the enlisted men tugged a heavy boat over the sandbar that blocked their way.[28]

At other points in the journey, there were so many animals that hunting was all fun. That made it a gentleman's entertainment. "Saw a great quantity of game of every species common here," Lewis wrote, reprising his collective vision of himself and his imagery of animals as steaks. "It is now only amusement for Capt. C and myself to kill as much meat as the party can consume." The only chore was keeping count—how many animals, their gender, species, weight, and the quality of the meat. Clark shot two buffalo on one of their outings and Lewis got only one, but Lewis's was, according to him, "the best meat."[29]

When the game was more elusive, excuses were part of keeping track. On one day Clark reported hunting with John Collins, who shot an elk. "I fired four times at one," Clark reported, "and have reasons to think I killed him, but could not find him." Lest the reader jump to the conclusion that Clark just plain missed, he let us know that conditions were less than ideal. "The mosquitoes were so troublesome . . . that I could not keep them out of my eyes." That explains it, except that Collins shot one despite the distraction.

By the time Clark rewrote the entry, he had come to terms with missing the elk: "I fired four times at one and did not kill him." He also had two excuses to replace the one. Not only were the mosquitoes insufferable, which may have explained why Clark missed, but not why Collins did not. "My ball being small, I think was the reason," Clark decided, meaning that he had brought the wrong rifle, a squirrel gun, which was inadequate for bringing down such formidable animals as the one he nearly got. In a convoluted way, then, Clark's miss was a brag against Collins's hit. Not only were mosquitoes swarming, not only did Clark hit his mark despite the interference with his vision, but the elk Clark shot was so big, bigger than Collins's, that it would have taken a more powerful weapon to kill "him."[30]

Clark persisted in this hunting habit, trying to kill the largest animals with the smallest-bore rifle he could. "I killed a fat buffalo this evening," he wrote; "little gun all my hunting." It was more sporting, more impressive, more daring, and more fun to shoot with the squirrel gun. The motive was the same as that of modern hunters, who use bows and arrows to hunt deer or a lightweight test line for fishing. Clark was testing his limits, his skill, his courage—in sum, his manhood.[31]

The pattern of reporting good hunting news in detail over bad news, which was entered either as an excuse or not at all, continued throughout the expedition. Where outcomes are unclear in the journals—either who did the killing or whether there was actually a kill—the reasonable assumption is that the kill was made by someone other than the journalist or that no animal was brought down at all. When Clark recorded that he and Lewis "went on shore to shoot a prairie wolf" or coyote, a careful reading reveals that the entry states their intentions but not the outcome. Indeed, we learn subsequently that they "made an attempt but could not get him."[32]

Sometimes, too, the hunters became the hunted. This, they quickly learned, could be exhilarating, but it was not fun. Being chased took the sport out of hunting for them. "A wolf bit Sergeant Prior through his hand when asleep," Clark reported. "This animal was so vicious as to make an attempt to seize Windsor, when Shannon fortunately shot him." Bears, snakes, and buffalo all took the explorers on during the expedition. The men did not always triumph in these encounters, but none of them lost his life in the combat. A beaver nearly killed Lewis's dog. A buffalo bull stampeded through camp when the men were asleep, nearly trampling several. More than one man was snakebit and there were any number of close calls.[33]

Snakes, bears, and wolves were the predators the explorers most feared. They constituted a special category of animals whose extinction the hunters gladly facilitated. These were also the animals with which the men most closely identified. These were their competitors for dominion over the wilderness. These were the animals that stood their ground or even pursued them for a good fight. These, then, were the animals the explorers considered "men."

Snakes were, of course, the most alien of Others, the least human and the animal the men most feared becoming. So snakes were masculine only by default of being genderless in cultural terms. There was nothing feminine about a snake, nothing human, except the temptation for humans to become snakelike.

The gendered presumption about bears and wolves was of a different order; masculinity was an active identity, rather than a default. The animals' manhood transcended biology. Grizzlies were "gentlemen" to the explorers even when they could see the difference. Wolves were "fellows" even when a suckling bitch protected her cubs. The appellations were complimentary, but also self-congratulatory. In hunting's complex triangulation of identity, the greatest challenge came from facing down yourself. Only another man could present the ultimate confrontation in which the hunter killed what was like him in order to prove who he was. He killed to live, to prove that he was a man.

This was a complicated identification, to be sure, and the notion of killing the animal with which you most closely identify has deep psychological significance that we can only ponder without fully plumbing. These bears and wolves were neither father nor mother to the hunters, as near as we can tell; they were them and not them in deeply troubling ways that the journals do not give enough clues to explore.

Especially since the grizzlies were neither "gentle" nor always "men," and since the explorers had little "fellow" feeling for the wolves they killed, we must accept the ambiguity of inversions that are embedded in fear. The complexity of such relationships with their prey is highlighted by the explorers' treatment of cubs. They displayed both affection and disdain without obvious incentive for either. The Field brothers "killed a young wolf and brought one home to camp for to tame" on the same day in June 1804. Perhaps they could not control two during their journey; possibly one was more responsive to them; maybe they thought that their goal could only be accomplished if they isolated the animal from others of its kind. This entry is typical of the unexplained, and perhaps inexplicable, randomness of the explorers' violence. We might presume that they eventually killed the other pup too.[34]

The hunters also regularly killed bear cubs without even counting them in their tallies. "The young cubs which we have killed have always been of a brownish white," Lewis explained in passing, "but none of them as white as that we killed yesterday." Dispassionately, Lewis mentioned a practice that the journals seldom remarked upon and that contravened the explorers' rule about shooting only what was of use. Killing a snake was more worthy of notice, apparently because the cubs presented no threat, provided no sense of accomplishment, and posed no challenge to hunting skills. Masculinity was not on the line, and may even have been undermined by the killing of animals that were cute, unthreatening, and insignificant sources of meat.[35]

The hunters identified with adult (male) bears. Indeed, they identified more closely with grizzlies than with any of the other animals, and most of the humans, they met on the expedition. "As we arrived in sight of the little wood below the falls," Lewis wrote in one of those entries that is more revealing than he intended, "we saw two other bear enter it." "Other" than what? Other than whom, perhaps; other than themselves, as Lewis mentioned no "other" bears in the entry. "This being the only wood in the neighborhood," Lewis continued, "we were compelled, of course, to contend with the bear for possession." "Of course," the wood was not big enough for so many "bear"—the singular form of the word is interesting too. They were precise competitors, of different species, to be sure—perhaps, better said, of different tribes at the top of the food chain.[36]

Mandan and Hidatsa informants told Lewis and Clark that bears were the most human of animals. They explained to the explorers that bears were the most formidable of foes—smarter and more ferocious than any warrior. Like humans, bears are omnivorous and will even eat us. Like us, according to the Indians, they lack tails—which is not literally true, but their tails are small, fur-covered, and often tucked in. When angered, scared, or sad, the bears cry out, making a sound like our own. According to the Indians whom Lewis and Clark met, the bears' footprints are human even though their feet have claws. This is often true of their hind paws because bears are, like us, plantigrade animals that walk on the flat part of their feet.[37]

Some Mandans believed that the bears' blessing was essential to the prosperity of their people. Hunting bears was a serious business, more steeped in ritual than other hunts, infrequent, and never undertaken lightly. Lewis and Clark attributed the Indians' attitude to blind fear. "Two of the Minetares [Hidatsa] have been killed and eaten up this winter on their hunting parties," Clark reported. The explorers thought the Indians timid and superstitious in any event, and prone to exaggerate the ferociousness of grizzlies in light of the Indians' inferior weaponry.[38]

Northern Plains Indians knew better; bears were their brothers, cousins, and grandfathers. The Cree called them "four-legged humans"; bears were their relatives. The Mandans sought the bears' spirit, and solicited the animals' favor in dreams and ceremonies. There were bear-dreaming societies composed of men upon whom the bear had bestowed his power. Bear shamans were the most mysterious of practitioners, sometimes even returning from the dead. Their magic could both cure and kill, depending upon the bear's temperament.[39]

The Indians' approach to bears was respectful, even reverential in some tribes. Hidatsa warriors did not fear death; they were not cowards. They solicited the bears' favor humbly and feared the consequences of displeasing the bears and endangering the spiritual well-being of their people. Some Plains tribes hung the bears' bones from the trees out of respect, a custom akin to resting human bodies aloft lest dogs and wolves gnaw on their relatives' bones. They talked to bears, asked permission to hunt them, apologized, and begged the bears not to be angry. Some used the most primitive weapons even when they had access to guns—out of respect, in ritual reverence, as an acknowledgment that they killed no bear without its permission. Other tribes refrained from hunting the bears altogether.[40]

Lewis and Clark dismissed Indians' "superstitions," exaggerated "fears," and "fantastic" stories. The explorers knew the difference between animals and men, dreams and consciousness, and spirits and reality. Bears were just animals—larger, perhaps, than other game, and more dangerous than "gentle" buffalo and elk. They could not imagine an animal that would not fall to their guns.

Then they saw some tracks "three times as large as a man's" and, they neglected to say, just as eerily human as the Indians had claimed. The Indians scared them with their bear stories, which the explorers did not like to admit—particularly in the journals, which they intended to be dispassionate testimonies of facts. Pierre Cruzatte shot at a grizzly one day when he was out alone. "He wounded him," Lewis dutifully recorded, "but being alarmed at the formidable appearance of the bear he left his tomahawk and gun." And ran, Lewis left out. Later the same day, Cruzatte also hid from a wounded buffalo in a ravine. He was spooked badly.[41]

Lewis was scared too, but he showed it differently than Cruzatte. By April 13, 1805, Lewis and most of the party had yet to see a grizzly bear, which gave their imaginations space to entertain the Indians' stories. "We saw also many tracks of the white bear of enormous size," Lewis recounted, "along the river shore and about the carcasses of the buffalo, on which I presume they feed." All they saw was tracks and the remains left by these hunters, which were spirits for all they knew. "The men as well as ourselves are anxious to meet with some of these bear," Lewis explained, distinguishing the emotional state of the enlisted men from the officers' but acknowledging that he and Clark were "anxious" too. "The Indians give a very formidable account of the strength and ferocity of this animal." The Indians' stories were now more "formidable" than foolish, more credible than fantastic, to Lewis, who had witnessed the tracks and the buffalo carcasses but made no direct sighting of the elusive predator.[42]

The Indians' problem was their weaponry, Lewis reasoned, and their bad aim, which led them to "fall sacrifice to the bear." Lewis was shifting conceptual ground, from the secular language of the confident hunter to the spiritual world of "sacrifice" that he formerly associated with timid, superstitious, less formidable men. "This animal is said more frequently to attack a man on meeting with him than to flee from him," Lewis recalled. At this point, he had no evidence to dispute the Indians' claim that this was an animal unlike any the explorers had ever faced. "When the Indians are about to go in quest of the white bear," Lewis concluded, "previous to their departure, they paint themselves and perform all those superstitious rights commonly observed when they are about to make war upon a neighboring nation." Now Lewis returned, he would have us believe confidently, to more familiar ground, where the Indians were superstitious and the hunters were the men with guns. It is easier to imagine, though, that at this point the explorers wished that they had bartered for some war paint.[43]

Clark saw two grizzlies on April 14. They were running away. "Those animals ascended those steep hills with surprising ease and velocity," Clark reported. The hunters' inability to engage the bears or even get close to them led Lewis to hope that the Indians' description of their aggressiveness was inaccurate. Since the animals hid or ran away upon seeing the explorers approach, Lewis surmised that "they are extremely wary or shy; the Indian account of them does not correspond with our experience so far." "So far." He was regaining his confidence, still nervous about their first meeting, impatient as a soldier can be on the eve of battle, but hopeful that the enemy had abandoned the field. At least, that is the pose Lewis took for the journals.[44]

Finally, two weeks later, Lewis killed his first grizzly. There were two bears; the hunters—Lewis does not say how many—let loose with a volley. One bear ran away; the other charged, badly wounded. "We again repeated our fire and killed him," Lewis explained. He examined the carcass thoroughly and described its testicles in detail. Yes, this was a male, although not fully grown, and it weighed over three hundred pounds. "It is astonishing to see the wounds they will bear before they can be put to death," he reported after examining the shot-riddled body. Now that he had killed one, Lewis was less impressed. "The Indians may well fear this animal," he reasoned, "equipped as they generally are with their bows and arrows or indifferent fuzees, but in the hands of skillful riflemen they are by no means as formidable or dangerous as they have been represented." They were just animals—not spirits, not men, and no match for hunters such as the explorers. What a relief, except that Lewis sounds disappointed. He would learn that he had been wrong to underestimate the grizzlies and the Indians, but not yet—for now he celebrated himself, his skill, and his technology. The testicles were impressive, though, so he had bested a formidable "gentleman."[45]

A week later, Clark and Drouillard shot the largest bear they had seen—probably weighing between five hundred and six hundred pounds, according to Lewis. "It was a most tremendous looking animal" and died a hard death, roaring in pain at the five shots in his lungs and five others lodged elsewhere in his body. Lewis, again, was impressed. This was truly a "monster," which shifts the linguistic ground again, back toward the Indians' view but with a vision of evil that justified the kill. In Lewis's spiritual universe, there were only angels and devils, and he knew where the soul of such a "monster" dwelled.[46]

The next day Lewis admitted that the men—not he himself, but his men—were scared by that encounter. "I find that the curiosity of our party is pretty well satisfied with respect to this animal," he wrote in a charmingly indirect admission of fear. "The formidable appearance of the male bear killed on the fifth added to the difficulty with which they die when even shot through the vital parts, has staggered the resolution [of] several of them." "Several" of the men were intimidated; "others, however, seem keen for action with the bear." These were the brave ones, the hunters—the men among the men.[47]

As for the rest, "I expect these gentlemen will give us some amusement shortly as they soon begin now to copulate"—the bears, that is, not his men. It was the male bears that interested them; those were the ones with which they identified. There were no Indian women around, so the "men" would just have to watch. Such shows would break the tension, provide some "amusement," reduce the bears to performers, and allow the men to explore the animals' masculinity from another angle. Perhaps it would even be good for a few laughs as they compared the bears' manhood to their own.[48]

Finally, after Lewis watched hopelessly as a grizzly chased one of his men and nearly killed him in the assault, he admitted that they had all had enough. "These bear being so hard to die rather intimidates us all"—not just "several" of them—"I must confess that I do not like the gentlemen and had rather fight two Indians than one bear." What a fascinating outright juxtaposition of hunting and war, hunting and fighting, and humans and animals. Grizzlies and Indians were the two Others of Lewis's life. The bear was, just as the Indians had told him, superhuman, with a powerful spirit that refused to die. Such a characterization only enhanced the hunters' appetite for killing, increased their disdain for the Indians, who they initially believed had exaggerated the bears' prowess, and led the explorers to celebrate themselves.[49]

Experience humbled the explorers, although not enough to make them approach the bear reverently. Meeting the grizzly only frightened them—they were not really as brave as the Indians or the bears—which led them, as always, to kill. "There is no other chance to conquer them by a single shot but by shooting them through the brains," Lewis concluded. Dominion was insufficient; the hunters broke both biblical constraints and their own rule against unnecessary kills. The explorers aimed to conquer bears and Indians. There was no middle ground of respect. Surrender and death were the only options for conquered "savages" and "monsters." Escape only postponed the conquest.[50]

It is significant that the expedition's first encounters with grizzly bears came when the explorers were totally out of touch with Indians. The bears replaced Indians as the principal triangulation point against which the explorers identified themselves. Bears were not just *an* Other but *the* Other for the hunters as they crossed what is today the state of Montana.[51]

The men became reluctant to leave camp alone. Lewis, intent on proving his courage to those who followed him, challenged his own fear. "I walked on shore this morning for the benefit of exercise," not venturing far, but armed with his rifle and espontoon—a half-pike upon which he rested the barrel to aim. "Thus equipped I feel myself more than an equal match for a brown bear provided I get him in the open woods or near the water, but feel myself a little diffident with respect to an attack in the open woods or near the water." Even fully armed, the hunter could become prey. "I have therefore come to a resolution to act on the defensive only, should I meet these gentlemen in the open country." This was another restatement of his hunting resolve, born of fear rather than guilt, but nonetheless difficult for the hunter to keep.[52]

They continued to shoot, no matter the circumstance, even without obvious cause. Gibson wounded a "very large" bear; the hunters saw three bears "which they wounded"; and "one of the party wounded a brown bear very badly, but being alone did not think proper to pursue him." And the bears fought back—one "tore François Labiche's coat; another attacked six men who had orchestrated their kill in military fashion.[53]

The latter bear posed no threat and was an old grizzly whose meat was of no use. Nonetheless, they snuck up on the bear, who had not even perceived their canoes passing, attacked him in two waves, some holding their fire until after the first rounds of the other four had wounded the animal. Two of the initial rounds penetrated his lungs. "In an instant," Lewis recounted, "this monster ran at them with open mouth." The other two fired, both hitting their mark and one of them breaking the animal's shoulder. The bear pursued his attackers and the hunters took flight. They split up and several reloaded, firing and hitting him several more times. The bear chased two of the men to a cliff overhanging the river by about twenty feet. They plunged and he dived after them. From the shore, another hunter took aim and this time hit the bear in the head. When they brought the carcass on shore, they discovered the eight balls. "The bear being old, the flesh was indifferent," so they took only the fleece. Lewis was thrilled that the men had escaped without serious injury, but was shaken by the event. "I cannot recollect [the scene]," Lewis explained, "but with the utmost trepidation and horror."[54]

Make no mistake about it; this was a war. The explorers pursued their enemy even when he was in repose. "Six good hunters" had used all their skill, according to Clark, and were still nearly "defeated" by this one bear. Clark chose appropriately the battlefield language of "defeat" in reference to the explorers' attack. The words capture well the spirit of engagement that was no longer just a hunt. "Use" was beside the point; they left the meat for vultures and wolves. This one old bear, whom they passed unperceived at two hundred yards' distance, did not threaten them. Something drew the men to battle the bear, but what?[55]

Bears possessed the explorers, who aspired to conquer the bear in themselves. "The mosquitoes [were] so troublesome to the men last night," Clark wrote in his journal, "that they slept but very little. Indeed they were excessive troublesome to me. My mosquito bear [sic, bier] has a number of small holes worn through [where] they pass in." The next day Clark walked a few miles from camp and "saw a bear of the white species walking on a sand bear [sic, bar]. I with one man went on the sand bear [sic] and killed the bear, which proved to be a female very large and fat." This was, not surprisingly, "much the fattest animal we have killed on the rout[e]." Clark did know how to spell "bar," if not "bier," but he fell under the spell of the bear.[56]

They killed a female grizzly, who showed physical signs that she was suckling cubs. Two days later, they shot another "through the heart," which nonetheless ran a quarter mile before it fell. Four days passed after that before they shot a grizzly that escaped them by drowning under some driftwood. Another week later, Drouillard killed a bear that almost caught him and Charbonneau. A week more and they killed two grizzlies on the same day. "At this place there is a handsome open bottom with some cottonwood timber," Lewis wrote, setting the scene. "Here we met with two large bear and killed them both at the first fire, a circumstance which I believe has never happened with the party in killing the brown bear before." The hunters ate those two bears in celebration, taking care to protect the meat from any wolves. That was a special day.[57]

Little wonder that the explorers named "White Bear Islands" during this stretch, although they do not tell us what distinguished these particular islands in that regard. On at least two occasions they did land on other islands solely for the purpose of hunting grizzlies. "We crossed to a large island nearly opposite to us," Clark explained, "to kill *bear*, which has been seen frequently on the island. We killed one bear and returned at sunset." Lewis called this recreational bear hunt a "frolic," but he ordered the men to sleep by their loaded guns and never to leave camp alone, and was greatly relieved when one of the

Field brothers returned to camp with only a cut hand, bruised knees, and a bent rifle after being chased by a grizzly. "The white bear have become so troublesome to us," Lewis explained, "that I do not think it prudent to send one man alone on an errand of any kind." Lewis's was an odd perspective considering that the hunters continued to go out of their way to "trouble" the bears.[58]

The explorers killed relentlessly. They were trying to clear the wilderness of grizzlies to make it safer for other white men. "These bears are very numerous in this part of the country and very dangerous," Patrick Gass wrote in his journal, "as they will attack a man every opportunity." The hunters had much evidence to the contrary—of bears running away, avoiding them when possible, of curious bears that were not always aggressive, and of personalities that varied as much as those of humans—but persisted in this view of the bears that they brought with them. So, in behalf of the civilization that was to follow them, and as a favor to the Indians whom they saw as the cowering victims of grizzlies, they went out of their way to hunt the bears down. They saw a grizzly eating a buffalo on a sandbar, fired two rounds into "him," followed the bear to shore, where they fired twice more, and then gave up their pursuit when darkness fell. "He bled profusely," Clark recalled. This bear posed no immediate threat to them, but as long as he lived the bear threatened the civilizing process that the explorers represented.[59]

The more bears they shot—and they killed them by the dozens—the more "mysterious" the animals became. Lewis fired at a buffalo and lacked time to reload before a grizzly pursued him. "She was not loaded," he explained, gendering his gun as the female instrument of a hunter's violence between the two males. The "monster" closed on Lewis quickly in great strides of massive feet, "the ground torn with his talons," obliterating the man's smaller prints. Lewis was in a race he knew he could not win. Suddenly, for reasons that Lewis found "mysterious and unaccountable," the bear turned and ran the opposite way at full speed. Lewis watched in bewilderment as the bear crossed three miles of open country, occasionally looking back to reassure himself that Lewis was not following. Perhaps "he" got a whiff of the hunter, but Lewis thought that the bear smelled him long before it fled. Indeed, the Hidatsa had told him the bear was a "myste-rious" creature, much like York, that bear of a man.[60]

Lewis learned nothing, although the lesson was open before him. He persisted in searching for a rational, observable cause. A catlike animal which Lewis first perceived to be a wolf then descended upon him. He fired; it disappeared. It did not just run away; it disappeared. What species the animal was, he could not say, and he could not find a discernible print. Very mysterious. Three bull buffalo separated from a herd and charged him. At a distance of about one hundred yards, the animals stopped, took a good look, and trotted away. "It now seemed to me," Lewis wrote in his journal, "that all the beasts of the neighborhood had made a league to destroy me or that some for-tune was disposed to amuse herself at my expense."[61]

Yes, the Mandan, Hidatsa, and Cree would say, the animals were in league against him. The grizzly, the cat, and the buffalo did not unite to destroy Lewis, though; otherwise they could have done the job that day when they had him alone. Any one of them could have killed him in revenge for their lost relatives. They aimed to warn him, but about what? Lewis knew if he only thought. He knew that the explorers hunted irresponsibly. He knew that they should not be killing more than they could use. He should have refrained from "frolics" against the grizzly and ordered his men to stop as well. They should not have troubled the bears. The hunters should have learned what it meant to be hunted; they should have accepted the gift of the game, given thanks, and moved on. They failed to learn, though, what the words in their journals taught.

Ultimately, Lewis had another chance to learn, but the hard way. One of his own men, Pierre Cruzatte, shot him in the buttocks. The shot passed through one and out the other without hitting a bone. Imagine the relationship between predator and prey that resulted in such a shot. Lewis wondered whether it was an accident. Initially, in the heat of the wounding, Lewis imagined that it must be Indians who had shot him. He panicked and he organized his men for battle against a foe that they never saw. Of course it was unintentional—there is no reason to believe otherwise, as Cruzatte had weak eyes—

but Lewis might have searched elsewhere for an explanation of what happened to him.[62]

The Mandans could have explained Lewis's misfortune, just as they could have interpreted the meaning of the grizzly running away, the disappearing cat, and the buffalo that feinted a charge. If Lewis had been willing to listen, they would have told him what the accident meant. They had rituals to perform before and after a hunt to prevent such mishaps. They had taboos against eating different parts of the bear's body. Women did not eat from the head or claws; men did not consume their grandfather's rump. Lewis's hunt was ritually deficient; quite likely he also overindulged when he ate. Too much bear was bad, impossible to digest spiritually. Bear was both an empowering and a disabling food.[63]

Lewis returned to civilization prone; he wrote while lying on the bottom of a boat. It was hardly a triumphant homecoming for an explorer. On his belly like a snake, growling in pain like a bear, Lewis floated on all fours. The explorers had become their own prey. In the end, the hunters literally hunted themselves.

CHAPTER EIGHT

Possessions

I F A M A N "found" a horse grazing freely on the Great Plains during the first decade of the nineteenth century, whose horse was it? In theory, both the Plains Indians and Lewis and Clark accepted the right to ownership established by prior possession. In other words, everyone acknowledged humans' predatory rights and no one entertained equine independence as a philosophical principle. The horse could be wild, but once captured it was immediately clear whether someone had "broken" the animal. If it accepted human dominance, the horse was someone's possession. So, if you saw a domesticated horse, whose horse was it when you caught it? Finders keepers, it seems.

To be sure, the Indian practice of releasing horses for whole seasons to graze freely compounded the practical and ideological problems of possession. Also, the frequent raiding of enemies' herds established a de facto rule on the Plains that recognized only the ownership rights of a man and his band. Lewis and Clark, too, believed that their horses were theirs, as were any horses they caught, but that anyone who found their horses and did not return them was a thief. Such ideologically inconsistent beliefs have no moral integrity, but Lewis and Clark were willing to kill or die in defense of their possessions nonetheless.

Possession objectifies creatures. It turns living beings into things. Possession is the product of creation, location, theft, gift, or purchase. In all but the case of creation, possession is the result of exchange. Which of these categories applies in any given situation is in the eye of the beholder. Whether an object is found or stolen, bought, lent, or *nothing is as it seems* freely given is a question of perspective, not a fact simply to be discerned. Possession is subjectively constructed and it is contested terrain.

The question of whether an object is found or stolen defines a fault line dividing possessors from the dispossessed. Lewis and Clark were not the first explorers to label natives savages and thieves, casting themselves by contrast as civilized respecters of property rights. Like others before and after them, Lewis and Clark defined themselves as propertied, and natives as impoverished. This was a subjective perspective based on the variety and value (by European estimation) of each culture's possessions. Like other explorers, including Columbus and Cook before them, Lewis and Clark applied a double standard that denied native ownership and claimed possession of all that they saw.

Indians were "inclined to thieve," according to John Ordway. "I had formed a camp on [an] eligible situation for the protection of our stores from theft," Clark reported on another occasion, "which we were more fearful of than their arrows." The explorers' vulnerability to theft was a persistent theme of the journals. As the journalists told it, they were under siege across the continent by Indian beggars and burglars who aspired to possess all that belonged to Lewis and Clark.[1]

In fact, closer to the opposite was true. The explorers took buffalo by the hundreds, elk and deer by the dozens, bears, birds, fish, fowl, and plants as if they were free. They stole horses, firewood, and a canoe. In return Lewis and Clark gave trinkets that neither they nor the Indians valued—medals, flags, and beads of the wrong colors. They were miserly with horses, tobacco, and weapons, which Indians wanted, imposed unequal trades where tribes tried to accommodate them, and used deception to steal supplies from people who were not duped.

The explorers portrayed themselves as victims but were often complicit in relations that broke down over possessions. On April 9, 1806, for example, they were pleased to find a pipe tomahawk that Clark had lost the previous fall. Since they recognized the weapon as

Clark's, expedition members felt fully justified in seizing it from the man who considered it his possession by right of purchase. According to John Ordway, the Indians "signed that they bought it below and appeared to be highly affronted at our taking it."[2]

Since Lewis and Clark had not met this band on their outward journey, the Indian's story about how he came to possess the tomahawk was quite possibly true. Ordway's generalization from the individual to the group—"they bought it below"—is typical of the explorers, who saw their possessions as personal but viewed Indian ownership as collective. This logic led them to hold individuals, whom they "made" chiefs, responsible for the actions of all their tribesmen. Apparently Lewis and Clark never considered purchasing the tomahawk or compensating its possessor. They simply took it and felt fully justified in doing so.

The next day, in what the explorers recorded as an unrelated event, they caught one of the Indians taking an ax. Whether it was the very Indian from whom they stole the tomahawk, the journals do not say, because the journalists did not distinguish either possession or action by Indians individually. "He," whoever he was, acted as an Indian, as a member of a tribe, but not, in the explorers' estimation, as an individual whose motives were personal. He had no identity apart from his gender, race, and tribal affiliation. "His" actions were "theirs."

The Indian's tomahawk was neither his nor any longer his band's, but Clark's. In passing from hand to hand, the tomahawk again became an individual's possession. Race and civilization conferred this personal ownership. The unnamed generic Indian's action was "theft" and blameworthy. The explorers' taking without permission was only right.

And yet the story of the stolen ax belies the explorers' sense of collective possession by savages. "One of the Indians stole an axe from us," Ordway reported—"one," a singular action. "Another one told one of our men and he followed him and took it from him." So the Indians were not acting collectively in this "theft," which Ordway recorded but neither acknowledged nor credited. Such facts do not alter the structure of the story or the nature of the generalizations that bind such stories together in the journals.

The explorer who followed the thief and relieved him of the ax "told him that was bad and he replied that he was &c.," according to Ordway. In other words, the Indian's admission of guilt vindicated the explorer's version of events. This is, of course, an outrageous tale of words exchanged between two men who did not speak each other's language. If there was a confession, which there was not, it would have been of frustration and outrage that taking possessions without permission was a one-sided game, which white men believed only they were justified in playing with their Indian hosts. But verbal confrontation was not this Indian's way; silence, surreptitious action, biding his time until he got another chance to take an ax, a knife, a gun, or a horse—whatever assuaged his anger over the uncompensated loss of his possession—was more likely his plan.[3]

[handwritten margin note: white guys play by different rules]

The equation of individuals and groups is apparent throughout the journals. In one entry, for example, Clark reported that "the Indians were detected in stealing a spoon and a bone." When Clark rewrote the entry, he accused an individual instead of the group: "[O]ne of the Indians was detected stealing a horn spoon."[4]

Both the bone and the accomplices are missing from the revised entry. The accusation about the bone, both its presence and its deletion, may give a clue to the motivation behind such petty takings. If the individual in question aimed to capture some of the explorers' power through their possessions—a bone that one of them had gnawed and a spoon from which he had eaten—those items had value beyond their material and functional worth.

The bone was not really worth mentioning since it was of no value and would have been discarded in any event, which is why Clark omitted the detail from his subsequent draft. The horn spoon, presumably crafted from an antler, was not beyond the ability of Indians to create. The Indian "thief" was capable of hunting his own elk or deer and crafting his own spoon. Indeed, it is likely that he was more skilled at both tasks than the explorers. Neither item would have been highly valued for rarity, beauty, or function in his culture. Both could have held spiritual power, though—"mystery" or "magic"—that would have increased their value to him. The items became valuable to the explorers only when the Indian took them. His act transformed the things into valuable signs for assessing the "Indian's" and "the Indians' " character. The bone and spoon became symbols of power by which the explorers expressed their intention to possess all that came under their purview, however intrinsically valueless.

Even when an Indian returned an item of his own volition, it was an occasion for the explorers' reiteration of the Indians' flaws. "One man brought me a tomahawk," Clark recorded, "which we expected they had stolen from a man of Captain Lewis's party. This man informed me he found the tomahawk in the grass near the place the man slept." Again, a solitary individual became plural—"one man brought"; "they had stolen."[5]

"Stolen" seems hardly the right term for an item returned under such circumstances. It is possible that the Indian found the tomahawk as he said; it is also plausible that he took it and then thought better of his act. There is an intermediate interpretation that the explorers might also have considered. It is conceivable that the Indian examined the weapon, perhaps to learn about its construction or to assess its comparative functional value. There is again the spiritual dimension to objects, which Lewis and Clark never grasped. It is possible that the Indian just held it or chipped off a splinter from the handle or a flake from the metal to add to his medicine pouch. Finding, taking, using, and returning would not, then, have been theft in his eyes.

Clark's entry implies other motives. Lewis's adds more details. "While Captain Clark was at these lodges an Indian brought him a tomahawk which he said he found in the grass near the lodge where I had stayed at the upper camp when I was first with his nation. The tomahawk was Drouillard's." Neither the "theft" nor the tomahawk had anything to do with Clark, which the Indian undoubtedly knew perfectly well. This makes it curious that the Indian returned the possession to Clark.

Lewis's account goes on to explain that Drouillard had missed the tomahawk when he awoke in the morning and that the party accompanying Lewis had searched for it unsuccessfully before returning to the main camp. We know from other entries that such searches were both thorough and rough. The explorers combed the living quarters and searched the bodies of Indians without permission and threatened physical retribution if they failed to recover the missing item. None of this "searching" produced the tomahawk, though, and they gave up.[6]

What this means is that the Indian who possessed the tomahawk, assuming that it was not lying on the ground undetected, as he claimed, was home free. "I believe the young fellow stole it," Lewis proclaimed, unwilling to accept the man's explanation. Perhaps the Indian offended Lewis by returning the tomahawk to Clark.[7]

There was a message implied in the return to Clark rather than to Drouillard or Lewis, but it is difficult to detect what it was. It may have been an attempt to curry favor with the white man who seemed the greater leader or in retaliation for Lewis's manner, methods, and tone. In any event, the tomahawk was voluntarily exchanged, undoubtedly in the hopes of promoting goodwill. Something was lost, though, in the translation of a possession's meaning between cultures that valued objects and ownership differently.

An unanticipated response to such a gesture could, of course, have the opposite of its intended effect. A deterioration in relations could result from a less than gracious acceptance of the returned item. Perhaps the Indian anticipated an exchange of gifts. Having acquired the tomahawk, by whatever means, and having retained it through Lewis's search, it certainly was his to keep. By gifting Clark with it, he made a gesture that required some form of reciprocation. A misreading of the cultural norms, or a refusal to abide by them, could lead to further takings—"thefts"—by the aggrieved party.

An unfair exchange or a gift inadequately reciprocated often led to problems that Lewis and Clark misunderstood. When Joseph Whitehouse prided himself on a sharp horse trade, for example, he misread the situation badly. "Previous to their departure," Lewis recorded, "one of our men exchanged an indifferent horse with one of them for a very good one." The next day Whitehouse could find neither horse.[8]

[margin, handwritten] unequal exchange

The explorers should have known better than to expect that the unequal exchange sealed the deal. Earlier in the expedition, Clark had explained the problem of assessing equivalency in transactions with natives. "Four Indians came from the upper villages," he wrote. "They offered us roots which we did not choose to accept of as their expectation for those presents of a few roots is three or four times their real worth."[9]

rejecting gifts

↓

theft

Rejecting a gift created its own problems, though, so Lewis and Clark made a mistake that time, too, which probably insulted their hosts and possibly resulted in some of the "thieving" they reported in the days ahead. Chronic takings led the explorers to conclude that these people were "forward and impertinent, and thievish," among the very worst in this regard that they had ever met.[10]

Such deterioration in relations manifested by the taking of possessions plagued the explorers throughout the expedition, but particularly among the Sioux on the Plains and the Clatsops of the West Coast. At no point did the journalists acknowledge their complicity in mutual "theft" relations with Indians, but in many places the explorers' participation in, indeed initiation of, such relationships is clear.

The explorers had a self-interested definition of theft, applying one standard to themselves and another to Indians. Lewis and Clark "found" things; Indians "stole" them. Patrick Gass recorded several possessions of horses within a three-week period early on. "Our hunters came in and brought with them a handsome horse, which they had found astray," Gass wrote. Two weeks later, they "found a gray horse." A week after that, "we found another horse on the bank of the river." Since the horses were neither branded nor confined, we should give the explorers the benefit of the doubt that they denied to Indians who "found" horses of theirs. On the other hand, the horses were domesticated and the explorers knew well that Plains Indians let their horses roam freely during part of the year. They recognized that

which part of the year?

someone had trained the horses and that someone—an Indian— considered the horses his possessions. Only a horse with an owner can wander "astray," so Gass's language reveals that he knew the explorers had stolen somebody's horse.[11]

We might also wonder why these three events were not recorded by either of the expedition's leaders. Finding a horse was not an insignificant event to these men who relied so heavily on the animals for transportation, as pack animals, and, in a pinch, as food. They were chronically short of horses and purchased many where none could be "found." Lewis and Clark omitted such events from the journals because they recognized them as thefts, which contradicted the self-image they wished the journals to portray and because stealing blurred the contrast between savagery and civility that previous explorers had taught them to draw.

stealing horses

"Thieving" went both ways. One of the expedition's hunters lost his rifle and a horse to six Indians—three men and three women, as he told it—when he turned his horse loose to feed. He pursued the thieves on another horse, catching them after what he estimated was a twenty-mile run. As he rode up beside one of them, he "jerked or caught hold of his gun and jerked the pan open losing the priming." This prevented the Indian from firing at him. "The Indian then let go and ran," according to John Ordway. "Our hunter then returned by their camp and took all their plunder consisting of service berries, dried different kinds of berries, and cherries, which were dried for food, also roots and a number of other kinds of wild fruit dried." He also stole several elk skins and "a number" of unnamed additional items.[12]

The Sioux apparently stole from Lewis and Clark first. Of course, we cannot know whether the explorers had "found" Sioux horses prior to the incidents recorded in the journals. Some Sioux bands had histories of bad relations with Europeans—Spanish, French, and English—which Lewis and Clark inherited through no fault of their own.

Lewis and Clark had heard that the Sioux were a "pilfering set" and their experiences only confirmed this precontact prejudice. Not only did the Sioux steal John Colter's horse in the fall of 1804, they destroyed a smokehouse the explorers created to preserve meat for the trail. "The Sioux burnt one of my meat houses," Clark recorded; "they did not find the other." Then about one hundred Sioux warriors attacked four of the expedition's hunters and took two of their three horses and two of their three knives.[13]

Clark misunderstood these thefts. The particular Sioux who harassed the explorers were not simply "robbers"; they were messengers who tried to communicate through the explorers' possessions. The Sioux did not fail to find the second smokehouse. They did not leave the third horse, as Clark believed, because they "feared being killed by our men who were not disposed to be robbed of all they had tamely." The Sioux outnumbered the isolated band of white men by about one hundred to four. They could have stripped the explorers or tortured and killed them. They could have taken all the horses, all the meat, and everything the white men carried and wore. The Indians' goal was not only to possess but also to warn Lewis and Clark off.[14]

It is interesting that the four men who lost the possessions estimated the size of the attacking force as precisely 105. Since the number was so large, events unfolded so swiftly, and the focus of the four was on defending themselves and their things, it is unlikely that they made such an exact count. They agreed that 105 "savages" attacked them, intent on murdering them and stealing all that they possessed. The number must have been significant to the four men in some way. Since they were outnumbered by over a hundred—101 to give their estimate the precision they bestowed upon it—the number must have vindicated their honor for losing their possessions to "savages."

The explorers lost more pride than objects in this encounter, though. The horses belonged to others—a fur-trading company and the army—at the fort where they wintered. They were humiliated, which was likely the intent of cutting off the horses' bridles and passing the animals "from one to another through several hands" in a symbolic showing of transferred possession. They were scared, which the Indians intended the "whooping and yelling" to increase, but the Sioux also challenged them.[15]

Lewis's and Clark's response was to pursue the "thieves," attempt to regain the possessions, and to kill the perpetrators of the theft if necessary to teach others a lesson. The threat of violence as retribution for theft was an equivalent to which Lewis and Clark adhered throughout the expedition. It was one that made sense in the moral universe they inhabited. This time they could not catch the "thieves," but on other occasions they warned Indians and delivered on their threat to kill those who tried to take their possessions.[16]

Although Lewis and Clark racially stereotyped all natives as thieves—a trope they learned from Columbus, Cook, and their own culture's prejudices—they believed that some Indians were worse than others and that the Sioux were among the worst of all. Their characterization of the Sioux is understandable in light of both the Indians' reputation among fur traders and their own experiences. On the other hand, the explorers engaged in reciprocal theft with the Sioux, misread messages delivered through their possessions, and reacted to thefts in ways that escalated tensions and had deadly consequences for the Americans who followed them.

The significance of Lewis's and Clark's struggles over possessions is too great, too complex, and too enduring to allow their perspective to substitute for historical analysis. We need to reckon with both Lewis's and Clark's self-deception in this regard and their conscious efforts to present themselves to readers as exploratory ideals. They were not just beleaguered by thieves. They stole and they fomented theft by relentlessly clamoring for what Indians possessed.

When Lewis and Clark stole firewood or canoes from Indians, they rationalized their thefts as necessary. As Joseph Whitehouse explained in his journal, "we found some wood on the island covered up with stones where the natives buried salmon every spring. Wood was so scarce that we made use of that which was covered so carefully with stone." This was neither driftwood nor scrap, but firewood carefully collected, cut or broken to size, transported, and saved for processing fish during the critical spring salmon runs. Lewis, Clark, and their men knew that they were stealing.

Whitehouse also recorded a similar event on the following day that Lewis and Clark omitted from their journals: "[We] passed several scaffolds of wood where it was put up [by Indians] to be saved for the use of their fishing in the spring. . . . No wood except an Indian's scaffold. We had to take some of the wood for our use this evening." It was cold; they could find no wood; they wanted to cook some food—all of which is understandable under the circumstances.[17]

The point is not to judge Lewis's and Clark's theft, which they reckoned as morally deficient. The idea is to acknowledge the explorers' capacity for theft on a regular basis, which both they and historians have denied. The goal is to understand better why the Indians "stole" from them. When Lewis finally did admit to a theft in the journals, he gave it another name. "We yet want another canoe," he wrote in his entry for March 17, 1806, "and as the Clatsops will not sell us one at a price which we can afford to give we will take one from them in lieu of the six elk which they stole from us in the winter."[18]

The reference to "theft" of the elk is a dubious construction of events that the Clatsops undoubtedly interpreted differently. True, the act of killing conveyed ownership, but abandonment of the carcasses abdicated rights of possession under the rules of the woods. As the explorers knew, the wilderness tradition made abandoned animals fair game for humans who "found" them dead. The expedition's hunters killed more game than they could carry back to camp and left the rest in the forest, where they planned to retrieve it later. Often they lost the rest to animal or human "thieves" who took what they found. In no obvious sense did the Clatsops' consumption of the dead elk justify stealing a canoe, at least by the laws of nature, American hunting traditions, or the Clatsops' culture.

Lewis already felt robbed before the elk incident by Indians who "pillaged" a beached whale "of every valuable part." There was no rational sense in which the explorers could see themselves as possessors of the whale, which was fair game for anyone who could exploit this gift from the sea. The Killamucks were more experienced, faster to the corpse, and more efficient in dealing with the remains before nonhuman scavengers took their share. Lewis felt frustrated, which led him to use the language of "theft" and to accuse the Indians of greed.[19]

When Reuben Field, one of the expedition's hunters, killed six (or seven) elk and left the meat in the open, Lewis worried again about being victimized by Indian thieves. "We are apprehensive," he wrote, "that the Clatsops, who know where the meat is, will rob us of a part if not the whole of it." This claim to possession makes a little more sense than Lewis's claim on the beached whale—the right to possession by killing has a logic and a history recognized in many cultures. The problem is that, by Lewis's admission, Field abandoned his kill to nature beyond the setting sun.[20]

no right of possession after dark

Early in the expedition Lewis and Clark learned that Plains Indians acknowledged possession of abandoned buffalo carcasses when the animals were clearly marked. As Clark noted in his journals, Lewis and a party of hunters killed fourteen buffalo on one day but were able to carry only five back to camp. When they returned for more, the carcasses were gone. "Those we did not get were taken back by the Indians," Clark explained, "under a custom which is established amongst them, i.e., any person seeing a buffalo lying without an arrow sticking in him or some particular mark takes possession." The mark indicated intent to return for the meat on the same day, since "all meat which is left out all night falls to the wolves."[21] Any meat not reclaimed by nightfall was fair game for animals or men, who recognized no right of possession beyond sunlight.

Olaus's sheep and wolverine

Since Lewis knew the customary limitations on possession, there was no rational reason for him to view harvesting abandoned corpses as theft by the time the expedition reached the Clatsops on the West Coast. If, on balance, the Indians claimed more of "their" meat than they did of any Indian tribe's, it was a consequence of different hunting practices. Sahaptan-speaking Indians usually killed in smaller, more portable quantities. The explorers hunted for fun as well as for meat, killing in quantities far larger than they could use in the time allotted before the rest of nature took its share. So Lewis's rationalization for their theft of an Indian canoe was born of panic rather than the morally justifiable notion of fair exchange that he claimed. Lewis also failed to weigh in the balance the large quantities of food and other assistance offered by the Clatsops to the explorers. Without the Indians' aid, Lewis and Clark would not have survived the winter.

The expedition's historians participate in the same rationalization for reasons that we have to surmise. When the editors of the most recent edition of the journals reach the canoe incident, for example, they acknowledge the undeniable event but imply that it was unique rather than part of a larger pattern of theft that the journals reveal. "The captains succumbed to temptation," the editors explain, "and violated their longstanding and consistently observed rule against stealing Indian property."[22]

The editors are being loyal, following their instinct to defend Lewis and Clark. The explorers' historians, who quite understandably admire their subjects, generally take this same advocacy pose. The expedition is vulnerable to charges that it constituted an imperialist extension of the American empire, an unlawful and immoral theft of native habitats. The connection between small-scale thefts and much grander continental designs is implicit in analyses of the explorers' thefts. Calling attention to less savory aspects of Lewis's and Clark's behavior also threatens the explorers' standing as heroes of the historical and mythical types.

Defenses precede anticipated assaults. "The natives demanded high prices for any food that they sold," the journals' editors explain, "and some of them could not resist stealing. The captains' patience was at low ebb." This one-sided take on relations both apologizes for the explorers' behavior and blames the Indians for provoking violence. It takes Lewis's and Clark's rationalizations as fact and neglects evidence that complicates and contradicts the explorers' version of events.[23]

When we pursue the canoe-for-elk story further in the journals, the explorers' (and historians') justifications for their theft becomes weaker still. Three or four days had passed before the explorers reached the carcasses to reclaim the meat. Clark now estimated the number of elk killed by Field as seven, one more than the six mentioned elsewhere in the journals. Of the six or seven elk shot by Field, the explorers recovered the meat of two and the skins of four. That is all that was left. "I find that those people will all steal," Clark concluded upon learning how much they got.[24]

About a week later, according to Lewis, a Clatsop man visited the explorers' camp. He brought with him "three dogs as a remuneration for the elk which himself and [his] nation had stolen from us some little time since; however the dogs took alarm and ran off. We suffered him to remain in the fort all night." It is unclear whether the explorers permitted the man to stay the night—"suffered" suggests grudging hospitality—or kept him captive while they renegotiated compensation for the elk, which the context implies. In any event, another ten days passed and Lewis reported that Drouillard accompanied some Clatsop people in their canoe "to get the dogs which the Clatsops have agreed to give us in payment for the elk they stole from us some weeks since."[25]

We have to imagine the recriminations, threats, and negotiations that occurred in the intervening period. The explorers accused the Clatsops of theft; the Clatsops had a different point of view and may even have been bewildered at first by the explorers' outrageous interpretation of events. In the end, though, it seemed advisable to exchange a gift for the meat that the white men claimed but failed to possess. So the Clatsops paid up, in dogs that the white men ate, and the explorers accepted the compensation as just.

Having been paid by their own account, how did Lewis and Clark come to the conclusion less than one month later that the Clatsops also owed them a canoe? They not only stole the canoe but had thoroughly alienated the Clatsops, who believed that the explorers' demands were unjust. If anyone had outstanding debts, it was the explorers, which were partially canceled by one of the Clatsops taking an ax shortly before the exchange of dogs.[26]

A final twist in this revealing story is that the canoe Lewis and Clark stole—rationalizing that the Clatsops owed them for elk that was not stolen and for which the explorers had already been repaid—did not belong to the Clatsops. When an Indian man caught up with them and demanded the return of his canoe, they learned that he was a member of another tribe. "He consented willingly to take an elk's skin for it," Lewis reported with no apparent sense of the irony of what they exchanged, "which I directed should be given him and he immediately returned." We cannot know whether the man was truly satisfied by the exchange, since he had no choice. His departure

[handwritten margin note: L & C at their lowest in Slaughter's eyes]

immediately after the transaction can be interpreted a number of ways.[27]

The canoe-for-elk incident also raises questions about Lewis's and Clark's interpretation of other Indian "thefts." What seems clear, in otherwise muddy interpretive waters, is that much of the taking was an attempt to redress imbalances in exchanges demanded by the explorers. The cultures of reciprocity were different. Lewis and Clark either misunderstood or declined to accept local customs, and hard feelings on both sides manifested themselves as increased tension over possessions.

The Clatsops refused to sell at a reasonable price, according to Whitehouse, who may have expressed the general view of the explorers. Other Indians were "great higglers in dealing," Lewis complained. By what right could Lewis and Clark demand sale or impose their sense of a fair price for canoes made and owned by Indians? The explorers' answer would undoubtedly blend descriptions of what they could afford, the greatness of their need, and rules of hospitality that they would have liked to impose on their hosts.[28]

So theft was rampant, but the stealing was going both ways. Clark, for example, used "magic" to scare Indians, at least temporarily, into giving him food. He hid a magnet in his palm to set a compass arrow spinning wildly. He threw a portfire match into a flame, which led the fire to change color and flare up. The tricks "astonished and alarmed these natives," Clark reported, "and they laid several parcels of wappato at my feet, and begged of me to take out the bad fire. To this I consented. At this moment the match being exhausted was, of course, extinguished and I put up the magnet." In the short run, Clark had craftily assuaged his men's hunger. The longer-term consequences of theft by magic are discernible in the attempts by Indians to recoup their losses. Clark, of course, considered himself shrewd, but not a thief. The Indians felt differently after the fire spirit had left.[29]

"Thieving" was often presumptive; whatever the explorers lost they assumed had been stolen. Horses, either left to roam or ineffectually shackled, were the primary focus of this logic. As living possessions inclined to wander, bolt, or seek better grazing, horses were often not where their owners had left them the night before. "This morning our horses were very much scattered," Clark reported in his journal. "They brought all except nine by six o'clock and informed me that they could not find those nine."[30]

Clark sent the men back out to scan a wider landscape. They returned without the horses an hour later, having circled six to eight miles without finding any evidence of the animals. "They had reasons to believe that the Indians had stolen them in the course of the night," according to Clark. Their suspicions were aroused by the quality of the missing horses. The best ones were gone; the worst ones were left. "I thought it probable that they might be stolen by some skulking Shoshones," Clark reasoned. The next day a search party found the horses, unattended by humans, "near the head of the creek on which we encamped, making off as fast as they could and much scattered."[31]

A week later, Clark used a similar logic to explain missing horses. Again he suspected Indians: "My suspicion is grounded on the improbability of the horses leaving the grass and rushes of the river bottoms of which they are very fond, and taking immediately out into the open dry plains where the grass is but short and dry." This time Clark may have been right; there were twenty-four horses missing and tracks leading out onto the Plains. There were signs of Indians and indications that the horses were running away from the explorers' camp at a considerable speed.[32]

Some of the theft by Indians would have happened no matter what. Stealing horses was part of Plains culture, in which the animals of your enemy were fair game and your enemy was anyone (generally outside your band) who had a horse you admired. The Indians on the Northwest Coast also had a very liberal sense of what belonged to them. Lewis's and Clark's expansive understanding of what "finding" a horse meant on their outward journey, though, only increased the license that others had for "finding" the explorers' horses—shackled or not—in the dead of night and eager for a good run.

The explorers' stealing of canoes, firewood, horses, and food was a contributing factor in the losses Lewis and Clark suffered in return.

The perception that the explorers were parsimonious and demanding also contributed to the contestation over possessions on the West Coast. The white men whined, begged, and bullied during winter, when everyone was hungry and "guests" breached etiquette by always expecting more. The explorers also did not share what they had, hoarding for a future that Indians never understood.

Indians also did not comprehend Lewis's and Clark's need for absolute control of their possessions when they were not being used. Such behavior was variously interpreted as rudeness, selfishness, and a desire to hide the "mystery" of what they had. The explorers offended one group of Indians by denying them permission even to examine visually or to touch their possessions. "Several of those from below returned down the river in a bad humor," Clark reported, "having got into this pet by being prevented doing as they wished with our articles, which were then exposed to dry."[33]

It is revealing that Indians and the explorers saw each other as "beggarly." The term, as used by Lewis and Clark, meant incessantly requesting more possessions than the possessor wished to give as a gift without offering something of like value in return. From a number of tribal perspectives, the explorers repeatedly breached guests' good manners by demanding more than their fair share of food during seasons of scarcity.

Clark extended a compliment to one tribe that reveals what he meant. "They are not beggarly," he explained, "and receive what is given them with much joy." Here Clark laid out his version of gift-receiving etiquette. You take what is offered with a smile and thanks, and leave it at that.[34]

In contrast, Lewis termed another tribe "great beggars" because they made demands for reciprocation. "Notwithstanding their hospitality, if it deserves that appellation, they are great beggars," Lewis wrote, "for we had scarcely finished our repast on the wappeto and anchovies which they voluntarily set before us before they began to beg." The Indians thought the explorers rude for consuming the food without offering something comparable in return. Lewis grudgingly "gave the first chief a small medal, which he transferred to his wife."

Not quite a rejection, but an indication that the "chief" (not to mention the rest of his party) may have found the explorers' exchange inadequate.[35]

Eventually, Lewis acknowledged that the explorers begged too. "As these people have been liberal with us with respect to provision," he wrote in the late spring of 1806, "I directed the men not to crowd their lodge [in] search of food in the manner hunger has compelled them to at most lodges we have passed." The order to desist from their usual begging for food came in response to a chief's complaint to Lewis that the begging "was disagreeable to the natives."[36]

This passage provides yet another clue to why Indians took so many of the explorers' possessions. Lewis's and Clark's men were constantly begging for food. They hung around Indian lodges during food preparation and meals clamoring for more. Undoubtedly they often ended up with more than the Indians wanted to give. Attempts to redress the balance were interpreted by Lewis and Clark as Indian "begging" and "theft."

At the heart of such mutual recriminations were cultural differences that the explorers and some of the Indians would not bend to accommodate. There were misunderstandings. There was also a stubborn resistance to learn, acknowledge, and accept differences as valid rather than as signs of racial inferiority. In the end, struggles over possessions revealed and deepened these fissures, resulting in violence and death.

Especially to Lewis, but to the other men as well, the assault on their possessions became more infuriating over time. By the end of the 1805–6 winter, patience was at a low ebb, the explorers were hungry, their supply of possessions was seriously depleted, and nerves were frayed. They were also frightened about the challenges remaining ahead. Always the most nervous, least patient, and most bellicose of the explorers, Lewis was now emotionally less stable than ever. His threats became more extreme; his retaliations became more frequently physical. He was a dangerous man.

On April 21, 1806, Lewis could take no more. One of the explorers' horses had disappeared, a tomahawk went missing, and he caught an

Indian taking an iron socket for a canoe pole. Lewis searched the bodies of those Indians upon whom he could lay his hands. He ordered "all the spare poles, paddles, and the balance of our canoe put on the fire as the morning was cold and also that not a particle should be left for the benefit of the Indians." Then he grabbed the one "thief" that he caught and "gave him several severe blows and made the men kick him out of camp." Finally, before the explorers broke camp, Lewis threatened more severe violence should he detect any more thefts. "I now informed the Indians that I would shoot the first of them that attempted to steal an article from us," Lewis raged, "that we were not afraid to fight them, that I had it in my power at that moment to kill them all and set fire to their houses."[37]

Patrick Gass also recorded the incident in his journal. According to Gass, "an Indian stole some iron articles from among the men's hands, which so irritated Captain Lewis that he struck him." Whether taking metal objects from the hands of the explorers was attempted theft is open to interpretation, but seems unlikely in this case. The men were loading up, perhaps anxious to get started for the day. The Indian was curious and possibly grabbed the iron socket to examine it.

Lewis lashed out for the hindrance to the group's departure. All were "struck" by the physicality of Lewis's explosion of temper, "which was the first act of the kind that had happened during the expedition." Gass implied the collective sense that this was an extreme and possibly dangerous event which might have ended "in a skirmish with them."[38]

Fortunately there was no retaliatory violence this time, but the episode reveals both how touchy possessions could be for the explorers, even when the objects were of such insignificance that they did not rise to the status of "articles" that Gass could name. The primary issue really was not the item's centrality to their survival. The specific value was less important than the general principle of possession. That is what the explorers defended, an abstract concept rather than a concrete thing—the very notion of possession more than an actual object they feared to lose.

The response from the "chiefs," as Lewis reported it, was to hang their heads and say nothing. The Indians, he implied, knew that he was right and feared the explorers' force. Clark reported it differently, though, including a detail that Lewis left out. "The chief from below," Clark wrote, "came up and appeared concerned for what had been done at his village." He was not pleased by the violence against one of his people and did not appreciate the threat to burn his village down. Clark was discreet and recorded no further comments. It seems likely that Clark defused the situation, placating the chief and calming Lewis.[39]

The next day, though, Lewis exploded again. One of Charbonneau's horses broke away and threw his load. They had to track the horse some distance before locating the animal and the saddle he threw off. Still missing was the blanket the horse wore on his back. After searching for some time, Lewis became convinced that "the Indians" stole it. He halted the party, sent the Shoshone woman ahead to request reinforcements from Clark, "being determined either to make the Indians deliver the robe or burn their houses. They have vexed me in such a manner," Lewis continued, "that I am quite disposed to treat them with every severity." Later, when he wrote the journal entry, Lewis claimed that he had decided to spare their lives as an act of mercy, not justice, being fully convinced that murdering the whole village was a fair response to the theft.[40]

Fortunately one of the explorers found the blanket in an Indian lodge before Lewis began his threatened carnage. The next day, in what Lewis reported as an unrelated event, an Indian brought Clark an "elegant white horse." Since Clark's ongoing role in defusing confrontations over possessions goes largely unreported in the journals, we can be sure that he was instrumental in calming all sides and preventing bloodshed, but we cannot know exactly what he did.[41]

Several days later, three young Indian men arrived at the explorers' camp with a steel animal trap that, according to Lewis, "one of our party had negligently left behind." As in the past, Lewis was not willing to generalize from such acts of generosity in the same way that he generalized about theft. "This is an act of integrity," Lewis grudgingly admitted, "rarely witnessed among Indians." There was no shaking either Lewis's assessment of Indians as dishonest or his anger, which remained close to the surface and hot.[42]

Violence continued that week, when Lewis threw a puppy in the face of an Indian who had teased him about eating dogs. Lewis responded in a fury and threatened the man with a tomahawk. Again, as discussed in the previous chapter, Lewis's violence was mostly bluster and others with cooler tempers extricated the explorers from the encounter without bloodshed.[43]

Not surprisingly, the only deadly engagement between the explorers and Indians came after Clark split off with some of the party, leaving Lewis without his calmer, more diplomatic, perhaps even less possessive coleader. During this period when Lewis led alone, he and Reuben Field each killed an Indian who threatened their possessions. It is important to emphasize that the immediate threat was not to the explorers' lives. This is clear from Lewis's description of events. Field killed in anger while regaining his rifle, not because an Indian threatened his life with the rifle. Lewis shot a man who had taken his horse.

Relations between the explorers and eight Piegans were tense before the thefts occurred. In other words, fear, distrust, and possibly some insult or misunderstanding preceded, if not precipitated, the taking of possessions. It is possible that whatever blunders the explorers committed could have been avoided or, at least, assuaged before they led to theft and violence if Clark was with them. It would be mistaken to assume that the "thefts" by Piegans were precipitating events. They were the consequence of relations that had already broken down.

John Ordway thought the Indians were fearful at first meeting on July 28. They also appeared friendly. The initial engagement was tense, as first meetings generally were, with each side eyeing the other for mannerisms they could comprehend.

Lewis and Clark had reputations by this time—three years into the expedition—that preceded the meeting. They carried the baggage of relations with other tribes, as well as the history of this band's dealings with other Europeans. Lewis and Clark had insulted some Indians, been rough, rude, and boorish with others, and they had gifted some with valued possessions.

The Indians made a request that the explorers thought they comprehended. The Piegans wanted Lewis and the other white men to visit their nation, which was about two days away and in the wrong direction as far as the explorers were concerned. Declining the invitation may have insulted the Indians. Perhaps they coveted "gifts" they knew the explorers had bestowed on other tribes. Lewis promised them a horse if the Indians went with the explorers to the place where they intended to meet up with Clark's party. A possession—a horse, perhaps a particular horse—was central to the conversation.

The Indians declined the invitation, Ordway said because "they were afraid of being killed by us." Possibly the Piegans saw the offered horse as a lure to a trap. Perhaps they resented the demand that they perform in some way to receive the gift. Other chiefs had received gifts from these white men without so much as leaving their tents. This could be an insult. Lewis gave one of them a medal, but it is not clear of what size, thereby "making" him a chief. Possibly this offended another member of the party. Perhaps the "chief" had seen a larger medal that Lewis had given another man in recognition of his higher status in Lewis's eyes. We cannot know any of this, but we do have good reasons to suspect that something went horribly wrong in the attempts to communicate through signs and that what happened the next morning was a consequence, not a cause, of problems between the two groups.

Joseph Field was on guard duty but had laid his rifle down next to his sleeping brother Reuben. Unperceived by Joseph, who we might guess had fallen asleep, an Indian slipped behind him and took his rifle and his brother's. Two others grabbed Drouillard's and Lewis's rifles at the same time. Joseph yelled out and his brother awoke to see an Indian running off with their guns. The brothers pursued the Indian, who could have stabbed them in their sleep if he had meant the white men any physical harm. They caught him after running about fifty or sixty paces, according to Lewis. The two of them wrestled the rifles from the lone Indian, and "R. Fields, as he seized his gun, stabbed the Indian to the heart with his knife. The fellow ran about fifteen steps and fell dead."[44]

The killing was in retaliation for the theft. Reuben Field took the rifle with one hand and stabbed the Indian with the other. The stab-

[margin handwriting: miscommunication due to language barriers can be complicated]

bing was not obviously necessary either to recover the rifle or to defend his life.

An Indian stole Lewis's rifle too. When Lewis awoke to the clamor and discovered his rifle missing, he drew his pistol and pursued the particular Indian who had taken the rifle. "I ran at him with my pistol," Lewis wrote in his journal, "and bid him lay down my gun (at the instant), which he was in the act of doing when the Field brothers returned and drew up their guns to shoot him, which I forbid as he did not appear to be about to make any resistance or commit any offensive act. He dropped the gun and walked slowly off." The immediate danger was past and Lewis's rifle and pistol rearmed him.[45]

Lewis then chased Indians who had taken possession of one of his horses. Precision is necessary here. Lewis clearly stated in the journal that he would not have been left horseless but would have lost one of an unnamed number of horses he considered his. "I pursued them so closely," Lewis recounted, "that they could not take twelve of their own horses but continued to drive one of mine with some others." In other words, Lewis had control of twelve of their horses and they had possession of one of his in addition to an unstated number of horses belonging to other members of Lewis's party. The issue here was not the need for horses to survive in the wilderness. Lewis was defending his abstract right of ownership against a challenge to his possession of a particular horse. "Being nearly out of breath," Lewis continued, "I called to them as I had done several times before that I would shoot them if they did not give me my horse and raised my gun. One of them jumped behind a rock and spoke to the other who turned around and stopped at the distance of thirty steps from me and I shot him through the belly."[46]

Lewis did not say why he shot the Indian. We do learn that the man was armed, but he fired only after he was hit by Lewis's shot in what may even have been an involuntary muscle contraction. In any event, the returned shot went past Lewis's head, as he told the story: "[H]e overshot me; being bareheaded I felt the wind of his bullet very distinctly." In other words, it was a close call. Lewis apparently wanted us to believe, then, that if he had not shot the Indian first, the Indian would have shot at him and would likely have had a better aim. The point of recounting the conversation between the two Indians that preceded the shooting was also to suggest a considered plot to kill him, which he foiled by quick thinking and good shooting.[47]

Maybe Lewis's interpretation is accurate. Perhaps his story is true. Possibly the Indian intended to surrender the weapon and the horse. We do not know whether the Indian understood the precise nature of Lewis's threat. Lewis certainly claimed no understanding of the conversation that passed between the Indians and undoubtedly would have told us if the Indian had actually pointed the rifle at him in a threatening fashion. Lewis felt threatened nonetheless. His nerves were on edge and he acted out of fear rather than a fully rational calculation to kill in retaliation for the taking of his horse.

It could be argued that in the wilderness environment certain possessions were truly the equivalent of life. In other words, a man left without a gun to hunt and defend himself was in mortal peril. A man without a horse faced an inhospitable environment on foot and was at a decided disadvantage against mounted enemies. The cases just described, though, do not rise to even a secondary definition of self-defense. They were not defenses at all, since recovery was not the precipitating motivation for the stabbing and shooting—the rifle was already recovered; the horse would never be. They were retaliations for the theft of possessions that served as extensions of selves.

The explorers' retaliation did not end with killing two Indians. They also seized the Indians' possessions—bows, arrows, shields, one rifle, and as many of the Indians' horses as they could catch. The goal here was not compensation, since they took none of the weapons with them and left most of the horses behind.

The Indian who took Lewis's horse, and whom Lewis killed in retaliation, was the same one whom Lewis had "made" a chief the previous day. In death he still wore the medal Lewis had given him. The explorers considered removing the medal from the body, but decided to leave it as an acknowledgment of their responsibility for the killing. Whether this was an act of bravado, intended to strike fear in their enemies, or an attempt to limit the focus of revenge is unclear. Whatever their goal, though, the next Americans who traveled that way would not get a fresh start in their relations with the Piegan.[48]

Of eight Piegan Indians whom Lewis and his men engaged, seven could be accounted for. Two were dead. Five got away on horseback. The Indians left behind one of their two rifles, four shields, two bows and quivers of arrows, buffalo meat, thirteen horses, and the flag Lewis had given them. They made off with one of Lewis's horses. Lewis's men recovered four of their own horses, but left one of them behind and took the four best Indian horses instead.[49]

In other words, the explorers had ten more horses than they could use in making their now hastened attempt to connect with Clark's party. Nonetheless, it was for the horses that Lewis feared. "I now told them," Lewis reported in his journal, "that it was my determination that if we were attacked in the plains on our way to the point that the bridles of the horses should be tied together and we would stand and defend them, or sell our lives as dear as we could." Lewis recognized that his previous violence left the explorers more vulnerable to their enemies, but he, at least, continued to value his possessions more than his life.[50]

Just as possession of the continent was an impetus for exploration, so were the accumulation and retention of possessions a primary goal of Lewis and Clark. They were collectors first of all. The idea was to bring things—living and dead, human, plant, and animal—back. They collected geographic knowledge in maps as possessions too. In those ambitions they reflected their acquisitive culture and its fear of impoverishment. One of the clarion calls to the American Revolution had been the imagined consequence of British taxation leaving colonists "naked in this cold country." Lewis and Clark displayed similar fears about exchanging possessions with Indians. Dependency frightened them and they were dependent on Indians throughout the expedition.

The shifting balance of valued possessions from the explorers to the "savages" threatened Lewis's and Clark's identities as "civilized" men. Who were they if they lacked things? Their packing lists revealed the extent to which they identified with objects. The things the explorers stole, their increasingly violent reaction to "thefts" by Indians, and their compulsive need to control their possessions reveal how much things defined them.

Over time and across space, as the explorers became more like Indians in the ways they looked, what they ate, and what they possessed, the scary prospect arose that they were becoming "savage." This contributed to their more violent behavior and to the rise of another fear. Perhaps their loss of possessions not only threatened to drag them across cultural identities, downward as they saw it; they also feared losing their humanity. Perhaps they were, as Indians told them, animals in their souls. They already feared that they were *dropping through heirarchies* lesser men than the great explorers whom they emulated, and grew to suspect that they were not even as brave or as powerful as grizzly bears.

They would have greatly benefitted by becoming more savage — or they would have never been there in the first place.

Reflections

S PACE IS MORE than a stage where people walk. Place is an actor, director, and author, not simply the ground where history is made. Like Lewis and Clark, Columbus and Cook failed to find what they sought. Columbus famously never found a western route to China. Cook searched for a great southern continent that was simply not there. Undeterred by geographical facts, as great explorers are wont to be, Cook and Columbus accomplished the impossible and found what they wanted to see. Columbus "landed" in Japan. Cook created a continent. Their journals and maps reflect those "realities."

For Lewis and Clark as well as Columbus and Cook, the explorers' every landfall had to be documented in writing; that is what their maps and journals did. These texts established the explorers' precedence: the journals and maps claimed possession of the discoveries that the explorers documented first. Explorers' right to name what they found could be established only in writing to a literate audience of "civilized" men. As explorers, Lewis, Clark, Columbus, and Cook also wrote different texts, which they delivered orally to the illiterate people they "discovered," speeches that explained what the "savages" could not comprehend—that they lived on white men's land and were subjects of monarchs—in the cases of Columbus and Cook—or an American president. That is why Thomas Jefferson's image was regally represented on a coin that Lewis and Clark insisted the "great chiefs" accept.

Jefferson peace medal. Jefferson image.
*"*TH. JEFFERSON PRESIDENT OF THE*
U.S. A.D. 1801." Distributed in two sizes*
to Indian chiefs during the expedition.
Department of Library Services, American
Museum of Natural History. Negative
number 2A 15302. Photograph by
Hollembeak.

Jefferson peace medal. Reverse. Hands
*shaking. "*PEACE AND FRIENDSHIP.*"*
Department of Library Services, American
Museum of Natural History. Negative
number 2A 15303. Photograph by
Hollembeak.

This was not a coin of the realm, for the republic had decided a decade before that imaging our living rulers was "monarchical," but the coin extended Jefferson's empire nonetheless. Jefferson was their "father," the Indians learned. As either biology or myth this was a nonsensical claim. Lewis and Clark told Indians that they could be peaceful "children" and please their father or suffer the consequences of his ferocious wrath. With the act of delivering the "chiefs" this coin—this possession—the explorers staked their claim to possessing the tribes—their sovereignty, land, allegiance, and the animals they hunted.

Gifts are like that. Acceptance creates debt, expectations, and responsibilities that the recipient may neither comprehend nor accept. Certainly the "chiefs" who declined the honor and had the coin forced insistently upon them faced unpleasant choices—rudeness to their rude guests or taking on the unspecified burdens, both spiritual and material, that the white men's gifts carried with them. The chiefs chose to err on the side of hospitality, which led Lewis and Clark to believe that the chiefs highly valued the symbolically laden possessions. Others learned differently as chiefs redistributed the coins among their enemies after Lewis and Clark left.

The differences between images and words are obvious to the beholder's eye if difficult to justify in the academic world of symbols and texts. There are points, though, where distinctions blur even before the naïve gaze. Lewis's description of a small fish is an interesting case, which raises the point—an ink sketch to life size, cast on a diagonal across a journal page, surrounded by words etched with the same pen. "I have drawn the likeness of them as large as life," Lewis wrote next to the fish's head; "it [is] as perfect as I can make it with my pen and will serve to give general idea of the fish."[1]

The drawing is a "perfect" likeness or, at least, that was Lewis's goal. The picture came first; the words supplement, surround, explicate, and authorize the sketch. Without the words, the drawing has no place in the journal. Even though the likeness is literal by Lewis's lights, the words are necessary to legitimize a fish of inconsequential size and significance.

with him two dogs. The chief and his party had brought
for sale a Sea Otter skin some hats, wappetoe and a species
of small fish which now begin to run and are 93
taken in great quantities in the Columbia R.
about 40 miles above us by means of skiming
or scooping nets. on this page I have drawn
the likeness of them as large as life; it
as perfect as I can make it with my
pen and will serve to give a
generals idea of the fish. the
rays of the fins are boney but
not sharp tho somewhat pointed.
the small fin on the back
next to the tail has no
rays of bone being a
= bonaceous pellicle.
to the gills have
each. those of the
eight each, there
are 20 and 2
that of the back
the fins are of
is of a bleuish
the the lower
is of a silve=
part. the
behind the
second of
the purple
a silver
and
like

thin mem
the fins next
eleven rays
abdomen have
of the pinnæ
half formed in front.
has eleven rays. all
a white colour. the back
duskey colour and that of
part of the sides and belley
of white. no spots on any
first bone of the gills next
eye is of a bleuis cast, and the
a light goald colour nearly white
of the eye is black and the iris of
white. the under jaw exceeds the uper
the mouth opens to great extent, folding
that of the herring. it has no teeth.
the abdomen is obtuse and smooth; in this
differing from the herring, shad anchovy
&c of the Malacapterygious Order & Class
Clupea

Lewis's eulachon. The American Philosophical Society. Lewis and Clark Codex J: 93.

From Lewis's writing it is unclear why he singled out this fish, a eulachon or anchovy as we now call it, above others for a more visually engaging representation. Lewis never drew a grizzly or a rattlesnake, and yet he wrote ever so much more about them. There is no implication that this diminutive fish had a standing comparable to that of buffalo, bears, or serpents in the explorers' hierarchy of species. They tasted the anchovy, but never expressed a taste for it that approached their craving for dogs. They seldom took up their pens to draw animals—prairie dogs, wolves, eagles, or terns—that they feared, ate or valued. We have no sketch of the Shoshone woman, York, Lewis's dog, or any of their horses. They never drew each other or Indians. Why, then, draw this fish?

Clark copied Lewis's words for his entry. The science, the voice, the language and words are those of the more literate, more book-educated, more "philosophical" of the captains. That does not necessarily mean, though, that Lewis drew the fish first. We have two drawings, which are not quite identical, although the intent was to copy the words and the drawing. The reflection is meant to be exact, with the placement of the fish on the page, the arrangement of the fins, and the size precisely the same.

Clark's shading is more careful and detailed; the features are more subtle and hued. Perhaps Clark took more time. Possibly he and Lewis worked together. Clark could have made a preliminary sketch as Lewis composed the words. They then could have serially copied the entry into their notebooks. Both were explorers; neither was an artist. Clark may have copied both the words and the drawing from Lewis's draft, rather than from a once living fish, but we do not know.

The reasons for transcribing the fish have less to do with its innate qualities and more to do with circumstance. It was late February during the explorers' long winter on the West Coast. They were at Fort Clatsop, on the banks of the Columbia River—hungry, bored, wet and depressed, but looking forward to spring and to returning home. They had nothing better to do. Drawing filled time as well as the page. It did not get them closer to any of their goals. The sketches added little to their ambitions or claims.

The drawings better reflected a stage in the explorers' journey than characteristics of the subject. The same is true for the journals' words. When the explorers wrote or drew and where—the temporal and geographical contexts—reveal more than the entries' contents. They might have drawn something else or nothing at all—as they did for months on end. As was typical of explorers, though, Lewis and Clark wrote more when less was happening. The detail of their descriptions was often in obverse relation to the subject's significance. There was less to do, less to see, nothing really happening, so they wrote and drew more about people, events, and small fish that in busier times they would have ignored. Just like those of sea voyagers, Lewis's and Clark's journal entries exploded with detail when they were becalmed; hence the particulars about this little fish. They were in their most reflective mood when they had less upon which to reflect.[2]

Mirrors

The eulachon's most estimable quality from the journalists' perspective was a coincidence of size. It filled the page. The fish fit perfectly into their notebooks. No larger specimen would do; no lesser one would do so well. At a time when they stretched for words to fill their days and their books, the fish helped fill them both. That is why Lewis and Clark drew this fish.

Lewis drew the eulachon because it was possible to represent it "perfectly." It fit on the page, almost filling the space from the lower left corner to the right top, sustaining Lewis's illusion about his journal that it represented reality literally. The sketch testified both to Lewis's aims and, at least subconsciously, to his success. The drawing is another one of those "incontestable" facts.

We should distinguish, though, between Lewis's reality and ours. It would be a mistake to see his decision to draw the eulachon as science, to treat the drawing as an objectified fact, to explain it as anything but a product of boredom, self-delusion, and circumstance. It is also an illusion—a fusion of symbol and text. It is an impression, representing a perspective that is both true to the artist and limited to his vision. The page—words and drawing together—is a piece of art.

fibers by means of which it attatches itself to the sides of the rocks. the shell is thin and consists of one valve a small circular apperture is formed in the center of the under shell. the animal is soft & boneless. –

The white salmon Trout which we had previously seen only at the great falls of the Columbia has now made its appearance in the creeks near this place. one of them was brought us to-day by an Indian who had just taken it with his gig. this is a likeness of it; it was 2 feet 8 Inches long, and weighed 10 lbs. the eye is moderately large, the pupil black with a small admixture of yellow, and iris of a silvery white, is a little turbid near its border with a yellowish brown. the position of the fins may be seen from the drawing, they are small in proportion to the fish. the fins are boney but not pointed except the tail and back fins which are a little so. the back fin and prime ventral ones contain each ten rays; those of the gills thirteen, that of the tail twelve, and the small fin placed near the tail above has no bony rays, but is a tough flexable substance covered with smooth skin. it is thicker in proportion to its width than the salmon. the tongue is thick and firm beset on each border with small subulate teeth in a single series. the teeth of the mouth are as before described. neither this fish nor the salmon are caught with the hook, nor do I know on what they feed. —

Lewis's coho salmon. The American Philosophical Society.
Lewis and Clark Codex J: 133.

There are other drawings in the journals, but only in those of Lewis and Clark. Many of them are clustered in time and space around the eulachon. The Fort Clatsop winter produced much of the explorers' art. "Not any occurrence worthy of relation took place today," Lewis wrote at the head of his long entry for March 16, 1806. So Lewis described unworthy occurrences in great detail and drew a coho salmon which he reduced in scale. It is unclear why he sketched this fish belly up or why it takes up a bit less of the page than the smaller eulachon does. It is also interesting, though, that the entry fills precisely two pages, fish and all. In other words, the composition neatly dictated length. Lewis compelled himself to fill two pages with unworthy occurrences, a discipline that dictated form. The content is secondary—unworthy of relation, Lewis wrote—to the primary motive, which was writing for writing's sake.

As with explorers' words, "original" drawings are not obvious. We do not know how many eulachon the explorers drew before the ones that they preserved. We cannot tell if or when they redrew the sketches and added the descriptions. The date of the entries is far from a sure guide. Although preliminary drafts of the fish do not survive, that does not mean that none ever existed.

The head of a California condor appears three times. Once, out of any apparent context, the disembodied head peers around the edge of Clark's map of the explorers' route from September 2 to 9, 1805. It also appears twice in the journals, once fully integrated with a journal entry for February 16, 1806, by Clark and again in an entry that Lewis wrote for February 17, 1806. The map sketch bears a closer resemblance to the one in Lewis's entry, so it appears that Lewis drew the bird on Clark's map preliminary to entering it in his journal.[3]

The occasion for the condor's portrait was again a coincidence of availability. Two of the men wounded a bird and brought it into camp still alive. Lewis and Clark believed the "large carrion crow or buzzard of the Columbia" to be the largest of North America's birds, which it is, and the size justified the time the explorers took to draw it over again. It was a "handsome bird at a little distance," but was "not in good order." The vulture was wounded, bleeding, scared—its mouth hung open and its tongue stuck out. When the hunter first approached the

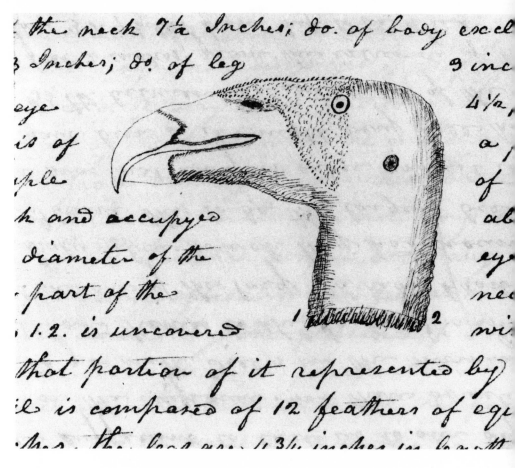

Lewis's California condor. The American Philosophical Society.
Lewis and Clark Codex J: 80.

bird after wounding it, the condor warned him off with "a loud noise very much like the barking of a dog." By the time Lewis and Clark saw the bird, though, it was gasping for air, perhaps from a wound to the lungs. It hardly posed while still alive, but we do not know how long the condor took to die.[4]

The bird's size, the captains' extra time and their need to fill pages, and the specimen's availability are the apparent reasons that they drew the condor. One of the men also brought in a gray eagle that day, but the explorers chose not to draw it. Possibly the eagle was

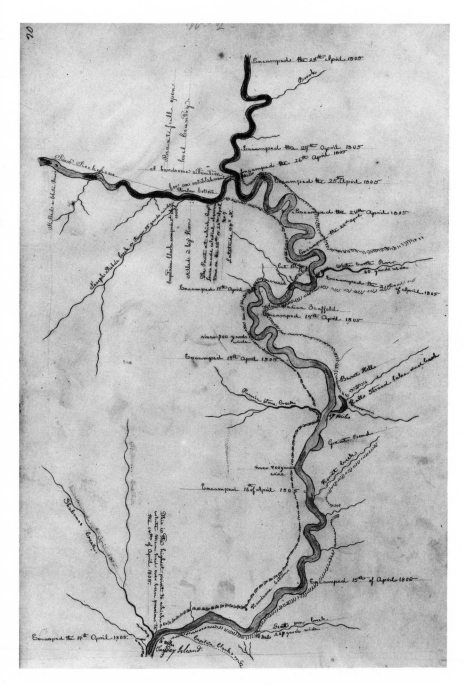

Clark-Maximilian map drawing. Sheet 20. Route from about April 14 to 28, 1805. Joslyn Art Museum, Omaha, Nebraska. Gift of Enron Art Foundation.

already dead, making it less interesting. It was a less impressive bird than the condor—smaller and gray—and more common in their experience. They aimed for novelty—the lifeblood of exploration and science. Anyway, they had already sketched one bird that day and had no need for another. Perhaps they drew the condor rather than the eagle because it came to them first.[5]

Maps also combined pictures and words, but differently than the animal sketches. The sixty maps drawn by the explorers covered unbound pages; they were not intended to fill a book, but to supplement the journals. Not even the edges of the paper confined the mapper's vision, as the explorers juxtaposed multiple maps to extend the limits of their gaze. Like the journals, Lewis's and Clark's maps had a narrative structure. Just like the journals, earlier maps composed drafts for revisions. Smaller maps became blueprints for larger ones that combined them and covered more space and time.

As symbolic depictions of terrain, maps are obviously about space. No less significantly, they are also about time. Lewis and Clark dated maps according to when they covered the particular ground that they drew. They included themselves within the maps' purview— a sketch of a boat to represent their small flotilla, a mark and legend where they camped for a particular night, a spot where they killed a grizzly, and the place where a buffalo rampaged among them while they slept.[6]

Like the journals, the maps' structure aims to be linear. The drawings represent movement toward a goal; laid end to end, more or less, the maps trace the whole route. In those drawn on the outward journey, three of the edges represent the unknown or, at least, the as yet unseen by them. The fourth extends their reach beyond the last map, from where they were to where they are in time and space. The preferred orientation is west at the top. They project themselves as moving up—climbing, straining, creating a straight line. They could not sustain the linearity, though.

Landscape did not cooperate. The mappers preferred straight lines from the bottom to the top and centered on their page. Deviations distracted and disoriented the explorers. Rivers became serpentine, meandering from Lewis's and Clark's directional goal, defying the

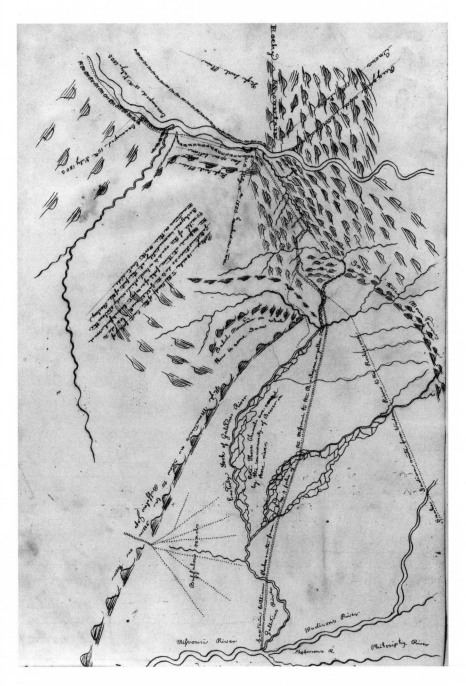

Clark-Maximilian map drawing. Sheet 26. Route from about July 12 to 16, 1805.
Joslyn Art Museum, Omaha, Nebraska. Gift of Enron Art Foundation.

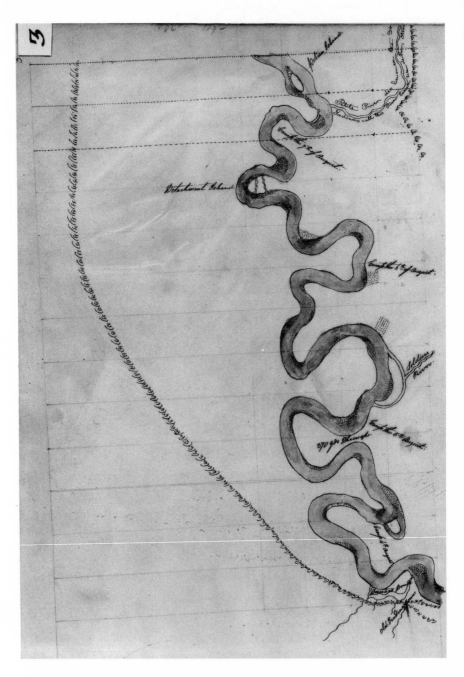

Clark-Maximilian map drawing. Sheet 3. Route from about August 3 to 8, 1804.
Joslyn Art Museum, Omaha, Nebraska. Gift of Enron Art Foundation.

explorers' ability to achieve control of their writing, never mind of their trip. Clark's maps covering the first two weeks of August 1804 show the Missouri doubling back on itself and on the explorers. The river refused to enter the map from the bottom; Clark could not force it to exit through the top. The drawing took on an intestinal shape, undigestible by pen and ink. Their route exploded out from the sides of the page, which threatened a reorientation of paper to represent greater width—north and south—than depth to their trip. Lewis and Clark did their best, as any explorers would do, to avoid such an admission in print and to themselves.

The Indians were no help. A map drawn on the West Coast in consultation with a Clatsop looks more like a circle than a straight line. Indeed, the river never leaves the page at all. Clark lifted his pen before the two ends connected; head and tail, east and west, beginning and end would have touched if he had allowed the Indian to complete his vision. The map thus starkly reflects the different orientations of the explorers and the people they explored. To the Indian, experience connected outside and in. Life and death, sleep and wakefulness, the spiritual and the profane were one and the same. Journeys were circles—never straight lines. The beginning and return were the same point.

Clark drew fifty-eight of the expedition's sixty maps. He was the mapper, the chronicler, the visionary, and the meticulous recorder of the journey in pictures and words. He drew where the explorers had been. He sat in a boat for days on end taking notes, sketching each bend and every sandbar of the Missouri as if they were permanent features on an unchanging landscape. This was a delusion, of course; the river moved with each season, and farther over longer stretches of time. Clark could see high-water marks over his head and dry riverbeds that once bore the mainstream, but he doggedly recorded the "facts" that would not long endure.

Clark's orientation would not outlast the trip; he edited out such details for his composite maps. Whether Clark considered his time wasted or filled is unclear, but he kept the explorers from losing their way. On any given day he could show the men where they were in relation to where they had been. He was the expedition's historian.

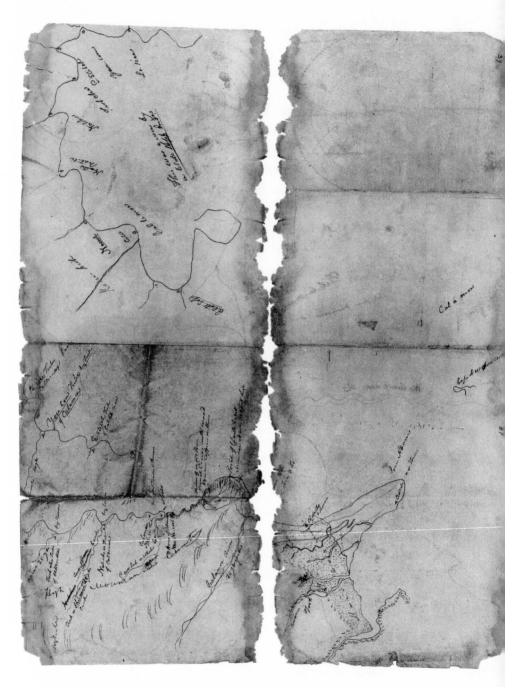

Clark's map based on information from a Clatsop Indian.
The Yale Collection of Western Americana,
Beinecke Rare Book and Manuscript Library.

This undoubtedly provided a sense of security—false to be sure, but reassuring nonetheless. They knew where they were going—to the Pacific Ocean by water—how far they had come—although Clark's estimates were way off—and what they had left behind.

When the maps disorient—as some of them do—and even when they do not, they represent Clark's interior landscape more literally than the earth's surface. They may reflect the state of mind of the other explorers too. The map of the expedition's route from August 24 to September 2, 1805, is a clear example of Clark's confusion. It is a mess, difficult to follow, with words entered every which way. It is disorganized and too detailed to be revealing. It reflects confusion, an inability to sort out significant details, and communicates poorly any sense of movement or scale.

Clark's maps collectively lose their orientation over the course of the trip—first north up, then west, rarely and randomly east, then again west on the way back as if they were returning downhill, and even the traditional north once more at the top. His words circle the lines, sometimes spinning the text. It can be difficult to tell where Clark was going, where he had been. Clark mapped his mind more fully, more accurately, than he mapped the continent. By the end, even sooner, Clark had more in common with the Clatsop Indian who narrated a circular river than he ever knew or would have liked to admit.

Lewis felt more disoriented than Clark, especially on the return. He had no place to go, no sense of future connections, only a vague notion of destiny dashed. Feeling himself a failure, he did not know where he was going and had no affection for where he had been. Lewis lacked the heart of a mapper, the constitution to write his own failure down. So it was Clark who persisted, ever the warrior, the better centered, the clearest imaginer of their enterprise.

The small, partial, "incomplete" maps were, of course, drafts. Clark intended them as notes for more ambitious composites showing the whole continent. There was more than one "final" map and those evolved over the years after the trip, reflecting information, speculation, and the desire not to let go of ambitions that had inspired the expedition. Lewis and Clark, and after Lewis's death Clark by himself, never let go of the mythical river route to the West Coast. Their maps continued to show that they found it or, at least, knew where it was.

The imaginary Multinomah saved the expedition from failure. Extending the fictional river south from the explorers' experience allowed the dream to persist and the mapmakers to delude themselves into thinking that they had found what they sought. Another El Dorado, the mythical Amazonian city of gold, although neither so credible nor ever so alluring, the Multinomah eventually disappeared. It was still there on Clark's map of 1810 and Nicholas Biddle's 1814 printing of it. Whether anyone still believed in the river that late, including Clark, is unclear, but it is unlikely that Lewis convinced himself that he had found a water route to the Pacific Ocean.

Perhaps Clark's peace of mind was constructed of illusions embedded in "facts." If so, his was an irrational sanity, an insane rationality documented in the expedition's journals and maps. Clark was a believer who convinced himself of success. The 1810 map and his journal entries testify to that. Lewis was the skeptic, trained well—too well by Jefferson—for his mental health. Lewis knew they had failed, which is why he could neither write nor draw on his belly as he floated back to St. Louis.

Lewis knew they had failed and could not cope; he lacked the capacity—spiritual, rational, or psychological—to construct the journey as a success. In the end, for all his attempts to delude himself and to deceive the readers of his journals, Lewis was not convinced. He was not "first" in any of the ways that he valued and he knew this at his end. Since he cast the exploratory ambition singularly—it was *his* expedition and *his* "first" that he sought—Lewis also experienced the failure personally. He failed Jefferson, his countrymen, and himself.

Other expedition members also constructed the expedition personally, but their goals were more flexible, more open, less rigid, less demanding, and more forgiving than Lewis's. Even without the Multinomah, Welsh Indians, or finding a lost tribe they could enjoy some sense of personal triumph and could relish being "first." They were all the first people they knew who had made such a trip and the

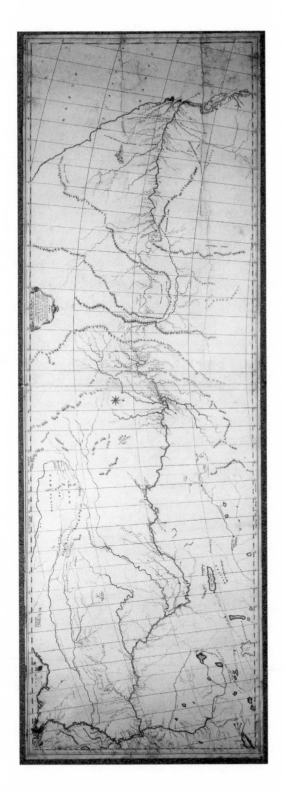

Robert Fraser map of route of
Lewis and Clark. 1807. Library of
Congress. G4125 1807. F Vault.

first to tell about it upon their return. Their stories secured them attentive audiences who admired their survival and perhaps envied their trip. The journey enhanced their prestige; they were not diminished by it in Lewis's sense. Several of them stayed west, extending their "firsts" for the rest of their days. Others may have returned.

In any case, the experience was replicable for all of the explorers save Lewis, who truly was lost. Whether in stories, return trips, or dreams to go back, the others returned to what for them were scenes of beauty, triumph, and personal accomplishment. They gained confidence in themselves and believed they could lead others to what they had found. They were mountain men, river men, trappers, and travelers. Porivo may have overcome her status as a slave, become by her choice a Comanche wife, by misfortune a widow, remained a mother, returned to the Shoshone, and again been a Snake. None of the expedition members would ever be an explorer again, although John Colter continued to explore the region as a fur trapper. "Explorer" was the principal identity only for Lewis and Clark.

Just like all mythical journeys, this one is also replicable for us—in the words, drawings, and maps of the explorers, and in the books, paintings, photos, and trips of countless Americans since. Tourists can repeat the journey in whole or in parts, in first-class accommodations or in a kayak. We can travel by donkey, cruise ship, SUV, or canoe. We can camp along the Columbia or Missouri and imagine ourselves in Lewis's and Clark's fleet. That we do so in so many numbers and with such joy attests to the expedition's success. It truly became our journey as a nation and a people, one that we cannot, and perhaps should not, let go.

the success / Lewis / couldn't grasp

The expedition's triumph had to be found. It got lost in words never read and stories not told for a century after the explorers' return. The success of the Lewis and Clark Expedition became a fiction treated as a fact transformed into history that created a myth. It is a story that we tell about ourselves, which makes our replications essential to our collective sense of self. The discovery of Lewis and Clark fills our need for frontier heroes, mastery of an alien environment, and prestige. Whether we consider it conquest depends on our mood, but we favor a version in which the good Indians welcomed

Lewis and Clark. The communal myth has broadened over the decades to include more people, becoming an interracial and transgender story about how "they" became "us."

Since the late nineteenth century, editors have organized the expedition's journals into chapters. This should be a clue that neither abridged nor "unabridged" editions are "original" texts. The journals, just like histories for which they are a principal source, are imaginative constructions of translation chains that run from the journal writers through editors, authors, and readers. Each of us adds to and selects from the "facts." The stories we tell are ever so different from the journalists' "original" intent. All of us are prisms through which the journals' light is refracted time and again.

As all travelers and explorers know, a journey can only be chaptered in retrospect. Until the trip ends, there is no telling what the story is and where chapters begin and end. Explorers lack the backward gaze that makes the reconstruction of the journey into chapters possible. That is also why we can retrace Lewis's and Clark's steps but never duplicate their trip—and neither could they.

Knowing that there is a next bend, never mind what is around it, changes the journey for all time. Willful ignorance cannot recapture the awe. We now know—rightly or wrongly—that the devils and monsters fail to appear for the likes of us. There are fewer snakes and fewer places for them to hide, although discovering just one is more than enough for most of us to recapture the fear that Lewis and Clark tried to keep to themselves.

There were about twelve thousand grizzlies living in the region that Lewis and Clark traversed. The explorers met up with thirty-seven. Since there are only six hundred to nine hundred grizzlies left in the wild, chances are that tomorrow's travelers will meet none in retracing the expedition's route. The grizzlies' range had already been restricted by the time of Lewis's and Clark's trip. The explorers saw none before reaching the western edge of the North Dakota Plains. Possibly white hunters had eliminated the bears any farther east. The grizzlies had already decided not to share their mystery with whites.[7]

Much the same is true of buffalo. Lewis and Clark sought the animals avidly, but found them only during part of their journey and

only on about 15 percent of the days when they were in buffalo country. The animals were, to them, surprisingly elusive, and generally
traveled in herds of fewer than fifty individuals. There were days
when they saw huge numbers, but those were remarkable. East of the
Dakotas, farmers had already hunted the buffalo down. They
believed that buffalo threatened their domestic cattle, fences, and
crops, so they killed them off in a process that would bring bison to
the brink of extinction in the century ahead. Still, the buffalo num-
bered 50 million or more when Lewis and Clark passed. Eighty years
later there were fewer than one thousand buffalo on the Great
Plains.[8]

The decline of the grizzly and buffalo was not Lewis's and Clark's
fault. In this sense, as others, their effect was minimal. The explorers
were harbingers of the future, but they did not cause it any more
than they could have stopped it had they the will. As individuals, they
were insignificant, except to the extent that they reveal the mind-set
of others who followed them. They were killers and they killed for
fun, for food, and to prove their self-worth. Make no mistake about it,
though: Indians contributed to the decline of buffalo too.[9]

We took the place of the buffalo and grizzlies in the American
West, so it is difficult for us to recapture the moment of a "first" sighting of those animals. We have seen them stuffed, in zoos, and in
books. None of these experiences prepares us adequately for stum-
bling upon a grizzly in the wild, which is still possible today, but less is
left to our imaginations than was true for Lewis and Clark, and shooting them with a small-bore rifle (or anything else) is now against the
law. None of us will ever see the great herds of buffalo that surpassed
750,000 and possibly a million or much more, but the numbers are
growing again.

We can dream of "first" sightings, but our dreams are more difficult
to sustain than the explorers' were then. In reveries we can reimagine,
and thus recapture, the awe of wilderness and the humility of our
place. As an opening to our imaginations, as facilitators of our connections to the past, nature, God, and the universe, Lewis and Clark continue to serve us, perhaps better than they served themselves. We are,
then, their progeny as well as their creators in a mythical sense.

like "Wild Horse Ranch" (handwritten margin note)

Reflections are never exact reproductions; they are never "facts" and can never be "first." Indeed, by definition they are second, at best. Sometimes reflections are, as in the case of mirrors, reversals of images—their opposites. Such reversals are revealing; at least those of us who use them in the morning take them for granted as true. Reflections are subjective, but neither any less true nor limited in perspective than a good mirror examined in clear light.

Plains Indians knew that reflections can enhance our self-knowledge. They can help us to know ourselves more deeply than the superficial gaze that allows us—backwards—to comb our hair. When we reflect on Lewis and Clark, our culture and ourselves refract back. During the twentieth century, Americans—generally white, usually male, often mythically inclined Americans—accepted such reflections literally, much as we accept the image of the person whose hair we comb. They saw the explorers and their journals as "facts" about "us," which is the most superficial view of the expedition.

In the twenty-first century, we have other options before us. We can meditate more deeply on the murky region within. Such self-examination is even scarier than a receding hairline, but can also be more revealing and hence true. There is no objective gaze into a mirror. We should not delude ourselves about that. Either choice—superficial or deep—is fraught with subjectivity. The more reflective path takes us to places where plausibility is our most defensible argument and implausibility is potentially our gravest offense.

John Logan Allen

In the end, though, the Lewis and Clark Expedition serves as a better guide to our souls than it has thus far to our skins. That is why we will keep returning to the journals even after we have plotted the location of every campsite, each encounter, and all of the bears, buffalo, and snakes the explorers killed. That is why we will keep repeating their journey over and over again.

Notes

INTRODUCTION

1. Stephen Ambrose, *Undaunted Courage: Meriwether Lewis, Thomas Jefferson, and the Opening of the American West* (New York, 1996); Bernard DeVoto, *The Course of Empire* (Boston, 1952). Burns's characterization appears on the dust jacket of Ambrose's book.

2. James P. Ronda, *Finding the West: Explorations with Lewis and Clark* (Albuquerque, 2001); Albert Furtwangler, *Acts of Discovery: Visions of America in the Lewis and Clark Journals* (De Kalb, Ill., 1993).

CHAPTER ONE: DREAMS

1. Maximilian, prince of Wied, *Travels in the Interior of North America*, ed. Reuben Gold Thwaites (Cleveland, 1906), 2:361–65; Martha Warren Beckwith, *Mandan-Hidatsa Myths and Ceremonies* (New York, 1938), 1–17.

2. The quotations are from Genesis in the 1611 edition of the King James Version of the Bible; Edmund Leach, *Genesis as Myth and Other Essays* (London, 1969); Anna Birgita Rooth, "The Creation Myths of the North American Indians," in *Sacred Narrative: Readings in the Theory of Myth,* ed. Alan Dundes (Berkeley, 1984), 166–81.

3. Gary E. Moulton, ed., *The Journals of the Lewis and Clark Expedition,* 13 vols. (Lincoln, Nebr., 1983–2001). Clark, November 2, 1804, 3:233–34; November 19, 1804, 3:238; undated, winter 1804–5, 3:485.

4. *David Thompson's Narrative of His Explorations in Western America, 1784–1812,* ed. J. B. Tyrell (Toronto, 1916; reprint, Greenwood Press, 1968), 361–62.

5. David Abram, *The Spell of the Sensuous: Perception and Language in a More-Than-Human World* (New York, 1996), 139–40.

6. Zoa L. Swayne, comp., *Do Them No Harm!: An Interpretation of the Lewis and Clark Expedition Among the Nez Perce Indians* (Orofino, Idaho, 1990), 105–6.

7. Ibid., 112–13.

8. Ibid., 113.

9. Abram, *The Spell of the Sensuous,* 140, 153.

10. *Journals,* Clark, October 17, 1804, 3:179, 180; November 2, 1804, 233–34; George F. Will, "Some Hidatsa and Mandan Tales," *Journal of American Folklore* 25 (1912): 93.

11. *Journals,* Clark, August 18, 1806, 8:308.

12. Abram, *The Spell of the Sensuous,* 199.

13. *Journals,* Clark, August 18, 1806, 8:308.

14. *Journals,* Clark, May 9, 1806, 7:234.

15. *Journals,* Clark, July 21, 1806, 8:213.

16. Matt Cartmill, *A View to a Death in the Morning: Hunting and Nature Through History* (Cambridge, Mass., 1993), 31, 36, 51; *Journals,* Gass, August 21, 1806, 10:270; Whitehouse, August 18, 1805, 11:276; Whitehouse, May 2, 1805, 11:143.

17. Maximilian, *Travels,* 2:258–59.

18. Kevin Dann, unpublished draft of an essay on the ceremonial functions of mirrors among Indians; Christopher L. Miller and George R. Hamell, "A New Perspective on Indian-White Contact: Cultural Symbols and Colonial Trade," *Journal of American History* 73 (1976): 311–28.

19. Kate C. McBeth, *The Nez Perces Since Lewis and Clark* (New York, 1908), 26; Swayne, *Do Them No Harm!,* 20; *Journals,* Clark, August 21, 1806, 8:313–14.

20. *The Manuscript Journals of Alexander Henry and of David Thompson,* 2 vols., ed. Elliott Coues (New York, 1807), 1:349–50.

21. Lee Irwin, *The Dream Seekers: Native American Visionary Traditions of the Great Plains* (Norman, Okla., 1994).

22. Ibid., 28.

23. *Journals,* Clark, August 18, 1804, 2:488.

24. *Journals,* Clark, August 22, 1804, 2:500; 2:502 n. 2.

25. *Journals,* Clark, August 24, 1804, 2:504.

26. *Journals,* Clark, August 25, 1804, 3:7–11.

27. *Journals,* Gass, August 25, 1804, 10:31; August 26, 1804, 10:31.

28. George Catlin, *O-Kee-Pa: A Religious Ceremony and Other Customs of the Mandans,* ed. John C. Ewers (1867; New Haven, 1967), 64.

CHAPTER TWO: BEING FIRST

1. *The Journals of the Lewis and Clark Expedition,* 13 vols., ed. Gary E. Moulton (Lincoln, Nebr., 1983–2001), Lewis, July 17, 1806, 2:112.

2. Johannes Fabian, *Out of Our Minds: Reason and Madness in the Exploration of Central Africa* (Berkeley, Calif. 2000); Paul Carter, *The Road to Botany Bay* (New York, 1987); Mary Louise Pratt, *Imperial Eyes: Travel Writing and Transculturation* (New York, 1992); James Belich, *Making Peoples: A History of the New Zealanders* (New York, 1996).

3. *Journals,* Lewis, April 7, 1805, 4:9–10.

4. *Journals,* Lewis, April 14, 1805, 4:36.

5. *Journals,* Lewis, April 26, 1805, 4:70.

6. Alexander Mackenzie, *Voyages from Montreal . . . through the Continent of North America, to the Frozen and Pacific Oceans* (London, 1801).

7. *Journals,* editor's introduction, 5:4.

8. *Journals,* Lewis, August 3, 1805, 5:37.

9. *Journals,* Clark, August 21, 1805, 5:140.

10. *Journals,* Gass, November 3, 1805, 9:145.

11. *Journals,* 6:14 n. 1; Clark, November 14, 1805, 6:15.

12. *Journals,* Clark, November 4, 1805, 6:17.

13. *Journals,* Clark, November 6, 1805, 6:27; 6:29 n. 15.

14. *Journals,* Clark, November 18, 1805, 6:62.

15. *Journals,* Clark, November 18, 1805, 6:62; November 19, 1805, 6:68; November 19, 1805, 6:69; December 3, 1805, 6:106; November 21, 1805, 6:74.

16. *Journals,* Clark, December 7, 1805, 6:114; 6:115 n. 14.

17. *Journals,* Gass, November 17, 1805, 10:172.

18. *Journals,* Clark, December 31, 1805, 6:147; Gass, November 23, 1805, 10:177.

19. *Journals,* 6:148 n. 3.

20. *Journals,* Clark, January 1, 1806, 6:155; Lewis, January 9, 1806, 6:186–87; Lewis, February 13, 1806, 6:302; 6:307 n. 2.

21. *Journals,* Clark, March 24, 1806, 7:10; 7:11 n. 8.

22. *Journals,* Lewis, March 26, 1806, 7:15–16; 7:17 n. 7.

23. *Journals,* Lewis, May 6, 1806, 7:216.

24. *Journals,* Clark, May 6, 1806, 7:218; 7:219 n. 3.

25. *Journals,* Lewis, August 12, 1806, 8:157, 158.

CHAPTER THREE: WRITING FIRST

1. James P. Ronda, " 'A Darling Project of Mine': The Appeal of the Lewis and Clark Expedition," in *Voyages of Discovery: Essays on the Lewis and Clark Expedition,* ed. James P. Ronda (Helena, Mont., 1998), 333.

2. Gary E. Moulton, "On Reading Lewis and Clark: The Last Twenty Years," in *Voyages of Discovery,* 281.

3. *The Journals of the Lewis and Clark Expedition,* 13 vols., ed. Gary E. Moulton (Lincoln, Nebr., 1983–2001), Clark, April 2, 1805, 3:328; Clark, April 9, 1805, 4:93.

4. *Journals,* Clark, [July 14–18], 1804, 2:373–74; Ordway, July 14, 1804, 9:25; 3:171–72 n. 7.

5. Reuben Gold Thwaites, "The Story of Lewis and Clark's Journals," *Annual Report of the American Historical Association for the Year 1903* 1 (1904): 107–28; *Journals,* Clark, August 29, 1804, 3:22; Clark, April 2, 1805, 3:328.

6. *Journals,* Clark, September 18, 1805, 5:213.

7. *Journals,* 5:214 n. 8, speculates that the red-ink changes were added in 1810, about five years after the entry's date.

8. *Journals,* Clark, December 16, 1805, 6:126–27.

9. *Journals,* Gass, April 5, 1805, 10:75.

10. *Journals,* Lewis, May 15, 1804, 2:229–30. Clark defines the date as a departure in his entry for the previous day. *Journals,* Clark, May 14, 1804, 2:228.

11. *Journals,* Clark, July 7, 1804, 2:355. For an example of Clark leaving a blank space for his hunting record, see Clark, June 14, 1804, 2:300.

12. *Journals,* Whitehouse, January 16, 1805, 11:121; June 14, 1805, 11:197.

13. *Journals,* Whitehouse, June 26, 1805, 11:212; June 26, 1805, 11:213; June 27, 1805, 11:213.

14. *Letters of the Lewis and Clark Expedition,* 2 vols., 2d ed., ed. Donald Jackson (Urbana, Ill., 1978), "Lewis to the Public," March 14, 1807, 2:385–86; "Prospectus" [ca. April 1, 1807], 394–97.

15. Donald Jackson, *Among the Sleeping Giants: Occasional Pieces on Lewis and Clark* (Urbana, Ill., 1987), 71.

16. *Journals,* 2:65, 66 n. 1.

17. *Journals,* Lewis, September 18, 1803, 2:84–85, and editor's note, 2:85.

18. *Journals,* Lewis, November 13, 1803, 2:86.

19. *Journals,* Lewis, November 14, 1803, 2:86.

20. *Journals,* Ordway, September 12, 1806, 9:361; 9:362 n. 4; Clark, September 17, 1806, 8:363.

21. *Journals,* Whitehouse, May 25, 1804, 11:13; Clark, May 26, 1804, 2:254.

22. *Journals,* 5:211, 213, 235.

23. *Journals,* 5:235.

24. *Journals,* Clark, November 7, 1805, 6:32; Lewis, March 19, 1806, 6:434–35.

25. *Journals,* Ordway, March 22, 1806, 9:279; 9:279 n. 4.

26. *Journals,* 6:34 n. 6, 440 n. 5.

27. *Journals,* Gass, November "[a]bout the 16th," 1804, 10:62.

28. *Journals,* 6:106, 107 n. 1.

29. *Journals,* Lewis, January 31, 1806, 6:255; 6:257 n. 6.

30. *Journals,* Lewis, September 14, 1803, 2:81; Lewis, June 17, 1806, 8:32; Lewis, September 14, 1803, 2:81; Lewis, September 15, 1803, 2:82.

31. *Journals,* Clark, [January 21, 1804?], 2:159–60.

32. *Journals,* Lewis, November 16, 1803, 2:87–90.

33. *Journals,* Lewis, November 16, 1803, 2:89.

34. *Journals,* Lewis, November 24, 1803, 2:110.

35. *Journals,* Lewis, November 28, 1803, 2:117.

CHAPTER FOUR: WHY SNAKES?

1. *The Journals of the Lewis and Clark Expedition,* 13 vols., ed. Gary E. Moulton (Lincoln, Nebr., 1983–2001), Clark, August 8, 1804, 2:459; August 5, 1804, 2:448.

2. *Journals,* Lewis, August 5, 1804, 2:449–51.

3. Herbert Leventhal, *In the Shadow of the Enlightenment: Occultism and Renaissance Science in Eighteenth-Century America* (New York, 1976).

4. *Journals,* Ordway, August 5, 1804, 9:34–35.

5. "Part of a Letter from the late Dr. Witt, of German town, in Pennsylvania, to Peter Collinson, Esq, dated ****," *Gentleman's Magazine* 38 (1768): 10.

6. J. Hector St. John de Crèvecoeur, *Letters from an American Farmer* (London, 1782; New York, 1981), "Letter X," 183.

7. Joseph Breintnall to Peter Collinson, February 10, 1746, *Philosophical Transactions of the Royal Society of London* 44 (1746): 147–50; John Bartram to Peter Collinson, February 27, 1737.

8. [John Lederer], *The Discoveries of John Lederer* (London, 1672), 12. Cotton Mather told this same story, also citing Indians as his source. See "An Extract of Several Letters from Cotton Mather to John Woodward," *Philosophical Transactions* 29, no. 339 (April–June 1714): 67. Like Lederer, John Clayton did not believe snake-charming stories. See Edmund Berkeley and Dorothy Smith Berkeley, eds., *The Reverend John Clayton . . . : His Scientific and Other Related Papers* (Charlottesville, Va., 1965), 111–21.

9. "Extract of a Letter from Dr. Kearsley to Mr. P. Collinson: dated Philadelphia, November 18, 1735," *Gentleman's Magazine* 36 (February 1766): 73–76.

10. Ibid.

11. Ibid. Sir Hans Sloane, an Irish-born physician and naturalist who was president of the Royal Society (1727–40), also believed that charming was the consequence of venom and that the victims had been bitten before the observers witnessed the scene. See Sloane, "Conjectures on the Charming or fascinating power attributed to the rattlesnake: grounded on credible Accounts Experiments and Observations," *Philosophical Transactions* 38 (1734): 321–23.

12. Benjamin Smith Barton, *A Memoir Concerning the Fascinating Faculty Which has been Ascribed to the Rattlesnake, and other American Serpents* (Philadelphia, 1796).

13. *Journals,* Lewis, February 11, 1805, 3:291.

14. *Journals,* Clark, June 7, 1804, 2:284–85.

15. *Journals,* Floyd, June 7, 1804, 9:378.

16. *Journals,* Whitehouse, June 7, 1804, 11:19.

17. *Journals,* Clark, June 24, 1804, 2:319–20.

18. *Journals,* Clark, June 26, 1804, 2:324; April 25, 1806, 7:168; Lewis, May 16, 1806, 7:265; August 4, 1806, 8:147; Ordway, June 7, 1804, 9:11; April 22, 1805, 9:136; May 18, 1805, 9:149; July 7, 1805, 9:181; July 15, 1806, 9:336; August 4, 1806, 9:345; September 15, 1806, 9:363; Floyd, August 5, 1805, 9:392; Whitehouse, June 7, 1804, 11:19; May 18, 1805, 11:160; July 8, 1805, 11:221; July 10, 1805, 11:222; Gass, April 16, 1806, 10:212.

19. *Journals,* Whitehouse, August 15, 1805, 11:270; Lewis, August 15, 1805, 5:98; Clark, August 15, 1805, 5:160.

20. *Journals,* Lewis, August 10, 1805, 5:64; Floyd, June 14, 1804, 9:380.

21. *Journals,* Whitehouse, July 11, 1805, 11:223, 224.

22. *Journals,* Clark, July 4, 1804, 2:347; Ordway, June 7, 1804, 9:11; Gass, July 9, 1804, 10:19.

23. *Pennsylvania Gazette,* January 6, 1730 (Philadelphia), October 28, 1731 (Connecticut), July 8, 1736 (Boston), December 26, 1752 (Delaware), February 5, 1761 (New Jersey).

24. James R. Masterson, "Colonial Rattlesnake Lore," *Zoologica* 23 (1938): 213–16.

25. Crèvecoeur, *Letters,* "Letter X," 181–82.

26. *Journals,* Clark, June 14, 1804, 2:301, 300.

27. Crèvecoeur, *Letters,* "Letter X," 180–81.

28. Thomas P. Slaughter, *The Natures of John and William Bartram* (New York, 1996), chap. 6.

29. D. Humphreys Storer, *Reports on the Fishes, Reptiles, and Birds of Massachusetts* (Boston, 1839); Jonathan Edwards, sermon at Northampton, 1739, quoted in Thomas Palmer, *Landscape with Reptile: Rattlesnakes in an Urban World* (New York, 1992), 121, 110; *Pennsylvania Gazette,* April 1 and May 9, 1751, September 19, November 21, and December 12, 1765, August 5, 1762.

30. "Rattlesnake and Its Congerers," *Harper's New Monthly Magazine* 10 (1854–55): 472, 278.

31. Nathaniel Hawthorne, "Egotism: or, The Bosom-Serpent," in *Nathaniel Hawthorne: Tales and Sketches,* ed. Roy Harvey Pearce (New York, 1982).

CHAPTER FIVE: PORIVO'S STORY

1. Rayna Green, "The Pocahontas Perplex: The Image of Indian Women in American Culture," *Massachusetts Review* 16 (1975): 698–714.

2. Ella E. Clark and Margot Edmunds, *Sacagawea of the Lewis and Clark Expedition*

(Berkeley, Calif., 1979), 7; *The Journals of the Lewis and Clark Expedition,* 13 vols., ed. Gary E. Moulton (Lincoln, Nebr., 1983–2001), Lewis, July 28, 1805, 2:7–9.

3. *Letters of the Lewis and Clark Expedition with Related Documents, 1783–1854,* 2 vols., 2d ed., ed. Donald Jackson (Urbana Ill., 1978), 2:638–39; Clara Sue Kindwell, "Indian Women as Cultural Mediators," *Ethnohistory* 39 (1992): 97–107; Åsebrit Sundquist, *Sacajawea & Co.: The Twentieth-Century Fictional American Indian Woman and Fellow Characters: A Study of Gender and Race* (Oslo, 1991); Marie Webster Weisbrod, "Sacajawea: Native American Heroine," *Journal of the West* 37 (1998): 25–33.

4. John C. Luttig, *Journal of a Fur-Trading Expedition on the Upper Missouri, 1812–1813,* ed. Stella M. Drumm (New York, 1964), 106; Helen Addison Howard, "The Mystery of Sacagawea's Death," *Pacific Northwest Quarterly* 58 (1967): 1–6.

5. Henry Marie Brackenridge, *Views of Louisiana* (Pittsburgh, 1814; Chicago, 1962), 202.

6. Both Henry Marie Brackenridge and his father—the writer and judge Hugh Henry Brackenridge—were not above changing a detail for literary effect. In this case, the contrast Henry Marie makes between "savagery" and "civilization" was best illustrated by characters known to his audience. "So true it is," Brackenridge wrote, "that the attachment to the savage state, or the state of nature, (with which appellation it has commonly been dignified) is much stronger than to that of civilization, with all its comforts, its refinements, and its security." The story of their "return" works better with one of Charbonneau's Shoshone wives than with the other, no matter which one Brackenridge actually met. Ibid.

7. The best recent illustrations of this form of heroic writing about Lewis and Clark are Stephen Ambrose, *Undaunted Courage: Meriwether Lewis, Thomas Jefferson, and the Opening of the American West* (New York, 1996), and Dayton Duncan and Ken Burns, *Lewis & Clark: The Journey of the Corps of Discovery* (New York, 1997).

8. Donald Jackson, *Among the Sleeping Giants: Occasional Pieces on Lewis and Clark* (Urbana, Ill., 1987), 40.

9. Gary E. Moulton, "On Reading Lewis and Clark: The Last Twenty Years," in *Voyages of Discovery: Essays on the Lewis and Clark Expedition,* ed. James P. Ronda (Helena, Mont., 1998), 287, 288.

10. Harold P. Howard, *Sacajawea* (Norman, Okla., 1971), 188–89, 191, 158.

11. Charles Burke to Charles Eastman, December 13, 1924; Doane Robinson, superintendent, State of South Dakota Department of History, to Charles H. Burke, Indian commissioner, March 18, 1925; March 23, 1925; March 27, 1925, and supplements, Central Classified Files of the Bureau of Indian Affairs for 1907–1939, file number 34936-1922-034, Shoshone, National Archives and Records Administration. Hereafter referred to as BIA files, NARA.

12. Grace Raymond Hebard, "Pilot of the First White Men to Cross the

American Continent," *Journal of American History* 1 (1907): 467–84; Hebard, *Sacajawea: A Guide and Interpreter of the Lewis and Clark Expedition* (Glendale, Calif., 1957).

13. BIA files, NARA; Eva Emery Dye, *The Conquest: The True Story of Lewis and Clark* (Chicago, 1902); Ronald W. Taber, "Sacagawea and the Suffragettes: An Interpretation of a Myth," *Pacific Northwest Quarterly* 58 (1967): 7–13; Donna J. Kessler, *The Making of Sacagawea: A Euro-American Legend* (Tuscaloosa, Ala., 1996).

14. Report of Charles A. Eastman to the commissioner of Indian Affairs, March 2, 1925, BIA files, NARA. On Eastman, a fascinating figure in his own right, see Charles A. Eastman, *Indian Boyhood* (Williamstown, Mass., 1975); Eastman, *From the Deep Woods to Civilization: Chapters in the Autobiography of an Indian* (Lincoln, Nebr., 1977); Marion W. Copeland, *Charles Alexander Eastman (Ohiyesa)* (Boise, Idaho, 1978); Raymond Wilson, *Ohiyesa: Charles Eastman, Santee Sioux* (Urbana, Ill., 1983).

15. Eastman, Report, BIA files, NARA.

16. Gary Anderson, *The Indians' Southwest* (Norman, Okla., 1999); Thomas W. Kavanagh, *The Comanches: A History, 1706–1875* (Lincoln, Nebr., 1996); T. R. Fehrenbach, *Comanches: The Destruction of a People* (New York, 1974).

17. Ibid.

18. Ibid.

19. Ibid.

20. Doane Robinson, State of South Dakota Department of History, to Charles H. Burke, March 18, 1925; March 23, 1925; and March 27, 1925, BIA files, NARA.

21. Hebard, *Sacajawea,* Appendix B, 225, 227.

22. Ibid., 232, 234.

23. Ibid., 237, 238.

24. Geoffrey O'Gara, *What You See in Clear Water: Life on the Wind River Reservation* (New York, 2000), 210, 212, 101.

25. Ibid., 102, 103.

26. Hebard, *Sacajawea,* 275–76, 250.

27. Ibid., 250; Fehrenbach, *Comanches,* 34.

28. Hebard, *Sacajawea,* Appendix B, 250 and passim.

29. Hebard, "Pilot of the First White Men," 467; Dye, *The Conquest,* 290; Taber, "Sacagawea and the Suffragettes," 8–9.

30. Hebard, *Sacajawea,* 249, 250, 255, 259, 279.

31. Ibid., 246, 247.

32. Sherry B. Ortner, "Is Female to Male as Nature Is to Culture?," in *Woman, Culture, and Society,* ed. Michelle Zimbalist Rosaldo and Louise Lamphere (Stanford, Calif., 1974), 67–87.

33. Sylvia Van Kirk, *Many Tender Ties: Women in Fur-Trade Society, 1670–1870* (Norman, Okla., 1983).

34. We know far less about Indian slavery and the slave trade in Indian women than we do about African slavery in the Americas. As more studies appear, we will no doubt be struck as much by the differences between Indian slavery and African slavery as we are by the similarities. Nonetheless, it is important to note that the trade in Indian women was widespread and was facilitated by the presence of European traders. It is also essential to recognize that the variety of "slaveries" in the Americas should not confuse us about the definitional appropriateness of labeling the practice of capturing, buying, and selling people as slavery. As James L. Watson explains, "the relationship characterized by slavery is by no means universal but it is 'special' in the sense that, wherever and whatever it appears, slavery is distinguishable from other forms of exploitation in the same society." "Slavery as an Institution: Open and Closed Systems," in *Asian and African Systems of Slavery,* ed. James L. Watson (Berkeley, Calif., 1980), 3. On the slave trade in Indian women on the Southwest Spanish borderlands, see Juliana Barr, "The 'Seductions' of Texas: The Political Language of Gender in the Conquests of Texas, 1690–1803," Ph.D. diss., University of Wisconsin, 1999. See also Leland Donald, *Aboriginal Slavery on the Northwest Coast of North America* (Berkeley, Calif., 1997), and James F. Brooks, *Captives and Cousins: Slavery, Kinship, and Community in the Southwest Borderlands* (Chapel Hill, N.C., 2002).

35. Watson, "Slavery as an Institution," 9; R. David Edmunds, "Unacquainted with the Laws of the Civilized World: American Attitudes Toward the Métis Communities in the Old Northwest," in *The New Peoples: Being and Becoming Métis in North America,* ed. Jacqueline Peterson and Jennifer S. H. Brown (Omaha, Nebr., 1985), 185–93.

36. *Journals,* Clark, August 14, 1805, 5:93.

37. *Journals,* Clark, August 17, 1805, 5:114.

38. *Journals,* Lewis, July 28, 1805, 5:8.

39. *Journals,* Lewis, August 19, 1805, 5:120.

40. *Journals,* Clark, November 24, 1805, 6:84.

41. *Journals,* Clark, November 30, 1805, 6:97; December 25, 1805, 6:137.

42. *Journals,* Clark, November 13, 1805, 6:44.

43. *Journals,* Lewis, January 6, 1806, 6:168.

44. *Journals,* Clark, April 23, 1806, 7:162; November 20, 1805, 6:72–73.

45. *Journals,* Clark, June 10, 1805, 4:277; June 11, 1805, 4:279; June 12, 1805, 4:281; June 14, 1805, 4:194; June 15, 1805, 4:197; June 16, 1805, 4:301; Lewis, June 16, 1805, 4:299; June 17, 1805, 4:303.

46. Hebard, *Sacajawea,* Appendix B, 235, 239, 240.

47. *Journals,* Lewis, May 16, 1805, 4:156.

48. Hebard, *Sacajawea,* 253, 279; Affidavit of Atsie McGhee of Dis-ha-yat-sie, born 1845, January 15, 1925; J.E.R.[?] to Grace Raymond Hebard, May 9, 1906; Charles Eastman, "Reply to Doctor Robinson's Letter: Supplement to the Original Report," undated, BIA files, NARA.

49. Grace Raymond Hebard to Charles Burke, April 29, 1925. In this letter Hebard claims that the journals were altered retrospectively and that the name was added in a red ink that the explorers did not carry with them on the expedition. Her conclusion is that the named references were inserted after the return to St. Louis. A check of the manuscript journals, though, shows that the named entries were made in the same ink and at the same time as the rest of the entries. The red-inked additions were apparently those of Elliot Coues, who was attempting to correct the explorers' spelling. I thank Robert S. Cox of the American Philosophical Society for his assistance with my examination of the manuscript journals.

50. O'Gara, *What You See in Clear Water,* 19 and passim.

CHAPTER SIX: YORK'S MYSTERY

1. Will of John Clark, July 24, 1799, and codicil, July 26, 1799, Jefferson County, Kentucky, Archives and Records Services; Robert B. Betts, *In Search of York: The Slave Who Went to the Pacific with Lewis and Clark,* rev. ed. (Boulder, Colo., 2000), 59.

2. *The Journals of the Lewis and Clark Expedition,* 13 vols., ed. Gary E. Moulton (Lincoln, Nebr., 1983–2001), Clark, December 26, 1803, 2:141.

3. *Journals,* Clark, June 5, 1804, 2:278; August 24, 1804, 2:504; January 1, 1805, 3:267; Lewis, July 7, 1805, 4:365; Clark, July 7, 1805, 4:366; October 26, 1805, 5:341; November 16, 1805, 6:53; November 18, 1805, 6:65; December 28, 1805, 6:140; Lewis, July 1, 1806, 8:74; Clark, December 8, 1804, 3:255.

4. Betts, *In Search of York,* 61–80; Vardis Fisher, *Tale of Valor* (Garden City, N.Y., 1958), 138; K. D. Curtis, "York, the Slave Explorer," *Negro Digest,* May 1962, 11.

5. *Journals,* Clark, May 1, 1804, 2:227.

6. Stephen Ambrose, *Undaunted Courage: Meriwether Lewis, Thomas Jefferson, and the Opening of the American West* (New York, 1996); Dayton Duncan and Ken Burns, *Lewis & Clark: The Journey of the Corps of Discovery* (New York, 1997).

7. *Journals,* Clark, June 20, 1804, 2:310.

8. *Journals,* Clark, December 7, 1805, 2:109.

9. *Journals,* Lewis, April 7, 1804, 2:9.

10. *Journals,* Clark, November 18, 1805, 6:65; December 28, 1805, 6:140; July 7, 1805, 4:366; August 24, 1804, 2:505.

11. *Journals,* Clark, October 9, 1804, 3:155.

12. *Journals,* Clark, October 10, 1804, 3:156–57.

13. *Journals,* Clark, October 10, 1804, 3:157.

14. Ibid.

15. *Journals,* Clark, October 15, 1804, 3:174.

16. *Journals,* Clark, October 28, 1804, 3:207–8.

17. Zoa L. Swayne, comp., *Do Them No Harm!: An Interpretation of the Lewis and Clark Expedition Among the Nez Perce Indians* (Orofino, Idaho, 1990), 38–41.

18. Ibid., 50–51.

19. *Letters of the Lewis and Clark Expedition with Related Documents, 1783–1854,* 2 vols., 2d ed., ed. Donald Jackson (Urbana, Ill., 1978), Nicholas Biddle notes from interviews with William Clark [1810], American Philosophical Society, 2:539.

20. *Journals,* Lewis, August 17, 1805, 5:112; *Letters,* Biddle notes, 2:503; Betts, *In Search of York,* 39.

21. *Letters,* Biddle notes, 2:503.

22. Alice B. Kehoe, "The Function of Ceremonial Sexual Intercourse Among the Northern Plains Indians," *Plains Anthropologist* 15 (1970): 99–103; Elliott Coues, ed., *The History of the Lewis and Clark Expedition by Meriwether Lewis and William Clark,* 4 vols. (New York, 1893; Dover, n.d.), 1:164; Betts, *In Search of York,* 70.

23. James J. Holmberg, "Summing Up," in Betts, *In Search of York,* 192 n. 1.

24. Ibid., 153–54.

25. William Clark to Jonathan Clark, November 9, 1808, Jonathan Clark Papers, Temple Bodley Collection, Filson Club Historical Society, Louisville, Kentucky, quoted by Holmberg, "Summing Up," 158.

26. William Clark to Jonathan Clark, December 17, 1809, quoted by Holmberg, "Summing Up," 162.

27. Ibid., 159.

28. William Clark to Jonathan Clark, May 28, 1809, quoted by Holmberg, "Summing Up," 162.

29. William Clark to Jonathan Clark, August 26, 1809, September 5, 1809, quoted by Holmberg, "Summing Up," 163; Edmund Clark to William Clark, September 3, 1809, Voorhis Memorial Collection, Missouri Historical Society, quoted by Holmberg, "Summing Up," 164.

30. John O'Fallon, Louisville, to William Clark, St. Louis, May 13, 1811, Missouri Historical Society, printed in Betts, *In Search of York,* 112–13.

31. William Clark Kennerly as told to Elizabeth Russell, *Persimmon Hill: A Narrative of Old St. Louis and the Far West* (Norman, Okla., 1948), 52–53.

32. *The Western Journals of Washington Irving,* ed. John Francis McDermott (Norman, Okla., 1944), 82.

33. Ibid.

34. *Adventures of Zenas Leonard, Fur Trader,* ed. John C. Ewers (Norman, Okla., 1959), 51–52.

35. Ibid., 52.

36. Ibid., 139.

37. Ibid., 147–48.

38. Ibid., 153.

39. Betts, *In Search of York,* 137–41.

40. J. Thomas Scharf, *History of St. Louis City and County,* 2 vols. (Philadelphia, 1883), 1:311; Richard Edwards and M. Hopewell, *Edwards's Great West* (St. Louis, 1860), 292.

41. Pierre Antoine Tabeau, *Tabeau's Narrative of Loisel's Expedition to the Upper Missouri,* ed. Annie Heloise Abel (Norman, Okla., 1939), 201.

CHAPTER SEVEN: HUNTING THEMSELVES

1. Matt Cartmill, *A View to a Death in the Morning: Hunting and Nature Through History* (Cambridge, Mass., 1993), 30, 50–51, and passim.

2. *The Journals of the Lewis and Clark Expedition,* 13 vols., ed. Gary E. Moulton (Lincoln, Nebr., 1983–2001), Lewis, May 5, 1805, 4:111; Clark, July 25, 1806, 8:224; Whitehouse, July 3, 1805, 11:217.

3. *Journals,* Lewis, May 5, 1805, 4:111.

4. *Journals,* Lewis, May 9, 1805, 4:130; May 25, 1805, 4:193.

5. *Journals,* Lewis, June 4, 1805, 4:255.

6. *Journals,* Lewis, April 27, 1805, 4:78; April 27, 1805, 4:79.

7. King James Version of the Bible, 1611 edition, Genesis 1:26.

8. *Journals,* Clark, December 10, 1805, 4:121.

9. Ibid., 255–56.

10. *Journals,* Lewis, May 9, 1805, 4:130; August 25, 1804, 3:12.

11. *Journals,* Clark, September 11, 1804, 4:64; Lewis, May 31, 1805, 4:227; Lewis, September 17, 1804, 3:80.

12. *Journals,* Lewis, October 16, 1804, 4:178.

13. *Journals,* Clark, April 13, 1805, 4:33.

14. *Journals,* Lewis, May 2, 1805, 4:100.

15. *Journals,* Lewis, April 22, 1805, 4:60; Clark, April 23, 1805, 4:64.

16. *Journals,* Lewis, July 29, 1805, 5:10.

17. *Journals,* Lewis, May 5, 1806, 7:209–10; Clark, May 5, 1806, 7:212.

18. *Journals,* Lewis, September 11, 1803, 2:79; September 14, 1803, 2:82.

19. *Journals,* Clark, September 9, 1804, 3:58; September 19, 1804, 3:90; Clark, November 16, 1805, 6:54.

20. *Journals,* Lewis, May 1, 1806, 4:96.

21. *Journals,* Clark, July 7, 1804, 2:355; July 20, 1804, 2:397.

22. *Journals,* Lewis, April 30, 1805, 4:88; Clark, August 9, 1806, 8:286.

23. *Journals,* Clark, December 7, 1804, 3:253.

24. *Journals,* Lewis, remarks following weather, December 1804, 3:265; Lewis, June 28, 1806, 8:60; Clark, June 28, 1806, 8:60.

25. *Journals,* Clark, February 3, 1805, 3:285; February 15, 1805, 3:296.

26. *Journals,* Clark, February 3, 1805, 3:285; February 15, 1805, 3:296.

27. *Journals,* Lewis, September 17, 1804, 3:80–81.

28. *Journals,* Lewis, September 16, 1803, 2:83.

29. *Journals,* Lewis, May 6, 1805, 4:118; May 9, 1805, 4:130.

30. *Journals,* Clark, August 8, 1804, 2:457, 459.

31. *Journals,* Clark, October 21, 1804, 3:189.

32. *Journals,* Clark, August 12, 1804, 2:471–72, 474.

33. *Journals,* Clark, August 7, 1806, 8:285; Lewis, May 19, 1805, 4:166; Clark, May 28, 1805, 4:213; Lewis, May 29, 1805, 4:215.

34. *Journals,* Ordway, June 7, 1804, 9:18.

35. *Journals,* Lewis, June 3, 1805, 4:287.

36. *Journals,* Lewis, July 16, 1806, 8:111.

37. Daniel J. Gelo, "The Bear," in *American Wildlife in Symbol and Story,* ed. Angus K. Gillespie and Jay Mechling (Knoxville, Tenn., 1987), 134–35.

38. *Journals,* Clark, undated [winter 1804–5], 3:482.

39. Gelo, "The Bear," 137, 139; A. Irving Hallowell, "Bear Ceremonialism in the Northern Hemisphere," *American Anthropologist* 28 (1926): 43, 44, 46.

40. Gelo, "The Bear," 136; Hallowell, "Bear Ceremonialism," 33–34, 36–37, 53–55, 73–74.

41. *Journals,* Clark, October 10, 1804, 3:188.

42. *Journals,* Lewis, April 13, 1805, 4:31.

43. Ibid.

44. *Journals,* Lewis, April 14, 1805, 4:36; Clark, April 14, 1805, 4:39; Lewis, April 17, 1805, 4:48.

45. *Journals,* Lewis, April 29, 1805, 4:84–85.

46. *Journals,* Lewis, May 5, 1805, 4:113.

47. *Journals,* Lewis, May 6, 1805, 4:118.

48. Ibid.

49. *Journals,* Lewis, May 11, 1805, 4:141.

50. Ibid.

51. *Journals,* editor's introduction, 4:2.

52. *Journals,* Lewis, May 12, 1805, 4:145.

53. *Journals,* Lewis, May 13, 1805, 4:149; Lewis, May 15, 1805, 4:156; Lewis, May 16, 1805, 4:157; Lewis, May 14, 1805, 4:151–52.

54. *Journals,* Lewis, May 14, 1805, 4:151–52. For a fascinating meditation on the significance of bears, see Calvin Martin, "Time and the American Indian," in *The American Indian and the Problem of History,* ed. Martin (New York, 1987), 192–220.

55. *Journals,* Clark, May 14, 1805, 4:154–55.

56. *Journals,* Clark, August 5, 1806, 8:281, 282.

57. *Journals,* Lewis, May 17, 1805, 4:159; May 19, 1805, 4:166; Clark, May 19, 1805, 4:168; Lewis, May 23, 1805, 4:184; Lewis, June 2, 1805, 4:242; Clark, June 4, 1805, 4:256; Lewis, June 12, 1805, 4:280.

58. *Journals,* Clark, June 17–19, 1805, 4:36; July 26, 1805, 4:433; Lewis, June 25, 1805, 4:311; June 27, 1805, 4:336; June 28, 1805, 4:338; Clark, July 2, 1805, 4:350; Lewis, July 2, 1805, 4:351–52; Clark, July 2, 1805, 4:352.

59. *The Journals of Patrick Gass: Member of the Lewis and Clark Expedition* (Missoula, Mont., 1997), ed. Carol Lynn MacGregor, May 14, 1805, 94; July 15, 1806, 204; *Journals,* Clark, July 31, 1806, 8:259; Lewis, August 1, 1806, 8:144.

60. *Journals,* Lewis, June 14, 1805, 4:292–94.

61. *Journals,* Lewis, June 14, 1805, 4:294.

62. *Journals,* Ordway, August 11, 1806, 9:347.

63. Hallowell, "Bear Ceremonialism," 68–71.

CHAPTER EIGHT: POSSESSIONS

1. *The Journals of the Lewis and Clark Expedition,* 13 vols., ed. Gary E. Moulton (Lincoln, Nebr., 1983–2001), Ordway, April 9, 1806, 9:288; Clark, October 22, 1805, 5:323.

2. *Journals,* Ordway, April 9, 1806, 9:288.

3. *Journals,* Ordway, April 10, 1806, 9:290.

4. *Journals,* Clark, December 21, 1805, 6:134.

5. *Journals,* Clark, August 21, 1805, 5:139.

6. *Journals,* Lewis, August 21, 1805, 5:138.

7. Ibid.

8. *Journals,* Lewis, June 11, 1806, 8:13.

9. *Journals,* Clark, December 30, 1805, 6:145.

10. *Journals,* Clark, December 31, 1805, 6:147.

11. *The Journals of Patrick Gass: Member of the Lewis and Clark Expedition,* ed. Carol Lynn MacGregor (Missoula, Mont., 1997), June 17, 1804, 43; July 3, 1804, 45; July 11, 1804, 46.

12. *Journals,* Ordway, August 22, 1805, 9:208.

13. *Journals,* Clark, undated [winter 1804–5], 3:482; February 15, 1805, 3:296.

14. *Journals,* Clark, February 15, 1805, 3:296.

15. *Journals,* Ordway, February 15, 1805, 9:114–15.

16. *Journals,* Clark, February 15, 1805, 3:296; February 16, 1805, 3:297; February 28, 1805, 3:305.

17. *Journals,* Whitehouse, October 15, 1805, 11:354; October 14, 1805, 11:352.

18. *Journals,* Lewis, March 17, 1806, 6:426.

19. *Journals,* Lewis, January 10, 1806, 6:193.

20. *Journals,* Lewis, February 3, 1806, 6:275.

21. *Journals,* Clark, December 7, 1804, 3:254.

22. *Journals,* editor's introduction, 6:4.

23. *Journals,* editor's introduction, 7:1.

24. *Journals,* Clark, February 6, 1806, 6:282; Lewis, February 6, 1806, 6:281.

25. *Journals,* Lewis, February 12, 1806, 6:299; Lewis, February 22, 1806, 6:336.

26. *Journals,* Lewis, February 22, 1806, 6:336. Clark, February 18, 1806, 6:327.

27. *Journals,* Lewis, March 24, 1806, 7:10.

28. *Journals,* Lewis, March 30, 1806, 7:32.

29. *Journals,* Clark, April 2, 1806, 7:58.

30. *Journals,* Clark, July 7, 1806, 8:169; July 9, 1806, 8:174.

31. *Journals,* Clark, July 9, 1806, 8:174.

32. *Journals,* Clark, July 21, 1806, 8:209; July 22, 1806, 8:210; July 23, 1806, 8:211.

33. *Journals,* Clark, October 27, 1805, 5:358.

34. *Journals,* Clark, October 17, 1805, 5:290.

35. *Journals,* Lewis, March 29, 1806, 7:28.

36. *Journals,* Lewis, May 10, 1806, 7:238.

37. *Journals,* Lewis, April 21, 1806, 7:152.

38. *Journals of Patrick Gass,* April 21, 1806, 178.

39. *Journals,* Clark, April 21, 1806, 7:153.

40. *Journals,* Lewis, April 22, 1806, 7:155.

41. *Journals,* Lewis, April 28, 1806, 7:177.

42. *Journals,* Lewis, May 1, 1806, 7:196.

43. *Journals,* Lewis, May 5, 1806, 7:210.

44. *Journals,* Lewis, July 27, 1806, 8:133–34; Clark, August 12, 1806, 8:294–95.

45. *Journals,* Lewis, July 27, 1806, 8:134.

46. Ibid.

47. *Journals,* Lewis, July 27, 1806, 8:135.

48. *Journals,* Ordway, July 28, 1806, 9:342.

49. Ibid.

50. *Journals,* Lewis, July 28, 1806, 8:137.

REFLECTIONS

1. *The Journals of the Lewis and Clark Expedition*, 13 vols., ed. Gary E. Moulton (Lincoln, Nebr., 1983–2001), Lewis, February 24, 1806, 6:342.

2. Paul Carter, *The Road to Botany Bay: An Exploration of Landscape and History* (New York, 1988).

3. *Journals*, Clark, February 16, 1806, 6:320; Lewis, February 17, 1806, 6:323; 6:67, map 68.

4. *Journals*, Clark, February 16, 1806, 6:318–21; Lewis, February 17, 1806, 6:321–23.

5. Ibid.

6. *Journals*, Clark, map 3a, route about November 25, 1803, 1; Clark, map 56, route about April 14–28, 1805, 1.

7. Daniel Botkin, *Our Natural History: The Lessons of Lewis and Clark* (New York, 1995), 59–75.

8. Ibid., 101–27.

9. Shepard Krech III, *The Ecological Indian: Myth and History* (New York, 1999); Andrew C. Isenberg, *The Destruction of the Bison* (New York, 2000).

Acknowledgments

Support for the research and writing of this book came from the University of Notre Dame, Rutgers University, the McNeil Center for Early American Studies at the University of Pennsylvania, and the Center for Advanced Study in the Behavioral Sciences (CASBS) in Palo Alto, California. I am grateful for the support of those institutions as well as to the Andrew W. Mellon Foundation, which funded my year at CASBS. I began the research in Palo Alto, started writing in Philadelphia, continued in New Jersey and Nova Scotia, and finished in South Bend. People in all those places helped me along the way.

Robert Cox and Roy Goodman greatly facilitated my research at the American Philosophical Society, as did James Green and Philip Lapsansky at the Library Company of Philadelphia, Andrea C. Ashby Leraris and Sharon Stevens at Independence National Historical Park, Anne Marie Menta at Yale University's Beinecke Library, Sharon Silengo at the State Historical Society of North Dakota, Charlotte Houtz at the Library of Congress, Nicole Wells at the New-York Historical Society, Larry Mensching at the Joslyn Art Museum, and special-collection archivists at the American Museum of Natural History.

Sam Baily, Mia Bay, Paul Clemens, Ziva Galili, Philip Greven, David Oshinsky, Stephen Reinert, and Mark Wasserman were longtime colleagues at Rutgers and are much missed friends. I miss the younger batch too, and regret not getting to know them better—Juliana Barr, Christopher Brown, Herman Bennett, and Jennifer Morgan. My loss, but Philip left us first—actually second, because Calvin Martin left us first—and Paul can pick up the slack for us all (as he always did anyway). Paul Clemens is undoubtedly unique in the history of collegial relations and carried me right through the ranks until I walked out the door. He would be justified in feeling that I betrayed him personally by leaving Rutgers, but that is not his way. His generosity and friendship are irreplaceable, and I will always miss him and my other New Brunswick friends.

My original conception of this project benefited from the questions of participants in the gender and family group at CASBS. Similarly helpful at a later stage were my fellow fellows at the McNeil Center who shared their reactions over one of our tasty brown-bag lunches. Colleagues who came for the annual McNeil Center picnic, but kindly arrived early to discuss chapter five, enlightened me on a number of subjects, but with persistent good humor on husbandry, wifery, and slavery.

Strangers as well as friends have helped me. Richard White generously read the entire manuscript and provided challenges and suggestions that improved it. Kenneth Lockridge read the proposal, an early draft of what became chapter five, and became a treasured correspondent on all things great and small. Having never met White or Lockridge, I am hugely grateful that they took the time to read and comment on my work.

Ken Lockridge and Mike Zuckerman must be two of the last historians who still write long letters by hand, and they are certainly among the high artists of the genre. Having known Mike for two decades, I am both sad to now live farther away from him, and hopeful that maybe I will get more of his letters.

I have met Bertram Wyatt-Brown and John Demos, once briefly each, so I am only slightly less amazed and no less grateful for their support of this project and its author over the past five years. James Green of the Library Company of Philadelphia read chapter two for me and enlightened me, as he has done in the past, with his unsurpassed knowledge of publishing, books, and the book trade in the eighteenth, nineteenth, and twenty-first centuries.

Camilla Townsend read chapter five and provided her usual insightful, sensitive, and empathetic insights to ways that my work could improve. Nancy Alvarez, Benjamin Fitzpatrick, and Tomasz Rzeznik read the whole manuscript and gave me useful advice on nuance and substance as I made final revisions. Tom also provided me with a list of editorial suggestions, which I much appreciate. Jessica Chamberlain tracked down the last elusive citation. Myrtle Doaks and Nancy Mitchell facilitated the completion of the project in a number of ways. Joyce Zurawski and LinDa Grams typed the manuscript with good cheer on short notice, which saved me from a computer bent on destroying all evidence that I had ever written this book.

I much appreciate Jane Garrett's support for the project at Knopf and greatly enjoyed working with her a second time. I am also grateful for the help of Jane's assistant, Sophie Fels; the book's production editor, Kevin Bourke; its production manager, Claire Bradley Ong; and its designer, Robert Olsson.

Louis Masur has read it all, more than once, and has suffered it and me as only true friends can do. Since this is the shortest book I have written, it is for Lou, with whom I have debated the comparative virtues of brevity, images, words, and preaching for almost a quarter century.

My family—Denise, Moses, and Jasmine—has not read a word, but has been there for me through some bad times, and some worse ones, during the life of this project. Nothing has been easy for us over the last six years, so the time they granted me to work on this book has been precious, but not as precious as they are and always will be.

Index

African-Americans, 115; *see also* York
Allen, John Logan, xiv
Ambrose, Stephen, xiii–xiv
American Philosophical Society, 20
American Revolution, 184
Anthony, Susan B., 101
Arapaho Indians, 94
Arikara Indians, 118, 121, 122
Astorians, 43
astrology, 67
Audubon, John James, 138
Austin, Stephen, 93

Bacon, Francis, 70
Barton, Benjamin Smith, 71
Bermejo, Juan Rodríguez, 29
Bible, The, 66; Genesis, 4, 5, 10, 66, 136, 137
Biddle, Francis, 55
Biddle, Nicholas, 55, 122, 123, 202
Blackfeet Indians, 130, 131
Black Pride, 115
Brackenridge, Henry Marie, 89, 95, 215*n6*
Brackenridge, Hugh Henry, 215*n6*
Breintall, Joseph, 69
Broughton, William, 42
Bureau of Indian Affairs, 92
Burnett, Finn G., 96, 109
Burns, Ken, xiii, xiv

Canada/Canadian, 38–9
Catlin, George, 24
Charbonneau, Toussaint, 37, 156, 179;
    Porivo's relationship with, 87–9, 92,
    102–10, 117, 215*n6*
charming, *see* fascination
Cheyenne Indians, 16
chief, 16, 86, 101, 111, 113, 176–9, 183, 186,
    188
Chinookan Indians, 59
Christianity, 21, 30, 33, 66
chronology, 28, 32, 59, 60, 110
Civil War, 94
Clark, Edmund, 126
Clark, John, 114
Clark, Jonathan, 123
Clark, William: ambition to be "first" of,
    34–6, 39–45, 47; bears and, 149–50, 152,
    155–7, 205; buffalo and, 205–6; commu-
    nication with nature of, 12–13; hunting
    practices of, 10, 134, 136–9, 141–7;
    idealization of, 116; Jefferson coins
    given to "chiefs" by, 186, 188; journals
    of, 48–53, 55, 57–64, 97, 102, 186, 190,
    191; linear sense of time of, 9; maps by,
    196, *illus. 197–8*, 199, *illus. 200*, 201–2;
    myth of, 204–5; naming of places by,
    41–2, 44–5; origin myths told to, 4–11,
    17; in ownership conflicts with Indians,
    160–77, 179–81, 184; Porivo and, 86–99,

227

Thomas P. Slaughter received his B.A. (1976) and M.A. (1978) from the University of Maryland and an M.A. (1980) and Ph.D. (1983) from Princeton University. From 1982 to 2001 he taught at Rutgers University. He is currently Andrew V. Tackes Professor of History at the University of Notre Dame. He is the author of *The Natures of John and William Bartram* (1996), *Bloody Dawn: The Christiana Riot and Racial Violence in the Antebellum North* (1991), and *The Whiskey Rebellion: Frontier Epilogue to the American Revolution* (1986), and editor of *Thomas Paine: Common Sense and Related Writings* (2001) and the Library of America edition of *William Bartram: Travels and Other Writings* (1996). He lives in South Bend, Indiana, with his wife and two children.

A NOTE ON THE TYPE

This book is set in Spectrum, the last of three Monotype typefaces designed by the distinguished Dutch typographer Jan van Krimpen (1892–1958), a recipient of the Gold Medal of the Society of Industrial Artists in 1956. Originally commissioned from him in 1941 by the publishing house Het Spectrum of Utrecht, Spectrum surpasses van Krimpen's other faces in both the elegance and versatility of the letter forms but shares with Lutetia and Romulus many qualities characteristic of van Krimpen's designs—fine proportions, sharp cut, and generous counters.

Composed by North Market Street Graphics, Lancaster, Pennsylvania
Printed and bound by R. R. Donnelley & Sons, Harrisonburg, Virginia
Designed by Robert C. Olsson